Forum 2010
Legal and Political Theory in the Post-National Age

Central and Eastern European Forum for Legal, Political, and Social Theory Yearbook

Edited by Jürgen Busch / Péter Cserne
Michael Hein / Miodrag Jovanović / Marta Soniewicka

Volume 1

PETER LANG
Frankfurt am Main · Berlin · Bern · Bruxelles · New York · Oxford · Wien

Péter Cserne / Miklós Könczöl (eds.)

Legal and Political Theory in the Post-National Age

Selected papers presented at the
Second Central and Eastern European Forum
for Legal, Political and Social Theorists
(Budapest, 21–22 May 2010)

PETER LANG
Internationaler Verlag der Wissenschaften

Bibliographic Information published by the Deutsche Nationalbibliothek
The Deutsche Nationalbibliothek lists this publication in the Deutsche Nationalbibliografie; detailed bibliographic data is available in the internet at http://dnb.d-nb.de.

Cover Design:
© Olaf Gloeckler, Atelier Platen, Friedberg

Printed with financial support of the Federal Ministry of Science and Research in Vienna, the University of Greifswald, the Jagiellonian University in Kraków and the Pázmány Péter Catholic University Faculty of Law.

ISSN 2191-8317
ISBN 978-3-631-61582-9

www.peterlang.de

Series Preface

This volume marks the start of a new book series, the Central and Eastern European Forum for Legal, Political and Social Theory Yearbooks. The idea of this book series grew out of the Central and Eastern European Forum of Young Legal, Political and Social Theorists, an initiative of a group of young researchers working at the University of Silesia in Katowice, Poland.

The principal idea behind the Forum has been unease with the currently dominant unidirectional flow of scientific ideas from Western Europe and the United States to Central and Eastern Europe and the related practice of following the research paths of others. Forum participants have started thinking about the broader context of these trends.

Through international academic mobility, researchers from Central and Eastern Europe enjoy new opportunities but also have to cope with new challenges. After 1989 both older and younger generations had the choice between different strategies. Among those who decided to remain in academia, some are working at universities in their home country, others study further or seek jobs at academic institutions in Western Europe or beyond, still others combine these strategies. At the institutional level, academic communities in the region have both to struggle with funding problems and to reinterpret their local and national traditions in light of an increasing internationalisation.

Somewhat surprisingly, these developments are combined with recurrent difficulties of Central and Eastern European scholars in finding contacts to colleagues with similar interests at other places in the region, even if they work in neighbouring countries. As a small-scale practical response, the Forum attempts to establish an academic community which allows for the mutual exchange of ideas. More ambitiously, it aims to create a competitive environment for scholarly investigations in legal, political and social theory, thus leading to independent and original developments which are linked to the Central and Eastern European region. Independence and originality, of course, should imply neither parochialism nor an academic *Sonderweg*. Instead, for some researchers it may mean putting a special emphasis on the impact of theoretical insights in national or regional contexts. For others, it may involve addressing local problems in a comparative manner or from a supra-national perspective.

Starting with a conference in Katowice in 2009, in the last two years the Forum has developed into an academic network, involving dozens of active participants from all over the region. As its most publicly visible activities, the Forum organises annual conferences (in 2010 at the Pázmány Péter Catholic University in Budapest, Hungary and in 2011 at the University of Belgrade, Serbia) and operates its own website, www.cee-forum.org.

In terms of research methodology, the Forum is open for both innovative and more traditional approaches and methods. Philosophical, historical, jurisprudential, comparative or empirical contributions on theoretical issues in law, politics and social developments are equally welcome. In geographical terms, we understand Central and Eastern Europe widely, thus including Albania, Armenia, Azerbaijan, Austria, Belarus, Bosnia and Herzegovina, Bulgaria, Croatia, Czech Republic, Cyprus, Estonia, Georgia, Germany, Greece, Hungary, Italy, Lithuania, Latvia, Macedonia, Moldova, Montenegro, Poland, Romania, Russia, Serbia, Slovakia, Slovenia, Turkey and Ukraine. Due to the enormous linguistic diversity of this region, the working language of the Forum is English.

No doubt, with the ease of online communication, genuine interest in and awareness of what colleagues from other countries in the region are working on can develop into fruitful research contacts and cooperation in a spontaneous manner. Still, the Forum is based on the idea that an institutional framework can and should give a further impetus to such cooperation and contribute to establishing ties and networks for future common projects. In any case, the term 'forum' indicates a common understanding that academic discussion should be based on free and respectful exchange of ideas.

Along with an explicit regional emphasis, from the beginning the Forum also has had a generational character. Experience suggests that the annual conferences of the Forum provide a unique opportunity for junior scholars to present their research in front of an international audience and discuss it in an open and non-hierarchical environment. On top of this pedagogical function of encouraging the participation of young researchers and initiating them to international academic life, the Forum has to play a role in socialisation in another sense as well.

It seems that at least in the post-communist countries of Central and Eastern Europe there is a generational gap in legal academia and the social sciences, with socialisation before or after 1989 being an important line of division. Our impression is that even some twenty years after the fall of Soviet-style socialism, the standards of academic interaction are changing rather slowly in this region. Hierarchical, not to say feudal reflexes, undue reverence to age and seniority seem to have a strong continuous impact on academic culture in Central and Eastern Europe. By providing space for open discussion in a non-hierarchical atmosphere, the Forum aims to contribute to important changes in this respect. We believe that Western standards of academic culture cannot be adopted quickly and mechanically; they should be learned through practice, in a slow process of socialisation. The effects will probably need several generations to be noticeable at the macro level. With its own means, mainly by showing an example, the Forum hopes to play a role in this change of academic culture.

While we believe that the uniqueness of this initiative lies in its combination of regional and generational aspects, it is neither parochial nor an academic kindergarten. The coming years will show how the Forum fulfils its goals and functions. Our hope and ambition is that this book series contributes to establishing a prestigious research Forum and a genuine community of legal, political and social theorists coming from, working in or doing research on Central and Eastern Europe.

We are also confident that by publishing a selection of papers presented at the annual Forum conferences, the CEE Forum Yearbooks will become a respected venue and an inspiring source of information for the international academic community to get familiar with research by Forum participants. The editors of the series are also open to discuss publication proposals from authors of original works in legal, political and social theory, beyond the formal confines of the Forum.

Jürgen Busch
Péter Cserne
Michael Hein
Miodrag Jovanović
Marta Soniewicka

Contents

Contributors

Jürgen Busch researcher, University of Vienna, Austria

Péter Cserne assistant professor, Tilburg Law School, The Netherlands; assistant professor, Pázmány Péter Catholic University, Budapest, Hungary

Goran Dajović lecturer, University of Belgrade, Serbia

Balázs Fekete assistant professor, Pázmány Péter Catholic University, Budapest, Hungary; junior researcher, Hungarian Academy of Sciences Institute of Law

Krisztina Ficsor assistant professor, University of Debrecen, Hungary

Mariusz Jerzy Golecki associate professor, University of Łódź, Poland

Anna Kalisz lecturer, 'Humanitas' University of Sosnowiec, Poland

Katalin Kelemen senior lecturer, University of Örebro, Sweden

Miklós Könczöl assistant lecturer, Pázmány Péter Catholic University, Budapest, Hungary; PhD student, Durham University, UK

Victor Negrescu PhD student, National School of Political and Administrative Studies, Bucharest, Romania

Máté Paksy assistant professor, Pázmány Péter Catholic University, Budapest, Hungary

Charis Papacharalambous assistant professor, University of Cyprus

Judith von Schmädel former researcher, University of Vienna, Austria

Marta Soniewicka assistant professor, Jagiellonian University, Kraków, Poland

Kamila Staudigl-Ciechowicz researcher, University of Vienna, Austria; researcher, Commission for Austrian Legal History, Austrian Academy of Sciences

Antal Szerletics senior research officer, University of Essex, UK

Adam Szot PhD student, Marie Curie-Skłodowska University of Lublin, Poland

Szilárd Tattay assistant professor, Pázmány Péter Catholic University, Budapest, Hungary

András Zétényi PhD student, Pázmány Péter Catholic University, Budapest, Hungary

Introduction

Péter Cserne and Miklós Könczöl

This volume comprises fourteen original essays written by young Central and Eastern European legal theorists and political scientists. Their first versions were presented at the international conference *Second Central and Eastern European Forum for Young Legal, Social and Political Theorists*, at Pázmány Péter Catholic University Faculty of Law in Budapest, Hungary, on 21 and 22 May 2010. In addition to the generational and regional commonalities, what is common to these contributions is their distinctively theoretical outlook. The authors are all committed to and engage in a scholarly discussion where what matters is not the age or national background of speakers but the strength of their argument. Whether they reflect on philosophical matters or more practical issues of law and politics, in their own ways all contributors take scholarship seriously. The overall aim of this collection is to contribute to ongoing discussions in legal and political theory in our post-national era.

Why post-national?

Using the term post-national in the title of this volume should not be seen as an over-ambitious attempt to re-orientate legal and political theory. Rather, it draws attention to the broader historical and cultural context of the scholarly fields to which these essays contribute and the potential impact of this context on the discussion in these fields.

At least in the last few centuries, we have been used to associate legal orders with nation states. Our stereotypical understanding of law assumes that it belongs to a particular political community with relatively well-defined boundaries: German law is valid in Germany, Polish law in Poland, and so on. International law has been primarily understood as inter-state law. In spite of its heuristic value, this state-centred view of the law has to face both practical and theoretical challenges.

On the practical level, the last decades witnessed social, economic, political and legal integration processes at the regional and even the global level. This has made the traditional linkage between law and the nation state less and less obvious. Within Europe, the birth and consecutive enlargements of the European Union raise questions as to how and to what extent a new European political community can emerge and be stabilised through legal instruments or other mechanisms.

These developments have not remained unnoticed in the otherwise conservative circles of academic legal scholarship either. Following upon other disciplines with some time-lag, there is now an extensive discussion in legal scholarship on the theoretical and doctrinal impact of globalisation, involving not only international and European law scholars but experts in other legal fields as well. With new buzzwords like trans-national, supra-national and trans-boundary law, the discussion revolves around how to conceptually grasp, critically reflect on and reasonably control new developments in the global legal arena.

These developments seem to highlight a slightly more abstract theoretical tension as well, between the general and the particular. Is law conceptually linked to the particular, i.e. certain geographically, ethnically or culturally rooted traditions, boundaries and communities? Or does the notion or ideal of law point at something more general, going beyond these contingent limits and constraints? Are there universal conceptual features of law, in spite of law as a social phenomenon being bound to space and time? It seems that law and politics are not only spatio-temporal phenomena but also local in the sense of being inherently linked to boundaries, inclusion and exclusion. On the other hand, philosophy and the social sciences typically pursue universalist goals, when their ambition is to theoretically explain and normatively evaluate particular legal and political phenomena from a broader, higher, non-parochial viewpoint. In one way or another, each contribution takes a stance on this broader issue as well.

The contributions

We divided the contributions into four thematic groups. The first group of essays focuses on conceptual and methodological problems that have proved to be central to modern legal theory. The first two papers are mainly conceptual; they discuss links between two pairs of basic concepts in legal philosophy. Szilárd Tattay reconstructs how a new understanding of the concept of rights was formulated in the late Scholastic legal philosophy of Francisco Suárez, and how he accommodated subjective rights in a philosophical system of objective natural law. Goran Dajović focuses on the conceptual linkages between the rule of recognition and the written constitution. He argues that while the two concepts are closely related, the former having primacy over the latter, the legitimacy of a constitution cannot derive merely from a rule of recognition.

Two further papers in this part address methodological problems of legal theory. Máté Paksy argues that while law itself is intrinsically connected to a given political community characterised by its culture and history, legal philosophy addresses 'basic questions' that can be 'transposed' to other legal cultures in order to understand the 'spirit' of the other legal system. Balázs Fekete scrutinises the emergence and promises of the cultural approach in the theory of comparative law, critically examining Pierre Legrand's arguments and highlighting post-Socialist legal *mentalité* as a potential field of application for cultural legal comparison.

Part Two addresses problems related to ethics and moral philosophy. The first two papers are more philosophical in character. Antal Szerletics outlines a novel approach to paternalism based on the ethics of care and virtue ethics. He argues that a reinterpretation of autonomy in terms of caring relationships also contributes to the moral justification of legal paternalism. András Zétényi's paper compares how the practical philosophy of John Finnis and Joseph Raz respond to the pluralism of modern Western societies. In particular, he argues that while the Razian view of social forms implies radical pluralism, Finnis's meta-ethical objectivism leads him to a moderate version of pluralism, i.e. a theory, which is nevertheless compatible with the idea of different ways of life pursuing basic goods.

The two latter pieces in this part show how legal reforms can raise serious ethical concerns. Both provide a critical outlook on legal concepts and techniques which address new technological or social developments in a morally controversial manner. Marta Soniewicka is concerned with the regulation of the use of genetic test results and other genetic information in various jurisdictions. She discusses genetic discrimination and the desirable scope of legal protection in education, employment and insurance.

Based on a thorough analysis of the case law of international criminal courts, Charis Papacharalambous discusses the radical change in the conception of responsibility brought about by the emergence of the notion of 'joint criminal enterprise' in criminal law doctrine. As he argues, this transformation of responsibility progressively lets a kind of 'collective guilt' resurface.

The third set of papers is concerned with courts and adjudication. The first two papers deal with judicial decisions and legal reasoning. In line with analytical legal theory, Krisztina Ficsor discusses the theoretical background and conceptual features of legal formalism. As she argues, formalism is a theory of adjudication which is closely linked to both legal interpretation and legal reasoning. In a comparative manner, Katalin Kelemen's chapter provides a broad historical overview on the institutionalisation of the dissenting opinion in various systems of adjudication, with a special emphasis on the role of dissent in East-Central European constitutional courts.

The next two papers focus on the interaction between national and supra-national judicial institutions. Starting from recent developments in the interplay between national courts and the European Court of Justice, Mariusz Golecki's paper provides a theoretical reconstruction of supra-national legitimacy. In particular, he argues that it is logically possible and institutionally feasible to interpret the European Union as a single complex legal order, a legal system based on circularity and self-reference. Anna Kalisz and Adam Szot scrutinise the interpretation of general clauses in national and supranational courts. Analysing Polish, European and international case law on public morals and public interest they argue that it is desirable to interpret these clauses as expressions of local and regional values.

The fourth set of essays focuses on theoretical issues related to international integration and cooperation. The paper by Jürgen Busch, Judith von Schmädel and Kamila Staudigl-Ciechowitz discusses the historical and biographical background of Hans Kelsen's theory of international integration, and compares his vision of world peace with Verdross's and Campagnolo's theories of the international legal and political order. Finally, Victor Negrescu focuses on the conceptualisation of 'co-operation for development' in various theories of international relations. He suggests that the notion reflects a complex interaction of national, international and humanitarian interests.

Acknowledgements

As editors of this book we would like to thank all participants of the Budapest conference for their contribution to the event, members of the CEE Forum Yearbooks editorial board for both fruitful discussions on institutional shape and academic contents of the Forum and their practical and timely help with securing the necessary funding for the present volume. Our particular appreciation and thanks are due to Jürgen Busch who has played a key role in organising the financial background of the publication. We are grateful to the University of Greifswald, Jagiellonian University in Kraków, Pázmány Péter Catholic University Faculty of Law and the Austrian Federal Ministry for Science and Research for their generous contribution, and to Peter Lang Publisher for the smooth collaboration in the preparation and production of the book.

Part I
Concepts and Methods in Legal Theory

The Subjective Concept of Right in Francisco Suárez

Szilárd Tattay

Abstract The Spanish theologians of the Second Scholasticism were the last great representatives of the medieval tradition of natural law and natural rights. They inherited the idea of natural rights directly from sixteenth-century Ockhamists. However, they were far from being nominalists; on the contrary, they were devoted Thomists. And Aquinas, their master, though certainly knew the subjective concept of right, seems deliberately to have avoided it. This clearly points out serious philosophical problems for any Thomist legal thinker who accepts the subjective concept of right: (1) Can the concept of *ius* as a moral faculty be reconciled with the authentic Thomist conception of *ius* as *id quod iustum est*? (2) How can a meaningful relation be established between subjective natural rights and objective natural law? In my paper I examine the answers that one of the leading figures of the Second Scholasticism, the Jesuit Francisco Suárez gave to these questions.

1

The Spanish theologians of the Second Scholasticism – the Jesuit Francisco Suárez, Luis de Molina and Gabriel Vázquez, the Dominican Francisco de Vitoria, Domingo de Soto and Bartolomé de las Casas, and others – were the last great representatives of the medieval tradition of natural law and natural rights. Their *oeuvre* thus constitutes an important link between scholastic and modern theories of natural law. They inherited the idea of natural rights directly from the sixteenth-century Ockhamists John Mair, Jacques Almain and Conrad Summenhart.[1] However, unlike their predecessors, they were very far from being nominalists; on the contrary, they were devoted Thomists – even if perhaps not without qualification.

1 This fact is especially emphasised by Quentin Skinner (1978, 176–178). For a useful survey and commentary of the texts of the representative authors of the Second Scholasticism (and some of their nominalist predecessors) on subjective rights, see Folgado (1960).

Aquinas, their master, though he certainly knew the subjective concept of right, seems deliberately to have avoided it. To be more precise, at times he uses *ius* in a subjective sense in the *Summa theologiae* (e.g., he speaks of *ius possidendi* and *ius dominii*),[2] but this usage is sporadic and marginal, and doing so he is only unreflectively following the common juristic terminology of his age, very far from thinking of developing a theory of natural rights (see Tierney 1997, 23).[3] As Annabel Brett points out,

> the scattered usage of the subjective construction of *ius* with the gerund does not affect the theoretical elucidation of *ius* as objective, which is indeed the sense that *ius* normally bears in Aquinas's text; nor does it necessarily imply a concept of subjective right as liberty.' (Brett 1997, 91 n. 12)

As a consequence, Dominican theorists in the sixteenth century were still quite moderate in the use of the subjective notion of *ius*. In his *Commentary on the Secunda Secundae*, in the Question '*De jure*' Vitoria, the greatest authority of the Dominican Order defines *ius* in a traditional Thomist way as *obiectum iustitiae*, the object of justice, and it is only later on in the same work that he introduces Conrad Summenhart's Gersonian, subjective definition of *ius* as 'a power or faculty pertaining to someone according to the laws'.[4] This cautiousness of Vitoria indirectly but clearly points out serious philosophical problems for any Thomist legal thinker who accepts the subjective concept of right:

(1) Can the concept of *ius* as a moral faculty be reconciled with the authentic Thomist conception of *ius* as *id quod iustum est*?

(2) How can a meaningful relation be established between subjective natural rights and objective natural law?

In my paper I will examine what answers the other leading figure of the Second Scholasticism, the Jesuit Francisco Suárez gave to these questions.

2

In *Natural Law and Natural Rights*, John Finnis sharply contrasts Suárez's subjective notion of *ius* with Aquinas's objective concept:

2 *ST* II-II q. 62 a. 1 ad 2: 'restitutio videtur locum habere praecipue in rebus exterioribus, quae manentes eaedem et secundum substantiam et secundum ius dominii, ab uno possunt ad alium devenire.' *ST* II-II q. 66 a. 5 ad 2: 'in parabola Evangelii dicitur, Matth. XIII, de inventore thesauri absconditi in agro, quod emit agrum, quasi ut haberet ius possidendi totum thesaurum.' For further examples, see Finnis (1998, 133 n. 10, 134 n. 12), and Aubert (1955, 91 n. 2).

3 Saint Thomas was well acquainted with law, and by the time he wrote his works, the subjective meaning of *ius* had widely spread in medieval legal language (cf. Tierney 1989; Tuck 1979; Berman 1983).

4 *De justitia* II-II q. 62 a. 1 n. 5: 'Conradus, qui fecit tractatum illum nobilem *De contractibus*, [...] dicit ergo quod jus est potestas vel facultas conveniens alicui secundum leges.'

> Aquinas prefaces his elaborate study of justice with an analysis of *jus*, at the forefront of which he gives a list of meanings of '*jus*'. The primary meaning, he says, is 'the just thing itself' [...] If we now jump about 340 years to the treatise on law by the Spanish Jesuit Francisco Suarez, written c. 1610, we find another analysis of the meanings of '*jus*'. Here the 'true, strict and proper meaning' of '*ius*' is said to be: 'a kind of moral power [facultas] which every man has, either over his own property or with respect to that which is due to him'. The meaning which for Aquinas was primary is rather vaguely mentioned by Suarez and then drops out of sight; conversely, the meaning which for Suarez is primary does not appear in Aquinas's discussion at all. Somewhere between the two men we have crossed the watershed (Finnis 1980, 206–207).

This is one of the rare points where Finnis appears to agree with the French historian of legal philosophy Michel Villey. According to Villey, Suárez turns completely upside down the legal philosophy of the *doctor angelicus*: 'the "just" of Saint Thomas [...] does not enter into his categories. But the subjective right [...] has a real existence for him' (Villey 1968, 379, 381). A third neo-Thomist legal philosopher, Louis Lachance goes even further by saying that Suárez confuses 'right' in the objective sense with the faculty of using it, and in doing so he falsifies the teaching of Aquinas: 'to define right as a moral faculty of the will and to set liberty as an end for it supposes that one makes human will and liberty the rule of morality [...] and this resembles a lot to Kantianism' (Lachance 1948, 294–295).[5]

René Brouillard, on the other hand, severely criticises this latter interpretation and claims that in associating *ius* with *facultas moralis*, Suárez 'in no way intended to substitute for or oppose it to the Thomist definition [...] In reality, in his thought one prolonged the other: the moral faculty was founded on and regulated precisely by the objective right in the Thomist sense' (Brouillard 1941, 2707). Likewise, Brian Tierney argues that though 'Suarez arrived at a subjective understanding of *ius* as a moral faculty inhering in a right-holder', he 'did not present this as an alternative definition, different from that of Aquinas. He seems to have assumed that this is what Aquinas meant all along' (Tierney 1997, 303).

3

Let us see what Suárez himself writes in his major legal work, *De legibus ac Deo legislatore* (*On Laws and God the Lawgiver*, published in 1612).[6] In general, he lays great emphasis on conceptual analysis. Immediately after the first chapter of the treatise, discussing the essence of law, he sets out to examine the question 'What *ius* means

5 Lachance's views are reiterated by Paul Van Overbeke (1958, 307–311).

6 In referring to the *De legibus*, I will quote the original Latin text from Suárez (1971–1981) and I will use the English translation to be found in Suárez (1944), unless otherwise noted).

and how it is to be compared with *lex*.'[7] He distinguishes between two etymological explanations of the word *ius*. The first derives the term from *iussum*, the perfect passive participle of the verb *iubere* (to command), the second from *iustitia*.[8] According to the first etymology, *ius* is the same as *lex*. Here, Suárez makes explicit a longstanding scholastic linguistic practice by declaring that '*ius*, in so far as it refers to *lex*, is used interchangeably with that term, and the two words are considered as synonyms.'[9] The second etymological explanation equates *ius* with '*iustum et aequum*': 'according to the last-cited derivation, *ius* has the same meaning as that which is just and equitable, this being the object of justice.'[10] In this sense, *ius* is nothing other than the just thing itself (*ipsum iustum*).[11] Following Aristotle, Suárez differentiates two meanings of the word 'justice'. In its generic meaning, *iustitia* stands for every moral virtue, 'since every virtue in some wise is directed towards and brings about equity', whereas in its specific sense it denotes 'a special virtue which renders to another that which is his due'.[12] Accordingly, *ius* as the object of justice has a double meaning, too. While in the general sense it may describe anything that is fair and reasonable, in its more specific meaning it refers only to 'the equity which is due to each individual as a matter of justice'. Suárez underlines that this latter usage of the term is more common, and this is the strict one.[13]

7 *De legibus* 1.2: 'Quid ius significet et quomodo ad legem comparetur.' In a way, this can be considered as a detour in a genuine treatise on law, but from another point of view it shows how much importance Suárez ascribes to the problem.

8 To be more accurate, Suárez mentions a third etymology as well, deriving *ius* from *iuxta* (close), but rejects it quickly as unconvincing. *De legibus* 1.2.1–2: 'Prius vero advertere oportet tres solere iuris etymologias assignari. Prima est, ut ius dicatur quod iuxta sit […] Eam enim omitto, quia mihi non probatur […] Secunda, et latinis magis recepta est, ut ius dicatur a iubendo; nam *iussum* participium est verbi *iubeo*, et si a participio *iussum* secundam syllabam demamus, ius relinquitur […] Tertia derivatio est ut ius a iustitia dicatur. Sic enim dixit Ulpianus: *Est autem ius a iustitia appellatum.*'

9 Ibid. 1.2.7: 'ius prout legem significat, cum illa convertitur et tanquam synonyma reputantur.'

10 Ibid. 1.2.4: 'iuxta ultimam etymologiam ius idem significat quod iustum et aequum, quod est obiectum iustitiae.' I have slightly modified the English translation.

11 Ibid. 1.2.9: 'nihil aliud est ius quam ipsum iustum'.

12 Ibid. 1.2.4: 'Considerandum est autem iustitiae nomen dupliciter accipi. Primo, pro omni virtute, quia omnis virtus respicit et facit aliquo modo aequitatem; secundo, pro speciali virtute tribuente alteri quod suum est.' For the original Aristotelian distinction, see *Nicomachean Ethics* 1130a–b.

13 *De legibus* 1.2.4: 'Utrique ergo significationi ius cum proportione respondet, nam primo ius significare potest quidquid est aequum et consentaneum rationi […] Secundo, potest ius significare aequitatem, quae unicuique ex iustitia debetur, et haec posterior significatio magis est in usu, nam ius sic acceptum ad propriam iustitiam referri maxime solet.'

4

So far, this is very close to what Aquinas said on the subject in his treatise on right and justice in the *Secunda Secundae* of the *Summa theologiae*. *Ius* is an objectively just thing or action; it is 'that which is in reality just and fair with regard to its object and, accordingly, with regard to its final, or formal and extrinsic cause.'[14] But now Suárez's discussion of *ius* takes a new direction. As James Tully has put it, the Aristotelian–Thomist concept of objective right 'is redescribed, in two elegant steps, in terms of two subjective rights' (Tully 1980, 67). First Suárez redefines *ius* as a moral faculty by means of the juridical notions of *ius in re* and *ius ad rem*. He illustrates the latter with Aquinas's classical example of just act, the payment of the due wage for a service rendered:

> According to the latter and strict acceptation of *ius*, this name is properly wont to be bestowed upon a certain moral faculty which every man has, either over his own property or with respect to that which is due to him. For it is thus that the owner of a thing is said to have a right in that thing, and the labourer is said to have that right to his wages by reason of which he is declared worthy of his hire. Indeed, this acceptation of the term is frequent not only in law but also in Scripture; for the law distinguishes in this wise between a right *in* a thing (*ius in re*) and a right *to* a thing (*ius ad rem*).[15]

Then he gives a similar paraphrase of Ulpian's famous definition of justice, reinterpreting Ulpian's '*ius suum*' to mean a legal claim right:

> Again, it would seem that *ius* is so understood in the *Digest*, where justice is said to be the virtue that renders to every man his own right, that is to say, the virtue that renders to every man that which belongs to him. Accordingly, this right to claim or moral power, which every man possesses with respect to his own property or with respect to a thing which in some way pertains to him is called *ius*, and appears to be the true object of justice.[16]

14 Ibid. 1.2.2: 'Nam priori modo verum est iustitiam derivari a iure (id est, ab eo quod in re iustum et aequum est) in ratione obiecti, ac subinde in genere causae finalis vel formalis extrinsecae.'

15 Ibid. 1.2.5: 'Et iuxta posteriorem et strictam iuris significationem solet proprie ius vocari facultas quaedam moralis, quam unusquisque habet vel circa rem suam vel ad rem sibi debitam; sic enim dominus rei dicitur habere ius in re et operarius dicitur habere ius ad stipendium ratione cuius dicitur *dignus mercede sua*. Et haec sinificatio vocis huius frequens est non solum in iure sed etiam in Scriptura; nam in iure hoc modo distinguuntur ius in re vel ad rem'. I have slightly modified Williams's translation.

16 Ibid.: 'Atque hoc modo sumi videtur ius in lege *iustitia*, ff. De iustitia et iure, cum dicitur iustitia esse virtus quae *ius suum unicuique tribuit*, id est, id tribuens unicuique quod ad illum spectat. Illa ergo actio seu moralis facultas, quam unusquisque habet ad rem suam vel ad rem ad se aliquo modo pertinentem vocatur ius, et illud proprie videtur esse obiectum istitiae.'

5

In Villey's interpretation, Suárez knows only two meanings of *ius*: *ius* as prescriptive law and *ius* as a subjective right (Villey 1968, 380; 1979, 222–223).[17] This interpretation is partly confirmed by Suárez himself: whenever he later returns to the problem of the etymology of *ius* in the *De legibus*, or in his other works touching the subject, he always gives a twofold definition.[18] However, if we read Suárez's analysis carefully, it can hardly escape our attention that in effect, the *doctor eximius* uses *ius* in three different senses. As Tierney pertinently observes, 'to a modern reader it will seem evident that Suarez gave three definitions – the original Thomist meaning, "the just" or "the object of justice"; his own understanding of *ius* as a moral faculty or subjective right; and finally *ius* as meaning law' (Tierney 1997, 303).[19] But why then has Suárez explicitly spoken of only two 'principal' meanings?[20] According to Tierney's – perhaps too benign – explanation, because 'he apparently regarded the first two meanings as merely different ways of saying the same thing' (ibid., 304). Dario Composta comes to a somewhat similar conclusion. He argues that although Suárez does not frequently use the expression '*res iusta*', this does not mean at all that he ignores Aquinas's objective concept of *ius*, but merely that he 'does not recognize it as a legal category distinct from that of the *moral faculty*' (Composta 1957, 26–27). Even Finnis acknowledges that although it is the subjective meaning of *ius* that becomes primary in Suárez's legal philosophy, that is to say, for him '*jus* is essentially something someone *has* [...] if you like, it is Aquinas's primary meaning of "*jus*", but transformed by *relating it exclusively to the beneficiary* of the just relationship' (Finnis 1980, 207).

6

It is extremely difficult to decide between these competing interpretations, for Suárez's usage of *ius* is far from being unequivocal. He does not make it clear what is the exact relationship between objective and subjective 'right'; instead he shifts from one meaning of *ius* to the other (as it was usual in medieval legal philosophy), without mentioning that he uses the term in these different senses. In general, he does

17 This is also the opinion of Reijo Wilenius (1963, 45–46) and Pauline C. Westerman (1998, 113). According to Westerman, Suárez 'abandons here the traditional Thomistic view of *ius* as "giving everyone his due". Rather, he identifies *ius* with *facultas* [...] *Ius* no longer refers to an overall regulative and distributive framework.'

18 Cf. *De legibus* 2.14.16, 7.1.9; *Defensio fidei catholicae* 4.9.11; *De religione*, tr. VII, 8.5.12.

19 Practically the same tripartite understanding of *ius* reappeared 13 years later in a clearer form in Grotius's *De iure belli ac pacis* (1.1.3–9).

20 *De legibus* 1.2.4: 'Iuxta has ergo duas vocis derivationes, nomen *ius* duas praecipuas habet significationes.'

not deal at length with the semantics of 'right' and 'justice'. This is comprehensible if we take into account that unlike many of his Dominican and Jesuit predecessors (among others Domingo de Soto and Luis de Molina), Suárez wrote not a *De iustitia et iure*, but a treatise *On Laws and God the Lawgiver*.[21] After all, I find more convincing the interpretation according to which by defining *ius* as a moral faculty Suárez intended to complement rather than to replace Aquinas's objective concept of *ius* as 'the just'. This reading seems to me more credible for several reasons. First, because, as we saw, Suárez identifies sometimes the objective, sometimes the subjective sense of *ius* with the object of justice. Secondly and more importantly, since Suárez constantly and consistently links the subjective notion of *ius* with the argumentation and the conceptual basis of Aquinas's discussion of objective right. The following passage is, I think, a perfect textual evidence of this:

> *ius* sometimes refers to the moral faculty to acquire or retain something, whether that faculty involves true *dominium* or merely a partial *dominium*; which is, as we learn from St. Thomas (II.-II, qu. 57, art. 1), the true object of justice. On the other hand, *ius* sometimes means law, which is the rule of righteous conduct; and in this sense it is that which establishes a certain equity in things, so that, as St. Thomas holds (ibid., art. 1, ad 2), it is the basis of right, that very acceptation of *ius* which we first noted.[22]

7

According to Villey, the reference to Aquinas is merely rhetorical in Suárez's analysis of *ius*; he employs Thomist terminology, but solely in order to disguise the nominalist, voluntarist elements inherent in the subjective understanding of the term (Villey 1968, 353).[23] The basic problem with this approach is that by Suárez's time, as Annabel Brett has shown, subjective right and objective right were no longer considered as direct opposites in scholastic thought at all (Brett 1997, 111–124, esp. 124). After Vitoria, the parallel use of the objective and subjective senses of *ius* became common among the members of the school of Salamanca who defended with

21 This is not to say that Suárez did not devote a special treatise to justice. He discussed justice in detail – and along predominantly Aristotelian–Thomist lines – in his disputation *De iustitia Dei* and in his lectures *De iustitia et iure* delivered in the College of Rome. However, in these works he does not speak much about *ius*.

22 *De legibus* 2.17.2: 'Ius enim interdum significat moralem facultatem ad rem aliquam vel in re, sive sit verum dominium, sive aliqua participatio eius; quod est proprium obiectum iustitiae, ut constat ex divo Thoma (II II, quaest. 57, art. 1). Aliquando vero ius significat legem, quae est regula honeste operandi et in rebus quamdam aequitatem constituit; et est ratio ipsius iuris priori modo sumpti, ut dixit ibidem divus Thomas (dicto art. 1, ad secundum)'. I have modified the translation at several points.

23 This is the view of Lachance (1948, 294), too.

the same determination moral and legal objectivism on the one hand and the rights of the Indians on the other. Certainly, to derive a subjective meaning from Aquinas's objective conception of *ius* is a difficult philosophical and linguistic manoeuvre.[24] But even so, Suárez had no reason to conceal his real sources, and he did not do so (as it is evident e.g. from his reference to Johannes Driedo's Gersonian definition of *ius*). Especially as Vitoria already created a precedent by interpreting Aquinas's dictum that law is '*aliqualis ratio iuris*' to mean that *ius* is 'what is licit by law' (*quod lege licet*), that is, a subjective right.[25]

Everything considered, we have good reasons to conclude that for Suárez there is an organic relation between *ius* as a moral faculty and the two other – objective – meanings of *ius*. What one has a right to is due to him according to the principles of justice, and law is the basis and measure not only of moral rectitude but also of rights. It is in that sense that Composta says that in Suárez 'objectivity does not cease to exist in the "moral faculty"', which remains identical with or closely related to 'the just and equitable', and conforms to the external order defined by laws (Composta 1957, 27). Tully also accentuates that Suárez can call the moral power to or in a thing a 'right', because

> the moral power cannot but be right in the objective sense. That is, the moral power is objectively right because it is a moral power with respect to what is right by definition: one's own and one's due. Thus subjective right is derived from and limited by natural law, the standard of what is objectively right. (Tully 1993, 105)

8

In the grounding of natural rights Suárez's conception of permissive natural law plays a primordial role. Suárez divides natural law into two parts: preceptive and

24 It should be noted that the Thomist notion of *dominium sui* served as an important conceptual basis for this manoeuvre. Janet Coleman argues (2006, 24–30), I think correctly, that scholastic conceptions of self-mastery or self-dominion must clearly be distinguished from the modern idea of self-ownership, as represented by Locke and Hobbes, seeing that medieval and modern writers had a very different understanding of the self.

25 *De justitia* II-II q. 62 a. 1 n. 5: 'Jus ergo, ut ex superioribus constat, nihil aliud est nisi illud quod licet, vel quod lege licet, id est jus est quod est licitum por leges. Patet hoc ex sancto Thoma supra, q. 57, a. 1 ad secundum, ubi dicit quod lex non est proprie jus, sed est ratio juris, id est, est illud ratione cujus aliquid est licitum.' Vitoria's discussion of *ius* was closely followed by his best pupil, Domingo de Soto. For a detaleid analysis of their concepts of objective and subjective right, see Brett (1997, 124–164). As regards Jesuit theologians before Suárez, Harro Höpfl underlines that albeit for them '*ius* was etymologically incapable of being permanently cut adrift from the generic notion of "what is right" [...] *ius* had also long ago acquired the sense of a personal entitlement, "faculty", a liberty, a "subjective" right [...] The idea of a subjective right was, however, easily derivable from the chronologically (and ethically) primary sense of *ius* as "what is right", or law as the source of rights' (Höpfl 2004, 265–266).

permissive.[26] The latter comprises certain recommendations of nature which are as valid as the commands or prohibitions of preceptive natural law, yet they are not absolutely binding. Permissive natural law thus defines an area within which human persons can licitly exercise their inherent power of free will and free choice. More concretely, when natural law permits an otherwise intrinsically good act, 'it not only does not prohibit it, but since it is good, it also grants a positive faculty or licence, or a certain right to it.'[27] It should be stressed that for Suárez there cannot be contradiction between the permissions and the precepts of natural law: permissive natural law can never permit or give right to immoral acts that are contrary to preceptive natural law. Thus the commands and prohibitions of natural law set bounds to the exercise of natural rights and prevent right-holders from abusing their rights (see Tierney 2002, 401, 405–406). Finally, what is perhaps even more important, preceptive natural law obliges others to respect the rights conferred by permissive natural law:

> The right to all these things is natural, that is they are all permitted by the law of nature. And in the same way the obligation of one person not to violate such a right of another is of natural law.[28]

To conclude, Suárez attaches natural rights to natural law in at least three ways. First, it is permissive natural law that constitutes their normative basis. Secondly, the commands and prohibitions of preceptive natural law set limits to natural rights and ensure their lawful exercise. Thirdly, the same law protects natural rights against violation by others.

References

Primary sources

Aquinas, Thomas. 1952–56. *Summa theologiae*, edited by Pietro Caramello, 3 vols. Torino: Marietti.

Aristotle. 1969. *Nicomachean Ethics of Aristotle*, translated by Sir David Ross. London: Oxford University Press.

Grotius, Hugo. 2006. *De jure belli ac pacis libri tres*. Hildesheim: Olms.

26 See *De legibus* 2.14.6, 2.14.14, 2.14.19 and 2.18.2.

27 Ibid. 1.15.11: 'Nam quando permissio dicitur de actu alias bono, non solum non prohibet illum: sed etiam cum sit bonus, dat positivam facultatem, seu licentiam, vel ius aliquod ad illum' (my translation).

28 Ibid. 2.18.7: 'Nam ius ad haec omnia naturale est, id est, haec omnia licita sunt iure naturae. Et eodem modo obligatio unius ad non violandum tale ius alterius, naturalis legis est.' I have modified the official translation.

Suárez, Francisco. 1858. *De iustitia Dei.* In *Opera omnia*, vol. 11, edited by Charles Berton, 515–582. Paris: Vivès.

Suárez, Francisco. 1859. *Defensio fidei catholicae.* In *Opera omnia*, vol. 24, edited by Charles Berton. Paris: Vivès.

Suárez, Francisco. 1859–1860. *De religione.* In *Opera omnia*, vols. 13–16 bis, edited by Charles Berton. Paris: Vivès.

Suárez, Francisco. 1944. *On Laws and God the Lawgiver* (selections). *In Selections from Three Works of Francisco Suarez*, vol. 2: *An English Version of the Texts*, translated by Gwladys L. Williams et al., 1–646. Oxford: Clarendon Press.

Suárez, Francisco. 1958. *De iustitia et iure.* In *Die Gerechtigkeitslehre des jungen Suárez: Edition und Untersuchung seiner römischen Vorlesungen De iustitia et iure*, edited by Joachim Giers, 29–122. Freiburg: Herder.

Suárez, Francisco. 1971–1981. *De legibus*, edited by Luciano Pereña et al., 8 vols. Madrid: Consejo superior de investigaciones científicas.

Vitoria, Francisco de. 1934. *Comentarios a la Secunda secundae de Santo Tomás*, vol. 3: *De justitia (qq. 57–66)*, edited by Vicente Beltrán de Heredia. Salamanca: Dominicos de la Provincias de España.

Secondary sources

Aubert, Jean-Marie. 1955. *Le droit romain dans l'oeuvre de saint Thomas.* Paris: Vrin.

Berman, Harold J. 1983. *Law and Revolution: The Formation of the Western Legal Tradition.* Cambridge (MA): Harvard University Press.

Brett, Annabel S. 1997. *Liberty, Right and Nature: Individual Rights in Later Scholastic Thought.* Cambridge: Cambridge University Press.

Brouillard, René. 1941. Suarez François: la théologie pratique. In *Dictionnaire de théologie catholique*, edited by Alfred Vacant, Eugène Mangenot and Émile Amann, vol. 14, 2nd part, cols. 2691–2728. Paris: Letouzey et Ané.

Coleman, Janet. 2006. Are There Any Individual Rights or Only Duties? On the Limits of Obedience in the Avoidance of Sin according to Late Medieval and Early Modern Scholars. In *Transformations in Medieval and Early-Modern Rights Discourse*, edited by Virpi Mäkinen and Petter Korkman, 3–36. New York: Springer.

Composta, Dario. 1957. *La "moralis facultas" nella filosofia giuridica di F. Suarez.* Torino: SEI.

Finnis, John. 1980. *Natural Law and Natural Rights.* Oxford: Clarendon Press.

Finnis, John. 1998. *Aquinas: Moral, Political, and Legal Theory.* Oxford: Oxford University Press.

Folgado, Avelino. 1960. *Evolución histórica del concepto del derecho subjetivo: Estudio especial en los teólogos-juristas españoles del siglo XVI.* San Lorenzo de El Escorial: Biblioteca La Ciudad de Dios.

Höpfl, Harro. 2004. *Jesuit Political Thought: The Society of Jesus and the State, c. 1540–1630.* Cambridge: Cambridge University Press.

Lachance, Louis. 1948. *Le concept de droit selon Aristote et S. Thomas*, 2nd ed. Ottawa and Montreal: Lévrier.

Overbeke, Paul Van. 1958. Droit et Morale: Essai de synthèse thomiste. *Revue thomiste* 58: 284–336.

Skinner, Quentin. 1978. *The Foundations of Modern Political Thought*, vol. 2: *The Age of Reformation.* Cambridge: Cambridge University Press.

Tierney, Brian. 1989. Origins of Natural Rights Language: Texts and Contexts, 1150–1250. *History of Political Thought* 10: 615–646.

Tierney, Brian. 1997. *The Idea of Natural Rights: Studies on Natural Rights, Natural Law and Church Law, 1150–1625.* Atlanta: Scholars Press.

Tierney, Brian. 2002. Natural Law and Natural Rights: Old Problems and Recent Approaches. *The Review of Politics* 64: 389–406.

Tuck, Richard. 1979. *Natural Rights Theories: Their Origin and Development.* Cambridge: Cambridge University Press.

Tully, James. 1980. *A Discourse on Property: John Locke and His Adversaries.* Cambridge: Cambridge University Press.

Tully, James. 1993. *An Approach to Political Philosophy: Locke in Contexts.* Cambridge: Cambridge University Press.

Villey, Michel. 1968. *La formation de la pensée juridique moderne: Cours d'histoire de la philosophie du droit*, 4th ed. Paris: Montchrestien.

Villey, Michel. 1979. Remarque sur la notion de droit chez Suarez. *Archives de philosophie* 42: 219–227.

Westerman, Pauline C. 1998. *The Disintegration of Natural Law Theory: Aquinas to Finnis.* Leiden: Brill.

Wilenius, Reijo. 1963. *The Social and Political Theory of Francisco Suárez.* Helsinki: Akateeminen Kirjakauppa.

The Relationship between Rule of Recognition and Constitutional Rules

Goran Dajović

Abstract In this paper the author deals with the concept of a rule of recognition and of a constitution and with their relation. In the first part, some of the essential properties of the rule of recognition as a theoretical concept are listed. One of such properties is that in a legal system with a written constitution, as a criterion of law's validity the rule of recognition commonly and at least partly, provides that norms which are duly enacted according to the constitutional procedure are valid law. The second part outlines an account of the most important features of the concept of a written constitution. Among them, the most striking ones are supremacy, judicial protection, durability and rigidity. Finally, in the last part a summary analysis of the possible and necessary relations between the two concepts follows. A few concluding remarks refer to the problems concerning the validity of laws, and the legitimacy and authority of a constitution.

1 Introduction

As it is well known, one of the key insights of Hart's jurisprudence is the idea that legal systems are not only comprised of rules but grounded on them, as well. In contrast to Bentham and Austin's idea of an unlimited sovereign who makes all legal rules, Hart introduced the idea that it is the rules that actually make the sovereign (see Shapiro 2009). In accordance with this theoretical turnabout, he also put forward the concept of the so-called rule of recognition (RR). This 'recognitional' rule is a special sort of social rule which determines the status of every rule as part of a certain legal system. It is a master rule that exists by virtue of the fact of its social acceptance and it establishes validity criteria for all other legal rules of the system.

In a system with a written constitution, RR as a criterion of law's validity, commonly and partly at least, provides that norms which are duly enacted according to the constitutional procedure are valid laws. Therefore, it is clear at first sight that the two concepts are closely related but they are also different and separate.

So, first, I shall list some of the essential properties of RR as a theoretical concept, concentrating on those that are important for the topic. Secondly, I am going to account for the most important features of the concept of a written constitution. Finally, I shall consider a few relations between the two concepts concerning the validity of laws, the contribution of a written constitution to the fulfilment of the function of the RR, and the legitimacy and authority of a constitution.

2 What is the rule of recognition?

A rule of recognition may be described most simply as a *social rule*[1] which is used to identify rules that are valid as law in a legal system. It is on the apex of a legal system: all other rules ultimately owe their validity, actually their *legal* status to RR. On the other side, being the ultimate rule of the system, the RR is not valid at all, for its existence is a matter of social facts. Namely, its existence has two necessary conditions: legal officials must *accept* and *follow* this rule. But what does it actually mean to 'accept and follow' the RR? First, officials *follow* the RR when there exists a common practice of identifying certain rules as valid legal rules. Second, officials *accept* the RR when they demonstrate a normative attitude towards that common practice. As Hart says, they take an 'internal point of view'[2] with regard to what they are practising, when applying the RR as the ultimate criterion of validity, and they criticise deviations from it by using normative terminology (Hart 1994, 55–57, 83–91, 102–3).[3]

So, the important step in the attempt to determine the nature of the RR is to describe the behaviour of legal officials that is regulated by the RR. I suppose that in order to answer the question about the nature and especially the bindingness of the RR, we must look at the structure of the relevant practice. As the simplest examples which illustrate the nature of this practice we can adduce Hume's two rowers having the common goal to propel the boat (Hume 2010 [1739], I. ii. 2), or

1 A social rule can be accepted for various reasons which do not need to be identical for all members of a social group. It is only important that there exists a convergent social behaviour and a widespread acceptance of the rule, from whatever reason, by most members of the group. On the other hand, a social rule is conventional when the general conformity of the members of a group to it is part of the reasons which every member of the group has for accepting the rule (see Hart 1994, 255).

2 The internal point of view with regard to a certain constant pattern of behaviour makes this pattern not only regular but regulated as well (by the accepted rule). The internal point of view makes a difference between two kinds of widespread social practice: social habits and normative social practices.

3 But it should be remembered that in Hart's opinion, acceptance does not mean moral *approval* (Hart 1994, 104–105; see Catania 1997, 149).

Margaret Gilbert's two walkers going for a walk together (Gilbert 1989). Although the practice which is regulated by the RR has some idiosyncrasy,[4] beyond doubt it is a common activity which demands cooperation and interaction[5] of the participants. When involved in such an activity, they keep an eye on their fellows' actions, comply with them and adjust their own actions to actions of the others. For instance, it is clear why a judge follows the very RR which is followed by his peers: he does not have a motive to abandon this RR because it would be otiose to follow some 'rule of recognition' which none of his colleagues does follow. So, other possible reasons for acceptance notwithstanding, there is always one such: the RR is accepted and followed by other members of the group. If they do not accept it, then this rule cannot exist and establish a practice.

Although it is clear what kind of behaviour the RR regulates and how it operates in the officials' practice, it would definitely be a mistake to think of a RR *only* as a sort of coordination convention.[6] As it is well known, coordination conventions are characterised by a so-called 'arbitrariness'. A conventional rule is arbitrary when the reasons for having a convention are more important to the members of the group than the reasons for preferring an alternative course of action (see Marmor 2001, 204). However, several authors (Coleman 2001, 94–95; Adler 2006, 750; Marmor 2001, 201; Shapiro 2002, 387, 426) set forth strong arguments for the opinion that the RR as a conventional rule is not arbitrary in this sense. For instance, Scott Shapiro argues that

> [M]ost Americans would [not] view the United States Constitution as an arbitrary solution to a recurring collective action problem… [M]any would believe that they had a moral obligation to heed a text that had been ratified by the representatives of the people of the United States, regardless of what everyone else did (Shapiro 2002, 387).

This means that usually, preferences for one particular form of the RR (which always solves the coordination problem, as well) is stronger than the preference for uniform conformity to whichever possible RR. After all, the RR can be accepted by officials both out of their desire and need to act in coordination with other officials and out of some substantive convictions. Now we are approaching a serious concern about the RR: is it a so-called duty-imposing rule?

4 Certainly, officials are not rowers or walkers, and their mutual relations are much more complicated.

5 Coordination through interactions – it is the way of operation of any group. Interaction between A and B exists when an act of A prompts an act of B and an act of B prompts an act of A (see Honoré 1987: 59).

6 A coordination convention is a concept introduced by David Lewis's famous book about conventions (Lewis 1969). On coordination conventions see also Postema (1982).

At first sight, it seems that the ultimate RR must be duty-imposing. If it were not then the RR could not fulfil its function, i.e. to bring certainty into a legal order. If legal officials only had an inclination or preference for one criterion of validity over another, if they were not bound by the rule which establishes such a criterion then in that society there would be no reliable 'landmark' to determine what is, what will be and what will not be the law. Consequently, one of the purposes of RR, that it provides a specific legal system with a measure of certainty would vanish!

However, the real issue is this: how is it possible that a fact (a practice, no matter how widespread) gives rise to a duty to abide by that practice? Hart has given one simple answer: the internal point of view towards a certain practice transforms that practice into a duty-imposing rule. Subsequent commentators have shown, however, that actually the internal point of view cannot do the job. As Jules Coleman explains:

> If each of 1.000 individuals separately applies criteria of validity comprised in RR, those separate acts do not impose any duty. For, it is not just that different judges decide individually and separately to apply some RR and thereby creating reason for their own actions that they can unilaterally extinguish. They are rather engaged in a practice that has a certain specific, so to say, normative structure, where, among other things, the fact that some judges apply criteria of legality is a reason for others do so (Coleman 2001, 91–92).

In short, such a practice is capable of creating not *just any kind* of reason for actions, but duties (as a *special kind* of reason for action). While it is a question for ethics and not for legal positivism to elucidate the nature of this conventional duty, it is important to emphasise again the *non-arbitrariness* of the RR. This suggests that the RR has in itself some qualities which in the mind of most officials prevail over the qualities of another possible RR. The RR is generally justified because it solves coordination problems amongst officials. But the answer to the question as to why *that specific RR* is binding, is not coming from this direction. At least for some, if not for most of the officials, the duty-imposing character of the RR can be based upon more substantive reasons than the need to coordinate mutual actions. It can ultimately be grounded in some normative theory. This also means that the *moral duty* to follow a *specific* RR ultimately must come, so to say, from outside the practice itself.[7]

[7] The question of the normativity of the RR is, of course, much more complicated than I sketch it here, and the conclusion which is presented is only provisional. But even in such an undeveloped form, it can serve as a useful 'device' for some further conclusions about the topics of this article.

3 What is a written constitution?[8]

The reason for referring in this paper only to *written* constitutions is that usually there is a strong connection and interdependence between the RR and this form of constitution, which does not exist between the RR and unwritten constitutions.[9] This argument was brought up by Joseph Raz, at least implicitly, when he pointed out that central features of a written constitution 'give rise to theoretical questions that do not apply, at least not to the same degree, to other law' (Raz 1998, 153) and, I would add, to unwritten constitutions either.[10] This is exactly the insight that motivates the analysis of the conceptual connection between the written form of a constitution and the RR in this paper. What are then these 'central features' of a written constitution?

The first and probably most important characteristic of a written constitution is its *normative supremacy*. It means that constitutional provisions prevail over ordinary legislation, i.e. the ordinary laws which conflict with these provisions are invalid. However, as I am going to explain in the next section, this does not mean that all laws derive their legal validity from the constitution.

Second, this supremacy must be, as it were, *institutionally strengthened*. Usually, this is done by entrusting the interpretation of a written constitution to the judiciary, either to specialised constitutional courts or to the regular court system. The essential point here is that there is a court that determines what the constitution means and which laws are invalid due to their unconstitutionality.

Further, at least in aspiration, a written constitution is meant to be of *long duration*. Since every constitution sets the basic structure of the legal and political system of a polity, it must be stable and intended to preserve the continuity of the political structure. Therefore, it is meant to apply well beyond the generation that created it. Owing to this aspiration, amending a constitution is a more difficult task than enacting and changing ordinary legislation. The more difficult it is to change the constitution, the more rigid the constitution is. *Rigidity* is closely tied to durability. If the constitution should be a long lasting document, then it must be relatively

8 Usually, *materiae constitutionis* encompass rules or conventions that determine who enacts laws and how, what are the structure and general principles of government, and nowadays also the general principles which, by establishing human rights, restrain government's overall power (see Marmor 2007, 69).

9 Moreover, the distinction between the RR and the customary, unwritten form of constitution is unclear. These two types of rules sometimes go on parallel lines, as is shown by the example of the English constitutional conventions (see Wade 1960, 74).

10 To note, an 'unwritten' constitution is not always customary or common law. In fact, usually some parts of it are written. In other words, 'unwritten' does not mean literally unwritten. My claim is that even when they are literally written in the same way as other written laws, statutes, by-laws etc., these constitutional laws do not have the features which are central for a written constitution in the sense explained in the main text.

difficult to amend it. Also, *judicial review* and the extent of its authority regarding constitutional interpretation depend considerably on the constitution's rigidity. The more rigid the constitution, the more lasting the power of judges to determine its content.

As we can see, all these features of a written constitution are in some way interconnected. Taken together, they make the concept of a written constitution important for legal practice. But they also make the study of its conceptual connections with the concept of RR interesting and fruitful.

4 The relationship between these two kinds of rules

In this section I compare these two kinds of rules, precisely these two concepts. Thus, my intention is not to offer an empirical analysis or provide information about the content of the RR in some specific legal system and the potential influence of its written constitution on that content. Comparing the two concepts is not an empirical but a conceptual task which consist in uncovering or pointing out interesting conceptual relations.

4.1 Constitution and the RR: identical or just overlapping?

It is sometimes ignored or forgotten that the RR and the written constitution cannot be identical. Conceptually, the RR is a social rule which may provide that one of the criteria of legal validity is conformity with the provisions of the constitution and that constitutional provisions are in some way superior legal norms. But the rule which sets some constitutional rules as superior legal rules cannot itself be a constitutional rule. Moreover, constitutional rules, unlike the RR, are always *valid* rules.[11] As a matter of linguistic convention, we have got used to say that a constitution is valid (or it was valid once). As all other valid laws, constitutional provisions are amended, changed or repealed by the procedure of constitutional revision and not by anyone's practice as is the case with social rules like the RR. And yet, of course, the provisions of the written constitution more often than not, report and describe part of the content of the RR. For instance, we can clearly see this in the US Constitution. Article VII (the so-called ratification clause) is part of the Constitution that it validates.[12] Therefore, it looks as if Article VII validated itself. However, although the Article's text is in the written constitution, its status as the (original) rule of recognition is external to the document and 'rests on its acceptance as the validating rule, not on its validation by having been ratified in accord with its terms'

11 Hierarchically, they are always immediately under the RR itself.

12 'The Ratification of the Conventions of nine States, shall be sufficient for the Establishment of this Constitution between the States so ratifying the Same' (US Constitution, Article VII).

(Alexander and Schauer 2008, 8). So the ratification clause itself is *not* the rule of recognition, rather it *records* or *describes* the rule of recognition.

Furthermore, it is not the case that *every valid legal rule* is valid on the basis of the provisions of constitutions. This is clearly the case in the US (but also elsewhere) where the authority of the decisions of the Supreme Court which it enjoys among other legal officials, is not immediately based on any constitutional provision, but is directly based on the conventional rule of recognition. Accordingly, the provisions of a written constitution which are part of the RR neither validate all the rules of the legal system nor are all valid rules in compliance with these constitutional provisions.

Finally, there may be rules of *constitutional character* which are not valid rules. In fact, they are not valid rules in accordance with any RR. For instance, as already mentioned, the conventions of the English constitution are social rules but still constitutional rules. Bearing this insight in mind, we can more easily explain the concept of the conventions of the English constitution and their alleged or authentic legal nature.

4.2 The RR as a remedy for the indeterminacy of the pre-legal order

Hart argued that the RR 'brings the certainty and knowledge in advance of the requirements of the law' (Hart 1994, 250), and that this is its crucial function.[13] The RR reduces uncertainty about the legal rules of conduct, by providing criteria for recognising these rules and by setting the conditions of their validity.

A written constitution strengthens this important advantage of the RR, i.e. that it brings certainty in social order and human relations. When a legal system gets a written constitution which usually *is*, at least partly, an effective social rule, i.e. a RR, then this 'strengthens' the function of the RR – at least that part of the constitution which, as I just explained, 'records' the content of *the* RR. The mere fact that through the articles of the constitution we can find some elements of RR in written form, surely improves the RR's capacity to diminish uncertainty and indeterminacy of the legal order. For it should not be forgotten that one of the functions of a legal rule as an authoritative verbal formulation is to rescue us from uncertainty engendered by different and often competing conceptions of justice or the good.[14]

13 But, as Shapiro points out, it is not the only function. He argues that 'the rule of recognition and the secondary rules more generally, also account for the law's dexterity, efficiency, normativity, continuity, persistence, supremacy, independence, identity, validity, content and existence' (Shapiro 2009, 1–2).

14 'Authoritative rules settle what to do in the face of that controversy, and by their formality, simplicity, and determinacy avoid the huge moral costs of moral controversy. Instead of being told

A written constitution also has another important function: to set limits to all branches of government. Historically, under the flag of constitutionalism, it gave rise to the movement for limiting the absolute power of rulers. Nowadays, this function of the constitution is slightly transformed but yet very appreciable. Even courts which, as I argued, play a distinct role in the interpretation and 'protection' of constitutionality, are limited in their decision-making. Namely, their discretion is usually to some extent constrained by the written constitution itself. We can see this if we look at one version of the RR in the US, as formulated by Kenneth Himma: 'Supreme Court Justices are obligated to decide the validity of duly enacted norms according to what is, as an objective matter, the morally best interpretation[15] of the [substantive norms] of the Constitution'[16] (Himma 2008, 21). This means that although the Supreme Court has some discretionary power to decide what is and what is not valid law, this discretion is substantially constrained by constitutional provisions.

Himma's formulation of the RR is very telling. It shows that there is a sort of 'synergy' between the RR and the constitution. They do the same job and they do it well in mutual combination.[17] So, the constitution will accomplish its task if and only if the RR generally works and fulfils its function of bringing certainty to the legal order. Without the RR, the constitution alone can do nothing about limiting the discretionary power of officials. As Himma himself concludes, the officials might not view the written constitution as binding at all. That is why in order to understand the role which a written constitution plays in determining what counts as law, we have to observe all the relevant practices of officials (Himma 2009). Larry Alexander and Fred Schauer draw a similar conclusion. After a scrupulous analysis of constitutional controversies in the US and the dependence of law on acceptance, they assert that

---

"do the right thing," the rule subject is told "in circumstance C, do X," where C and X are relatively easy for rule subjects to comprehend and ascertain' (Alexander and Schauer 2008, 18).

15 Himma's formulation draws attention to the importance of the practices of constitutional interpretation as well. It should be noted that, for instance, Kent Greenawalt thinks that if judges are bound to follow some standards of interpretation in deciding what the Constitution means, these standards need to be accorded some place among the ultimate or derivative criteria for determining the law (Greenawalt 1987, 655–656).

16 Note that this does not mean that the Court must reach the objectively correct decision that reflects the morally best interpretation in a given case, or even in any case. The Court must merely ground its decisions in an attempt to determine the morally best interpretation. The Court's discretion is constrained, 'by what the other officials are prepared to accept from the Court in the way of validity decisions' (Carey 2009, 1182).

17 As a matter of fact, the RR alone, i.e. without a written constitution can be a proper 'device' for limiting the power of rulers (I emphasise, *can* be) but for the moment this doesn't matter. What matters is that without the RR, the constitution itself cannot accomplish this task. This point is very clearly put forward by Himma (2008) and Alexander and Schauer (2008).

> once we appreciate the unavoidable and dizzying fragility of a legal system's non-legal foundations, we discover that the security and stability that constitutionalism is alleged to bring depends less on constitutionalism itself than on the pre-constitutional understandings that make constitutionalism possible. Some such understandings will make constitutionalism more stable than others... It will be a useful reminder that constitutionalism of any sort resides not in a constitution, but in the pre-constitutional commitments that make any form of constitutionalism possible (Alexander and Schauer 2008, 25).

4.3 Authority of the constitution and the rule of recognition

In some sense the RR helps the constitution in performing its function. Just as the RR can be seen as a duty imposing and in some sense normative practice, so is the case with the constitution. The written constitution has a possibility to be normative, *i.e. to be the reason for action of officials*, thanks to the normativity of the RR itself. (This latter normativity was briefly explained above, in section 2.) Yet, does the constitution have *legitimate authority* over the officials and broadly over the citizenry? This is a very important and frequently posed political and jurisprudential question. Can the concept of the RR give at least a hint to the answer to that question?

First of all, it should be emphasised that the RR cannot transmit anything to the written constitution that it does not possess itself: a *moral justification* for the legal system of which the RR is the existence condition. The moral reasons for obeying the constitution cannot be derived from the rules that determine what the law is. If there is a moral 'ought' to play the game by the specific RR, so to speak, then this 'ought' cannot be expected to come from the function which the RR serves, because every imaginable RR can do it. The moral obligation to play by a specific RR, or in other words, to follow the valid law must come from other sort of considerations.

However, we need some qualification here. It is important to remember what has been said about the nature of the RR. Conventions like these are not arbitrary conventions and they have their own value, at least for those whose practice reflects the RR. Such conventions not only give the answer, as Marmor says (2001, 215–216) as to 'how' such a practice must proceed. They also go some way towards explaining 'why' *this* practice is more valuable than any other. In an activity in which participants accept the specific RR for the values it offers them, specifically for some kind of substantive normative reason (not simply because others accept and follow it), the RR can be located in the moral and political arena. In other words, it may be cited to support, justify and perhaps even legitimise aspects of the Constitution itself. Even so, this does not mean that each and every RR can be used in this way. In fact, this process of justification is always done with reference to some normative theory which stands in the background of both the RR and the Constitution.

5 Conclusion

The analysis of the connections between the concepts of RR and written constitution has revealed, I hope, some interesting conceptual insights which can further elucidate some already known properties of written constitutional rules. First, although normative supremacy is the characteristic of a written constitution, the constitution *as a whole* is not the supreme rule of a legal system. It is not even necessarily a *supreme valid* rule. Second, one of the crucial and original functions of a written constitution and the function of the rule of recognition are in a sense complementary. However, the latter has a sort of primacy. Finally, the perennial problem of the legitimacy of a constitution cannot be solved by merely referring to the rule of recognition. Rather, the authority of the constitution, even for officials, lies in the normative field where also can lie, at least partly, the reason why the RR is accepted. Here again, the 'destiny' of the RR and the written constitution overlap. This remind us that they are closely related not only as concepts but as phenomena too.

References

Adler, Matthew. 2006. Popular Constitutionalism and the Rule of Recognition: Whose Practices Ground U.S. Law? *Northwestern University Law Review* 100: 719–805.

Alexander, Larry, and Schauer, Frederick. 2008. Rules of Recognition, Constitutional Controversies, and the Dizzying Dependence of Law on Acceptance. *University of San Diego School of Law Research Paper* No. 08–066 [http://ssrn.com/abstract=1235202].

Carey, Stephen. 2009. What is the Rule of Recognition in the United States? *University of Pennsylvania Law Review* 157: 1161–1197.

Catania, Alfonso. 1997. Acceptance in the Thought of H.L.A. Hart. In *Law and Language. The Italian Analytical School*, edited by Anna Pintore and Mario Jori, 147–163. Liverpool: Deborah Charles Publications.

Coleman, Jules. 2001. *The Practice of Principle.* Oxford: Oxford University Press.

Gilbert, Margaret. 1989. *On Social Facts.* London: Routledge & Kegan Paul.

Greenawalt, Kent. 1987. The Rule of Recognition and the Constitution. *Michigan Law Review* 85: 621–671.

Hart, Herbert. 1994. *The Concept of Law.* 2nd edition. Oxford: Clarendon Press.

Himma, Kenneth Einar. 2009. Understanding the Relationship between the U.S. Constitution and the Conventional Rule of Recognition. In *The Rule of Recognition and the United States Constitution*, edited by Matthew D. Adler and

Kenneth Einar Himma. Oxford: Oxford University Press. [http://ssrn.com/abstract=1269748]

Honoré, Tony. 1987. *Making Law Bind.* Oxford: Clarendon Press.

Hume, David. 2010. *A Treatise of Human Nature* [1739]. [http://www.gutenberg.org/files/4705/4705-h/4705-h.htm]

Lewis, David. 1969. *Convention: A Philosophical Study.* Cambridge (MA): Harvard University Press.

Marmor, Andrei. 2001. Legal conventionalism. In *Hart's Postscript: Essays on the Postscript to The Concept of Law*, edited by Jules L. Coleman, 193–217. New York, Oxford: Oxford University Press.

Marmor, Andrei. 2007. Are Constitutions Legitimate? *Canadian Journal of Law and Jurisprudence* 20: 69–94.

Postema, Gerald. 1982. Coordination and Convention at the Foundation of Law. *Journal of Legal Studies* 11: 165–203.

Raz, Joseph. 1998. On the Authority and Interpretation of Constitutions: Some Preliminaries. In *Constitutionalism: Philosophical Foundations*, edited by Larry Alexander, 152–193. Cambridge: Cambridge University Press.

Shapiro, Scott. 2002. Law, Plans, and Practical Reason. *Legal Theory* 8: 387–441.

Shapiro, Scott. 2008. What is the Rule of Recognition (and Does it Exist?) *Yale Law School, Public Law Working Paper* No. 184 [http://ssrn.com/abstract=1304645].

Wade, Emlyn Capel Stewart. 1960. *Constitutional Law.* 6th ed. London: Longmans.

On Hartian Questions of Legal Philosophy

Máté Paksy

Abstract In a broader research project my principal aim is to analyse contemporary French legal philosophy and to highlight its historical origins and its connections to other legal cultures. The framework is based on Hart's 'persistent questions' whereas the content consists of the 'would-be answers' of French legal philosophers. With regard to these Hartian questions, this paper develops the following argument. Although law itself is intrinsically connected to a given political community characterised by its culture and history, legal philosophy recommends an abstract and general approach to law. 'Abstractness' and 'generality' urge the legal philosopher to treat basic legal problems independently of this or that legal system. I shall argue that this 'independence' requires analysing the spirit of the legal system rather than positive law. The pursuit of legal philosophy seems feasible if legal philosophers can elaborate sufficiently 'basic questions' that can be 'transposed' to other legal cultures and if by answering these they can understand the spirit of the other legal system. My claim is that Hart's 'persistent questions' meet these criteria.

Le plupart de mes collègues détestent la philosophie. (Villey 1989, 25)

Since fairly long, lawyers, students and scholars coming from different legal cultures have known Hart almost by heart.[1] Also the perplexities at the beginning of his *The Concept of Law* have become commonplaces: 'How does law differ from and how it is related to orders backed by threats? How does legal obligation differ from, and how is it related to, moral obligation? What are rules and to what extent is law an affair of rules?' (Hart 1961, 13).

In this essay I am going to argue that these questions arising from his 'perplexities' may be considered as 'general problems of legal philosophy'. It would be, without doubt, somewhat far-fetched to say that these are *the* general problems of

1 Author's thanks go to all who made comments on this text, either during the round-table discussion, or afterwards in the course of writing this essay, especially to Péter Cserne and Miklós Könczöl.

legal philosophy. My claim here is more modest and necessarily abstract, which may account for the title. I shall merely plead for the feasibility of legal philosophy, adding that Hart's 'perplexities' can be conceived of as its 'basic' questions. I hope to provide logical arguments while trying to avoid contingent historical and/or sociological explanations. This is necessary since authors often come up with lists of 'basic questions of legal philosophy' without justifying the elements of these lists.[2]

1

Any serious theoretical attempt in the field of social philosophy that seeks to understand the 'point' of any regulation of human behaviour in a given society has to face the following problems. On the one hand, a normative system is intrinsically connected to a given political community with its particular culture and history. On the other hand, social philosophy must be an abstract and general approach to normative systems or else it cannot be called 'philosophy'. No one has seriously questioned that legal philosophy has certain features in common with social (or practical) philosophy.

By virtue of the 'abstractness' and 'generality' of legal philosophy, its basic problems have to be treated independently of the content of a given legal system. 'Independence' requires the scholar to analyse not positive law but the 'spirit' of the legal system. The pursuit of legal philosophy is feasible only if legal philosophers formulate questions that are sufficiently 'basic' and capable of being 'transposed' to other legal cultures, and if by answering these one can understand the 'spirit' of the other legal system as well. 'Spirit' is something less than the 'essence' but more than the 'content' of the law. Usually, it has a political character, and is shaped by contingent factual circumstances and crystallised from the social practice and institutional framework of a given legal system. Nonetheless, 'spirit' is something that needs to be elaborated in a formal and abstract way.

One may state for example that the 'spirit' of French law has to be defined with reference to 'equality' (*égalité*). This is a highly abstract concept which calls for an abstract philosophical explanation. Still, if one really seeks to understand it, one must not forget to take into account the contingent criteria of its application – or, as Rawls or Dworkin would put it, the various conceptions of the concept of 'equality' – throughout French history since the Revolution or even before it.[3] Positive

2 See for example Le Fur (1937).

3 Cf. Hart (1963, vii): 'justice is a concept of complex structure within which we should distinguish a constant formal element and a varying material element. This distinction might be presented in terms used in recent English moral philosophy as one between the constant *definition* of justice and the varying *criteria* for its application [...]' See also my discussion of the Dworkinian theory of justice in a French context (Paksy 2009).

legal rules of the French legal system of a given period contain these criteria of application. One should take these into account but one should also bear in mind that without philosophical explanation they are insufficient to demonstrate the 'spirit' of that system. Obviously, a particular French theory of justice as equality without reference to legal rules says nothing legally relevant about the 'spirit' of French law either.

2

One can formulate many kinds of arguments (sociological, historical, etc.) for the very existence of legal philosophy. Here I take into account only those using (or being compelled by logic to use) philosophical justifications. I would like to show that even an 'empirical' legal theory cannot dispense with philosophy.

Let me give two examples. Reading Kelsen's apologetic essays on the purity of legal science as opposed to the 'impure' philosophy of justice, one can discover without much intellectual effort that the author uses a simplified neo-Kantian framework coupled with an even more oversimplified anti-cognitivist meta-ethics (which are, by the way, inconsistent with one another) (see Kelsen 1960). Now, in the light of subsequent criticism, it is a commonplace today to state that the whole Kelsenian enterprise is nothing but 'normative metaphysics.' In Kelsen's case, the reader finds no serious justification for the choice of the philosophical framework (why 'purity'?) or for its possible meta-ethical corollary (why 'impurity'?).

The second example may be less known to those not familiar with French legal philosophers. According to Léon Duguit, scholarly research in the field of law has to focus on the facts if it is to avoid metaphysics. Like Ross does it later, Duguit argues that normative concepts are meaningless, since they have no facts as their semantic references. Although the original targets of his criticism were Rousseau's notion of the 'general will' and German doctrines of subjective rights (these theories were rejected by Kelsen as well), his anti-metaphysical stance clearly opposed him to the author of the *Pure Theory*. For Duguit, only an individual will can be considered as empirical fact. It is not some imaginary social contract but solidarity that integrates these individuals to a human community. Solidarity is a social fact and it is based on the empirically observable sense of justice. This sense being the same in the case of every individual, one can reformulate it by using general patterns. In order to justify that general principles of justice are empirically well-founded, Duguit simply claims that the authors of the best theories of justice, like Aristotle and Thomas Aquinas, were sociologists. What counts for our purpose, however, is the very fact that Duguit's argument for empiricism is clearly 'philosophical'. It goes without saying that he pays a considerable price with the argument of 'Aristotle and Thomas Aquinas were sociologists' when he tries to avoid metaphysics in this highly superficial way. In fact, it would have been more adequate and less controversial to accept that the notion of solidarity implies normative – not empirical – research in the field of legal theory (or philosophy) (see Duguit 2003 [1901] and 1927).

For our present purpose, it suffices to see that even 'positivist' and/or empirical legal theory implies philosophical argumentation. In this sense, 'philosophical' simply means that the research is not purely empirical. And, on the other hand, if it is feasible, it is not necessarily counter-factual either. I shall not analyse the second option here, for now I am going to focus on Hart who did not use this theoretical 'trump'.[4]

It seems that Hart's famous perplexities have an overlapping area, namely, the problem of normativity. His major contribution to legal philosophy consisted in finding a middle way between empiricism and idealism with regard to the problem of normativity and his theoretical path was justified in a philosophical way. When speaking of 'perplexities', he seems to be using the methodological tools of ordinary language philosophy (see Green 1997, 1688, n. 1). Yet he is not satisfied with a possible conclusion which would state that the task of legal philosophy is to 'clarify' or 'correct' the ordinary language of lawyers (see Bayles 1992, ch. 1).

I am far from saying that this is unproblematic. Kelsen would separate the 'ordinary' discourse of lawyers from the language of legal science, separating 'what the law should be' (lawyers' 'impure' discourse) from 'what the law is' ('pure' discourse on lawyers' 'impure' discourse). This is one reason why Kelsen could not come to the problem of normativity through linguistic analysis. Duguit would say, following Comte, that legal discourse has no meaning, since in this discourse 'meaningless' metaphysical concepts are used. However, if the normative discourse is 'pointless' or 'meaningless', the problem of normativity is necessarily excluded from scholarly research on law. Hart's argument against Scandinavian realists can be used, *mutatis mutandis*, against Duguit as well (see Hart 1955).

Hart's first problem ('How does law differ from and how it is related to orders backed by threats?') can be interpreted to raise the question of whether the 'vagueness' or 'open texture' of ordinary and legal language calls for 'philosophical' arguments or not. Perhaps 'vagueness' implies discretion in the case of the application of law, or 'perplexities' if the concept of law is in question but it is the very problem of normativity which cries for philosophy. The question of how and why rules are to be followed is independent of the question of whether these rules are vague or not. Methodologically the same distinction can be made between the vagueness of a concept of law and the discretionary character of legal adjudication, caused by the open texture of legal rules. Whenever an official is obliged to slot some empirically observable fact into a legal category ('Is the atheist church a church at all?'), (s)he does not use logic but decides and, for the sake of legitimacy, develops a rea-

[4] Counter-factual theories are e.g. those proposed by Rawls or Habermas.

soning in order to justify his or her decision. Legal philosophy should show for what reasons an official is obliged to decide. This is a sufficiently general and abstract question, independent of the cultural or political context of the given legal system. An official is obliged to decide, regardless of whether it is explicitly or – as Article 4 of the French Civil Code stipulates it – implicitly prescribed by law. In the latter case, legal philosophy is able to transform the latent obligation into a manifest one.

Hart's legal philosophy is characterised by himself as 'descriptive sociology' seeking to describe law as a complex system of rules from an internal point of view. Still, one may object that the 'generality' of legal philosophy is highly questionable because of the uniqueness of legal systems. As mentioned earlier, 'uniqueness' here stems from the particularities of national history and political culture. Is legal philosophy an impossible pursuit then? I think this is not the case. But my claim about the spirit of the legal system notwithstanding, I would agree with someone saying that no legal philosopher can elaborate a position independent of his or her own legal culture. Indeed, *The Concept of Law* is an important contribution to one's legal discourse – provided one has a 'common law mind'. Are the 'perplexities' mentioned at the very beginning of Hart's book too 'British' to be considered as 'general problems' of legal philosophy? Let us now have a look at this question.

A purely contextualist theory of legal scholarship would take a sceptical attitude. One could claim that Hart was a product of his time and socio-economic context and that *The Concept of Law* is nothing but a reflection of that. Simplistic as it is, such criticism is sometimes formulated against others, like Kelsen ('The pure theory is in fact impure, because it is Austrian'). In France, many scholars argued that the 'pure theory' may well fit the federal system of Austria, but it would lose its plausibility if someone applied it to describe the legal structure of the French Third Republic. This attitude changed when French scholars faced the problem of constitutional adjudication during the Fifth Republic. In this situation they had to re-read Kelsen in a decontextualised way in order to justify this new and strange institution.

There is an obvious reply to this kind of objection: a purely contextualist reading may backfire, as it cannot justify for what reason it and it alone is not a product of its socio-economic context. And even if there are such reasons, it cannot be shown that these are not products of their socio-cultural contexts...

It seems clear on the other hand that the opposite, i.e. a 'pure' analytical legal theory, is impossible, too. Even in its purest form, it reflects to a certain extent at least the prejudices of its author. Complete 'generality' can never be obtained. Even within the common law family, one can observe different institutional frameworks: 'constitutionalism' or 'Rule of Law' can be justified in various ways in different common law systems with a rigid written constitution (USA), with no written constitution (UK), or with a written but more or less flexible constitution (Canada) (see

Corcoran 2010). In France, a scholar who has been trained in the field of (uncodified) administrative law necessarily has a different attitude towards codification than a civilist who, at least in some respects, regards the two hundred years old Code as the 'holy scriptures' (see Steiner 2010). A moderate Cartesianism is still plausible: the observer should always take a critical self-reflective position in terms of his or her own scholarly enterprise.

3

On the basis of the above arguments, it seems feasible to write an essay with Hart's 'persistent questions' as the theoretical framework, with the content consisting of 'would-be answers' of French legal philosophers.

3.1

One of the 'persistent questions' concerns the difference between the brigand's and the legislator's commands. I do not claim that the following is the only way to 'translate' this question and to put it into a French context. It is nevertheless possible to discuss the problem this way without seriously misinterpreting either Hart or the French legal culture.

For Hart and other English-speaking theorists, the 'gunman' is nothing but a methodological construction (or analytical tool), since these political communities (UK, USA, Canada, New Zealand, etc.) have never really experienced a 'brigand-state' under the rule of 'gunmen', namely, a totalitarian and/or authoritarian régime. The case was, however, different on the Continent. The Vichy government (1940–1942) in France may be seen as a régime governed by a group of 'gunmen'. Even though their *coup d'Etat* was justified by certain of the relevant French constitutional theories, they were nothing else than 'gunmen' as their commands were obviously and – to use Gustav Radbruch's terminology (cf. Radbruch 2006 [1946], 7) – intolerably unjust. One of the questions for a legal philosopher is related to the positivist attitude of the professors of that time: does legal positivism mean that a professor, like Maurice Duverger, is incapable of criticising these commands? According to Danièle Lochak, this attitude was one of the Vichy government's main sources of legitimacy, and she puts the blame on legal positivism in general. Michel Troper, in turn, defends legal positivism and accuses these lawyers of 'anti-positivism' (see Lochak 1989; Troper 1989).

The 'Duverger case' is obviously different from the debate that took place between Hart and Fuller. In English-speaking legal cultures, where constitutionalism has been continuous, professors of law have not been forced to justify their arguments with references to *science*. During the 19th and 20th centuries, in Continental literature the 'science' of law somehow replaced the constitution itself (in Germany) or the authority of the constitution (in France). In Anglo-American legal philosophy the central theoretical question was that of the obedience to unjust laws, while on the Continent professors accused one another of providing additional legitimacy for the tyrannical legislation when writing commentaries on inadmissible statutes. By contrasting these debates, it becomes apparent that the problem of normativity is formulated in different ways.

3.2

In *The Concept of Law*, Hart develops a theory of interpretation according to which interpretative power must be conferred on the official when applying law because of the open texture of normative texts. The very notion of 'open texture' is culturally independent, and for British and French legal cultures at least, it is true that the original idea was to establish a strictly limited judicial authority which gives effect to the legislative intent as formulated in normative texts. In the common law tradition, canons guiding statutory interpretation have been justified from both apexes of the institutional hierarchy. On the one hand, the ideology of parliamentary sovereignty requires that judges give full effect to the legislative will. On the other hand, legislative penetration into the local *ius commune* (the common law) have been considered as an exception and for this reason judges can and should limit this somehow 'illegitimate' legislative activity.

Montesquieu's famous metaphor of the judge who should be the 'mouthpiece of the law' (*la bouche de la loi*) seems to be a common point for both continental and common law cultures. As it is well known, Montesquieu used this metaphor in the chapter of his *Spirit of Laws* where he 'described' the British constitutional system. The original French text uses the term *loi*, which translates as 'statute' (*lex*) rather than 'law' (*ius*), and it was true that judges tried to limit themselves to the 'plain meaning' when performing statutory interpretation. Montesquieu deliberately avoided the term *droit* (law), for it is obvious that the metaphor would not be plausible for case law or equity (cf. *L'Esprit des Lois*, Ch. 11).

However, in Montesquieu's theory it is the legislation that is regarded as the centre of gravity in social regulation. According to him, the best case would be if the legislator were able to remove the citizens' prejudices, and in this way, the judges being at the same time citizens, they might lose their prejudices, too. With this argument in mind, it does not really matter whether the term *loi* or *droit* was used by Montesquieu. Reading the chapter on the British legal system in that way, one is compelled to interpret it as normative political philosophy or utopia hidden in a descriptive sociological text. In this sense, Montesquieu's claim was that in an enlightened society – and the Britons were certainly closer to this than feudal France – the judicial power should not be a power at all. The question of whether it is a plausible claim or not is still discussed by legal philosophers of both legal cultures.

Be this as it may, 'open texture' has not been perceived as a problem in France for long, neither in public nor in private law. As for the interpretation of the written rule of recognition, it was not so much about the meaning of the rule, as about its extension and place within the legal system.

In the Third Republic, the question was whether a bunch of statutes could be considered as the constitution. This was the 'longest Republic' until now and during this period the British and French legal systems were very close to one another as regards their structures and institutional operations. The rule of recognition or the *ultima ratio* of the validity of legal rules was in both cases the principle of parliamentary sovereignty. This institutional framework was termed 'legal state' (*l'Etat légal*) by Carré de Malberg. In this context, his criticism of the pyramidal structure of law as developed by Merkl and Kelsen questioned the 'generality' and 'abstractness' of legal philosophy. Carré de Malberg argued that the *Stufenbaulehre* cannot be right, since in the absence of a constitution the normative structure of the Third Republic does not fit into this theory at all. The only basic (and 'unwritten') norm is the provision to respect the will of the majority. If the pure theory cannot be applied to the French system, then it is a wrong theory (see Carré de Malberg 2007 [1932]). Otto Pfersmann rejects Carré de Malberg's argument and writes that a particular social practice (the one which existed during the Third Republic) cannot invalidate an abstract theoretical construction, like the one elaborated by Merkl and Kelsen (see Pfersmann 1997).

By the time historical circumstances gave birth to substantive constitutional adjudication in the Fifth Republic, in 1971, interpretive attitudes towards the rule of recognition had been well established in French legal mentality and practice. For a legal philosopher, the basic questions of legal interpretation and the justification of constitutional adjudication are still open for discussion. Yet one should be very careful when discussing canons of constitutional interpretation. French, British and American textualist ('originalist') schools, for example, show similarity in terms of their conclusions but they justify these in different ways. In addition, an analysis can show why the Dworkinian theory of 'moral reading' cannot be transplanted into the French legal culture (see Paksy 2009).

3.3

The last Hartian problem is related to the difference between a legal and a moral obligation. According to classical French doctrines, the ultimate reason to obey the law cannot be identified in the field of legal science. If the question is dealt with in a normative way then it is political philosophy that has a 'scholarly' competence, while for a descriptive approach it is sociology. Rather than speaking of a rule of recognition, French scholars tend to use the notion of a 'constituent power' (*pouvoir constituant*). This notion would be the theoretical substitute for the social contract, a 'hypothetical basic norm' in the Kelsenian sense, even though the same concept came into play in political and/or legal discourses during the Enlightenment (see Klein 1996). In the French Republican tradition, arguments from natural rights had never been plausible until the last decades of the 20th century. Instead, such rights were considered as political programmes.

For Hart, the rule of recognition as the ultimate criterion of legal validity is neither valid nor invalid itself: it is merely accepted by the courts (at least). In the French context, the existence or non-existence of some distinguished social fact, like an accomplished revolution, determines whether the commands of the parliamentary majority are obligatory for the officials or not. The interpretation of these social facts is always a political question. The 'Frenchness' of the French legal system can be defined as the adherence in its spirit to the idea of 'equality', understood in its material sense in most cases.

If 'validity' means that a given legal norm makes part of the legal system, French doctrines can be divided into at least three main groups: normative, sociological and moral theories. Carré de Malberg gave a Kelsenian answer to this problem, Duguit followed Durkheim's path, and Maritain elaborated the natural lawyer's perspective. The potential of Hart's legacy is shown in this field, too: his criticism of normativism (pace Kelsen), realism (pace Ross) and the 'old fashioned' way of natural law thinking can help to understand why French doctrines fail to justify the obligatory force of law.

Let us see three French strategies intended to avoid the very problem of normativity. These may be described as strategies of (1) exclusion, (2) transformation and (3) saturation. (1) In order to save 'scientific' purity and objectivity, Carré de Malberg excludes the *ultima ratio* of normativity from the field of scholarly research. In the case of French law, this *ultima ratio* would be the 'constituent power'. For Carré de Malberg this notion is not legal, which means by virtue of the negation that it is political and this is the reason why one cannot discuss it at all. (2) Duguit argues that social sciences like jurisprudence should deal with social facts. The solidarity which creates societal links among individuals and is recognised by the legislator as law is a social fact, too. To explain this notion, he transforms classical theories of justice – like those of Aristotle or Thomas Aquinas – to sociology. It is due to their 'scientific' character, he argues, that a scholar can take these theories into account. Still, one cannot analyse the normativity of law or morality in scientific terms, since facts have no normativity. (3) Among these three scholars, only Maritain takes the problem of the obligatory force of law 'seriously'. Yet his theory, which claims that law is necessarily connected to morality and the unjust law is not a law at all, fails when it tries to explain why the validity of legal norms has to be saturated by morality or what kind of 'overlapping' morality can be built upon different individuals' ideological engagements in a pluralistic society.

4

In this essay I argued that the three Hartian questions formulated at the outset of his *Concept of Law* can be seen as general problems of legal philosophy. It goes without saying that one can formulate these questions or 'perplexities' in different ways, too. My claim was that legal philosophy, i.e. a non-empirical analysis of basic legal problems, is a legitimate enterprise and this position is supported by a philosophical explanation. For the sake of this argument, I used the concept of 'spirit'. I do not claim that other general problems different from Hart's perplexities cannot exist. One can find others like the gaps and other inconsistencies of legal systems, the relation between law and economics, literature or religion, etc. One can discuss whatever seems important but what one cannot do is to neglect the very problem of normativity, at least if one claims that what one does is legal philosophy. Research in the field of French legal scholarship can show certain paths which in most cases try to avoid the problem of normativity. Yet, if someone scrutinises their final axioms, one will discover that these ways are logically impossible or lack the force of rhetorical plausibility.

References

Bayles, Michael. 1992. *Hart's Legal Philosophy. An Examination.* Dordrecht, Boston, London: Kluwer.

Carré de Malberg, Raymond. 2007 [1932]. *Confrontation de la théorie de la formation du droit par degrés avec les idées et les institutions consacrées par le droit positif français relativement à sa formation.* Paris: Dalloz.

Corcoran, Suzanne. 2010. Internalisation and Statutory Interpretation – Looking Wide and Looking Deep. In *The Internalisation of Law. Legislating, Decision-Making, Practice and Education*, edited by Mark Hiscock and William van Caenegem, 38–54. Cheltenham and Northampton, MA: Edward Elgar.

Duguit, Léon. 1927. *Traité de droit constitutionnel I. La règle de droit – le problème de l'Etat.* 3d ed. Paris: Boccard.

Duguit, Léon. 2003 [1901]. *L'État: le droit objectif et la loi positive.* Paris: Dalloz.

Green, Leslie. 1997. The Concept of Law Revisited. *Michigan Law Review* 94: 1687–1717.

Hart, Herbert. 1955. Review of *Inquiries into the Nature of Law and Morals*, by A. Hägerström. *Philosophy* 30: 369–373.

Hart, Herbert. 1961. *The Concept of Law.* Oxford: Clarendon Press.

Hart, Herbert. 1963. Introduction to *The Idea of Justice and the Problem of Argument*, by Chaïm Perelman, vii–xi. London: Routledge & Kegan Paul.

Kelsen, Hans. 1960. The Pure Theory of Law and Analytical Jurisprudence [1941]. In *What is Justice? Justice, Law, and Politics in the Mirror of Science, Collected Essays*, 231–256. Berkeley and Los Angeles: University of California Press.

Klein, Claude. 1996. *Théorie et pratique du pouvoir constituant.* Paris: P.U.F.

Le Fur, Louis. 1937. *Les grands problèmes du droit.* Paris: L.G.D.J.

Lochak, Danièle. 1989. La doctrine sous Vichy ou les mésaventures du positivisme. In *Les usages sociaux du droit*, 252–285. Paris: P.U.F.

Paksy, Máté. 2009. Review of *La vertu souveraine*, by Ronald Dworkin. *Droit et Société* 72: 503–507.

Pfersmann, Otto. 1997. Carré de Malberg et la 'hierarchie des normes'. *Revue française de droit constitutionnel* 31: 481–509.

Radbruch, Gustav. 2006. Statutory Lawlessness and Supra-Statutory Law [1946]. *Oxford Journal of Legal Studies* 26: 1–11.

Steiner, Eva. 2010. *French Law. A Comparative Approach.* Oxford: Oxford University Press.

Troper, Michel. 1989. La doctrine et le positivisme (à propos d'un article de Danièle Lochak). In *Les usages sociaux du droit*, 286–292. Paris: P.U.F.

Villey, Michel. 1989. Le droit dans les choses. In *Controverses autour de l'ontologie du droit*, edited by Paul Amselek and Christophe Grzegorczyk, 11–26. Paris: P.U.F.

Cultural Comparative Law?

Balázs Fekete

Abstract The main aim of this paper is to discuss some recent developments in comparative law. Many scholars – including Pierre Legrand, David Nelken and Csaba Varga – declared that comparative law is in need of a 'cultural turn.' They advocate a wide application of the concept of culture in comparative legal studies instead of relying on the classical legacy of functionalism and the notion of 'legal families' coined by Zweigert/Kötz and David. The paper presents cultural comparatism by examining Legrand's theses and formulates some critical remarks. In conclusion, it is argued that the premises of cultural comparatism can be fruitfully applied in comparative law but this should be done with a modest and critical attitude since some points of culturalism imply unrealistic assumptions. The final claim of the paper is that a potential field of application may be the research of post-Socialist legal *mentalité* in Central Europe.

1 'Cultural revolution' in comparative law?

The focus of this paper is on a full-fledged methodological question: how to compare legal systems. Obviously, this question is very broad in itself; therefore, it will be discussed from the aspect of a recent development in comparative law. Recent trends in comparative legal studies suggest that the basic tenets of comparative law – which were widely applied and shared in the last fifty years[1] – have undergone a decisive transformation. This process may be termed as the 'cultural turn' or 'cultural revolution' in modern comparative law theory (cf. Whitman 2003, 312–313).

1 This 'classical' approach in modern comparative law can be related to the widely known handbooks of Konrad Zweigert/Hein Kötz and René David. Both approaches, even though they differ on many points, share the same premises. First, they consider the taxonomy of legal systems of the world as the primary aim of comparative law. Second, they accept the starting points of the so-called functionalist approach in their methodology (see Zweigert and Kötz 1998; David 1964).

This 'revolutionary'[2] process has started in the nineties, and one can find three scholars who played a prominent role in the application of cultural premises in comparative legal studies. They were Pierre Legrand, David Nelken and Csaba Varga. Legrand was appointed in Tilburg as a professor of comparative legal cultures in 1996; Nelken as professor of sociology of law taught classes entitled 'comparative legal cultures'; and Varga tried to integrate the so-called cultural approach into his legal theory curriculum.[3]

The titles of their papers may indicate that a process of renewal has started in the theory of comparative law.[4] The question marks they use are also very telling, since they express the openness of this debate as well as its unfinished nature. Throughout the debate, various authors made serious efforts to restructure the bases of comparative law from a theoretical point of view and they also declared that the concept of legal culture must play an outstanding role in this.

2 Some antecedents of the cultural approach

Before going into details, it has to be mentioned that this wave of the cultural approach was obviously inspired by certain theoretical achievements of the eighties. First of all, one should mention the oeuvre of Lawrence Friedman who devoted several decades of his professional life to the research of legal culture, mainly in the context of the US. He laid down such basic tenets as for instance that legal culture consists of different attitudes towards the law; that legal thinking is necessarily bound to its culture, and legal culture determines the limits within which legal thought can change; or that there is a differentiation between 'internal' and 'external' legal culture. The internal legal culture is the culture of legal professionals, while external legal culture consists of attitudes to law shared by those outside of the official sphere of law (see Cotterrell 2006, 83–86). So, many statements of today's cultural comparatists can be traced back, implicitly or explicitly, to the concepts of Friedman.

2 The extent to which this 'cultural turn' can be regarded as revolutionary is doubtful indeed. However, if one takes into account Thomas Kuhn's thesis about the development of science, it is not too difficult to interpret this proliferation of cultural elements as the sign of some anomalies forecasting a scientific revolution, i.e., an imminent paradigm shift (cf. Kuhn 1996).

3 Obviously, scholars other than Legrand, Nelken and Varga also widely used the concept of legal culture. However, these experiments were rather fragmented and also relatively incoherent. The main difference between the three above mentioned authors and others is the fact that Legrand, Nelken and Varga developed their approach coherently and consistently – they even reflected on each other to a certain extent – in a series of publications.

4 As for instance: Legrand: *How to compare now?*; *Comparative legal studies and commitment to theory.* Nelken: *Disclosing/invoking legal culture: an introduction*; *Using the concept of legal culture.* Varga: *Legal traditions? In search for families and cultures of law*; or *Comparative legal cultures?* (Legrand 1995; Nelken 1995 and 2004; Varga 2005 and 2007).

Another very important source of inspiration was the work of Günther Frankenberg. In the mid-eighties, Frankenberg published one of the first post-modern, that is, diversity- and culture-oriented critiques of modern comparative law characterised by functionalism and looking for legal families. In his fundamental study he laid down the main lines of a plausible post-modern critique by focusing mostly on the methodological premises of functionalism. In doing so, he strongly criticised what he called the 'false neutrality' of legal comparison implied in functionalism and pointed out convincingly that it is impossible to find an external point of view from which different legal rules could be compared neutrally. He also emphasised that it is insufficient to focus on legal rules in comparative research, since the social context of legal institutions, the culture as it were, also has to be integrated in the inquiry (see Frankenberg 1985).

Reading the articles of Legrand, Nelken and Varga carefully, it is not impossible to find almost all these points and theses in their original or partially restructured forms. Thus, the 'cultural comparatism' of the nineties has its roots, besides other factors, in the legal sociological approach of studying law in its cultural context as well as in the critical attitude of post-modernist legal theory.

3 Legrand's arguments

Because an in-depth and comprehensive discussion of the above scholars' articles is obviously impossible in such a brief contribution, the focus of this paper must necessarily be sharpened. Therefore, as an illustration, it will briefly discuss Legrand's ideas concerning the necessary cultural shift in comparative law.

Legrand's starting point here is his dissatisfaction with the recent state of affairs in legal comparison. Comparative law is a really fashionable subject, Legrand asserts, but 'self-styled comparatists' normally hardly do anything else than simply putting legal rules from different legislations next to one another and trying to find similarities and differences (Legrand 1996a, 234). As Legrand aptly describes this phenomenon, 'they do not compare, they contrast' (ibid.). Therefore they are unaware of even the most fundamental questions of legal comparison.

In order to change this unfavourable situation, correction has to come and start from the very basics, that is to say from the theoretical background. First of all, in doing comparison one must be committed to theory. It means that in order to find relevant insights, elementary questions focusing on the basic problems of law have to be discussed. For instance: where does law begin and where does it end in a given society? Where are the boundaries of law among the many normative phenomena? These questions – mainly related to the ontology of law – can lead us towards an empathic and in-depth understanding of legal cultures and this is the point where, in the eyes of Legrand, real comparative work can start (ibid., 235).

Secondly, comparatists also have to be committed to interdisciplinarity. They should do this because, as Legrand argues, 'law does not exist in a vacuum,' in the middle of nowhere. Law is obviously part of a much broader context, and it can only be properly understood through interdisciplinary research. Legrand emphasises the importance of anthropology, linguistics and cognitive psychology (ibid., 238), while other authors add such traditional fields of study as economics, sociology, political science and history,[5] since law can be found at the meeting points of these social phenomena.

So, comparative legal studies must turn towards the study of the foundations of legal cultures, that is, a plausible concept of law as well as the interdisciplinary dimensions of law in a given legal culture. That is why Legrand uses the example of a French painting – one by Jacques-Louis David – which depicts Napoleon drafting the Code civil by candlelight (see Legrand 1996a, 235). In Legrand's eyes this painting properly illustrates 'the historically-conditioned relationship between legislative and judicial powers in France.' Thus, for this approach French law is a cultural phenomenon having different cultural (interdisciplinary) layers besides the traditional view that it is the binding law of France (ibid., 236).

In conclusion, Legrand argues that comparative law should turn towards the different legal *mentalités* (cognitive orders) of legal systems, as the concept of *mentalité* is able to grasp and describe law as a cultural phenomenon (Legrand 1996a, 238; see Legrand 1996b, 60–64). Therefore, it is a real mistake to speak of 'legal families' in comparative law. Instead of the odd taxonomy of legal families, various legal *mentalités* must be studied as for instance the civil law mentality, the common law mentality or even the Far Eastern mentality.

As an example of the capacity of this cultural approach, one can mention Legrand's discussion of the convergence between civil law and common law. There is a general opinion in Europe shared by many leading comparatists that a new legal order has been emerging since the establishment of the European Community of Coal and Steel, the *corpus iuris Europaeum* or *ius Europaeum*. And, within the framework of this 'European law,' the gradual convergence of civil and common law has also begun. This is the so-called 'convergence thesis,' elaborated and defended by scholars like Patrick Glenn or Basil Markesinis (see Legrand 1996b, 54–56). Both of them are leading scholars of today's comparative law.

However, as Legrand points out, if we approach the convergence thesis from a cultural point of view, fundamentally different conclusions can be reached. The

5 Varga argues that 'the part [legal culture] always remaining the component of a broader whole, legal culture too is inevitably embedded in the general social culture, being formed in interaction with it.' This statement implies that legal culture can only be rightly understood if one studies the economic, sociological, political and historical aspects of a given general culture (see Varga 2005, 183, and cf. Legrand 1996, 236).

common law *mentalité* is, according to Legrand, 'irreducibly' different from the civil law *mentalité*, and therefore it is impossible to speak of the convergence of these two *mentalités* (ibid., 81). This divergence is due to many factors, all of which are analyzed by Legrand in detail.[6] The main points are the following:

(i) The nature of legal reasoning. Common law thinking is essentially inductive and empirical, while Continental law always prefers a deductive and theoretical approach. In Max Weber's terms, in the common law world law is perceived 'as craft,' whereas on the Continent it is mostly regarded 'as science' (ibid., 64–65).

(ii) The role of systematisation. The legal thinking of common law has little interest in theorising because it mostly finds this way of thinking useless. Modern civil law, in turn, is based on a rational systematisation of legal concepts, as it is perfectly expressed in several modern codes (ibid., 65–67).

(iii) The character of rules. In strict terms, one can find no abstract formulation of legal rules in common law, since law can only be inferred from cases, mostly on the basis of their *ratio decidendi*. In contrast, a civil lawyer always regards law as a set of precise rules having generalised meanings (ibid., 67–68).

(iv) The role of facts. Common law thinking is strongly related to the particularity of cases, that is, this tradition is convinced that legal knowledge emerges fundamentally from facts (*ex facto ius oritur*). Civil law mentality, however, is based on a different attitude, since it has made serious efforts to eliminate the factual dimensions of legal rules in order to create handy abstract concepts (*ex regula ius oritur*) (ibid., 68–70).

(v) The meaning of rights. The formula 'no writ – no right' perfectly expresses that in common law rights are related to actions before courts. 'Rights' have no abstract meaning in this sense, as legal actions are based on a factual and concrete wrong rather than an abstract and independent right. Civil law follows an essentially different line of thinking, it acknowledges the 'existence' of subjective rights independent of actions or other external factors (ibid., 70–71).

(vi) The presence of the past. Lastly, one should not forget that common law has a strong historical perspective, as it dates back its origin to immemorial times. This historical attitude has formed the customary and communitarian dimensions of English law. On the contrary, Continental law is not historical in this sense, because it purports to organise the relationships of the present and close future independently of the influence and force of the past (ibid., 71–74).

6 Other authors advocating a new model for comparative law identified partially similar elements of the legal culture. For instance, in the eyes of van Hoecke and Warrington, a legal culture is based on the following points: (i) a concept of law; (ii) a theory of legal sources; (iii) a methodology of law; (iv) a theory of argumentation; (v) a theory of legitimation of law; and (vi) a basic ideology (see van Hoecke and Warrington 1998, 514–515).

The main conclusion of Legrand is very simple: due to these fundamental differences, it is simply unrealistic to speak of convergence between common law and civil law at the level of *mentalités*. Moreover, this hypothetical convergence would also mean the reduction of the plurality of European legal thinking, which would be obviously undesirable since these divergent *mentalités* mean different approaches to reality. So, convergence could make us definitely poorer in this sense (ibid., 80–81).

4 Critical remarks

Legrand's theses (and those of the other authors mentioned) seem to be very convincing, and they adequately highlight many problems inherent in modern comparative law. Yet they can also be criticised, as every scientific statement can (and should) be. In this sense, three critical claims can be made here.

The first argument is very simple. Is the integration of cultural dimensions of law into the theoretical background of comparative law really a new enterprise? An inquiry based on the history of ideas can show that culture has already been used as a starting point of legal research for centuries. The concept of culture or the cultural approach has its roots in 18th century Romanticism (see Whitman 2003, 315). Western Romanticism was a reaction to the pressure of Enlightenment trying to rationalise and systematise the whole world in the name of Human Reason. In order to escape the generalist tendencies of the Enlightenment, Romantic authors advocated a return to individuality, nature, emotions, people and nation (see Szerb 2000, 402). Among others, the birth of Romanticism also meant the revival of history in scientific thinking, as opposed to the ahistorical attitude of the philosophy of Enlightenment.

This transformation of general thinking had a certain influence in the field of legal thinking, too. For instance, Friedrich Carl von Savigny already relied widely on the concept of *Volksgeist* (hard to translate perfectly: maybe the spirit of a nation) in his oeuvre. By stressing the role of *Volksgeist* in the formation of law, he emphasised the decisive role of special cultural factors such as history or public thinking in legal development (see Whitman 2003, 316). Furthermore, well-known figures of comparative legal studies in the early 20th century – the German Joseph Kohler and the Russian-English Sir Paul Vinogradoff – also explicitly referred to the role of culture in law. Kohler pointed out the importance of the so-called legal postulates which emanate from the conditions of a given culture and argued that these postulates determine the content of the legal rules (see Pound 1912, Elison 1961).[7] Vinogradoff asserted that all aspects of law can only be known by the so-called synthetic method

7 It may be worthwhile recognising that this is exactly the same statement about the relationship of law and culture as the point made by Friedman.

which regards law as an historical phenomenon. He argued that research into historical, sociological and economic factors is inevitable if one wants to know legal development in its entirety (Vinogradoff 2000). Although Kohler died in 1918 and Vinogradoff in 1920, in the light of recent cultural developments in comparative law, these authors can be regarded as very modern ones, or to be a bit provocative, slightly more modern than for instance Konrad Zweigert or Hein Kötz were in their time. In other words, modern cultural comparatism is certainly not an absolute novelty, it has its ancestors in Romanticism and in early 20th century legal thinking.

The second comment is related to the concept of legal culture. What is legal culture? Can we define it on a really scientific level? Roger Cotterrell argues that this concept has many deficiencies and therefore its scientific explanatory value or potential is strongly questionable. By analysing Friedman's oeuvre, Cotterrell highlights many ambiguities within the concept of legal culture. One weak point is that we can speak of levels of legal cultures. For instance, according to Friedman in the US the poor and the rich, the black and the white all have their own legal culture. So, it is a pluralistic concept (Cotterrell 2006, 84). The extension of the term 'legal culture' is also problematic. Does it only contain attitudes towards law or the main features of legal thinking are also relevant? (Ibid., 83 and 85) Cotterell argues that it is extremely hard to describe a legal culture in a genuinely scientific way. Therefore, the term has more of an artistic than a real scientific function, since it allows the researcher to formulate the general tendencies of law in a given society (ibid., 87). Thus, in order to avoid this vagueness a very strict and serious definition is needed, if one wants to use the concept of legal culture in a scientific way.[8]

The last reflection is related to the interdisciplinarity embedded in the idea of cultural research. It can be regarded as the key issue, since the integration of interdisciplinary elements into the comparison of legal systems makes this cultural approach qualitatively different from modern comparative law relying mainly on premises stemming from a positivist, so to say mostly rule- and institution-oriented approach. Interdisciplinarity also sounds very well, since it is a quite fashionable topic in contemporary scientific discussions. However, it has its own problems, too, since a real interdisciplinary approach is very much, perhaps even excessively demanding. Imagine that, in order to meet the criteria of the aforementioned interdisciplinarity, a lawyer has to become an expert in anthropology, linguistics and cognitive psychology, moreover he or she should be a real political scientist, economist

8 It must also be mentioned that when the original version of Cotterrell's criticism was published in 1997, Friedmann answered to some of these critical remarks in the same volume. He argued that the concept of legal culture is 'no worse' than other concepts of social science. Then, he also pointed out that it contains many elements that can be exactly measured, so it can be applied in a scientific way (see Nelken 2004, 8).

and historian. This seems to be simply unrealistic, and one person, even if extremely talented and intelligent, may never achieve that (cf. Palmer 2004, 6). So, cultural comparison should be a bit more modest. This means that comparatists should be aware of the non-legal, so to say cultural dimensions of their work and they should try to integrate as much of these elements as they responsibly can. Here the problem of dilettantism is a real danger, since by being very or extremely interdisciplinary, the researchers risk losing the real scientific value of their work.

5 Concluding points

Firstly, the community of comparatists should recognise that something has been changing in the theory of comparative law for at least twenty years. This transformation means an obvious departure from the classical premises of Zweigert/Kötz and David, so it seriously affects all legal research having comparative aspects. In the focus of these changes one can find the concept of legal culture, and it is also more than obvious that cultural comparatism offers an alternative which consists of valuable ideas and elements. However, this cultural approach also has its internal problems and we should be aware of them. So, the theses of culturalism cannot be integrated into comparative law without reflection, without criticism.[9]

Secondly, there is a problem which might be interesting for the researchers of Central Europe. To put it bluntly: can we speak of a so-called post-socialist legal *mentalité*? Or in other words, are our legal systems completely similar to the civil law systems? Obviously, at the level of legal rules it is very hard to find qualitatively new and different features, mostly because from the early nineties, the aim of EU accession considerably influenced these countries to voluntarily introduce many Western institutions and solutions. Human rights, the rule of law, constitutional review, consumer protection, ombudsman and environmental law: it is unnecessary to continue this line symbolising the process of reception that took place in the region during the last twenty years. However, cultural comparatism teaches us that the similarity of rules can only have a limited relevance in the understanding of a legal system, since one must also discover the deep structures of the given system or systems in comparison.

Without explaining them in detail some related points must be highlighted here. These may suggest that this question needs a much more detailed and deeper analysis. It is well known that the region of Central Europe[10] has a unique history charac-

9 This criticism has already begun, since – for instance – Jaakko Husa comprehensively discussed the applicability of such classical concepts as legal family and functionalism and proved that with some modifications they can be useful for further research (see Husa 2003 and 2004).

10 Jenő Szűcs, a leading Hungarian historian argued that in Europe between the regions of the West (*Mundus Occidentalis*) and of the East (*Mundus Orientalis*) there is another one with unique fea-

terised by a constant drift between the Western and Eastern poles of Europe. Could this mean that behind the layer of legal rules one can find attitudes and motives which distinguish this region from general Western patterns?

(i) Below or, perhaps, beyond the official culture of law mostly comprised of the attitudes of legal professionals one can also recognise certain 'hidden cultures'. These 'hidden cultures' cannot be recognised at first sight but due to their norm-generating nature they have a serious influence on the everyday functioning of law. For instance, one could talk about a 'culture of legal scepticism' in the region. It has its roots in the Socialist era when law clearly served political goals. As a response, citizens developed an attitude towards the law characterised by a deep institutional scepticism (see Los 1996, 475). This scepticism could really hinder or even impede the traditional functioning of Western style legal institutions and mechanisms.

Besides scepticism, another element of this 'hidden culture' may be the overemphasised welfare expectations. Citizens of the region clearly count on social security benefits in their everyday life. These social justice expectations not only create a strong pressure on the legislature, they may also lead to a considerable dependence on the state. Therefore, it is highly questionable whether autonomy, one of the underlying ideas of Western law, could properly work in such a context. More specifically, these expectations can also lead to an unusually broad interpretation of social rights (see Los 1996, 476; Sajó 2004, 208–212).

(ii) Another unique feature of post-Socialist *legal mentalité* can be the existence of a special kind of legal pluralism. In Western legal systems state norms generally have a prominent place among normative phenomena. This is clearly expressed in the comprehensive scope of constitutionalism, as well as in the superiority of such values as rationalism, certainty, universalism and order. In post-Socialist legal systems, however, one can find a fairly different setting. Here, contrary to the Western model, besides the central position of state law other competing normative systems can be recognised.

This post-Socialist legal pluralism has both an internal and an external dimension. Internal pluralism means that private orders try to influence state law to reflect their system of rules. Basically, some particular normative orders become, due to successful lobbying strategies, generally valid legal rules since the legislator enacts

tures, the region of Central Europe. The process of differentiation has already started from the early Medieval Age. The outlines of Western style societies got solid contour in this region during this period; for instance, the formation of nobility and bourgeoisie as well as the unification of the different positions of villeinage were finished at the end of the 14th century. However, these Western patterns were also deformed to a certain extent. Some of them remained unambiguously incomplete (e.g. the development of cities), others were even slightly overdeveloped (e.g. the nobility) compared to the general Western tendencies. So, from a historico-social aspect this region has always been a special alloy of Western and Eastern models and influences. This could also help in understanding the unique features of East-Central European legal development (see Szűcs 1996).

them as general state norms. From an external point of view, legal pluralism in transition societies implies that there are existing normative orders besides the sphere of state law. These normative orders are related to traditional communities which were able to preserve their own customs during even the socialist era. The best example for this is the so-called gypsy legal system being independent of state law and having its special processes and rules (see Sajó 2003, 14–20; Loss 2005).

(iii) As a last example, the comprehensive presence of ethno-nationalism in the region should be mentioned. In the nineties ethno-nationalism swiftly revived in all East-Central European countries as a natural reaction to the internationalist and imperialistic policies of the Soviet bloc. Under the influence of revival, many special – unusual in Western terms – legal rules have been enacted. For instance, in the Baltic countries language and citizenship laws openly discriminating against Russian inhabitants were enacted (see Roth 1996, 276–278); in the constitutions, including the preambles, one can easily find articles related to the principles of national self-determination and sovereignty (see ibid., 278–281; Sajó 2004, 197–198); furthermore, a system of what could be called 'status laws' for the preferential treatment and protection of co-national minorities living outside of a given country has also been emerging in the last decade (see Halász, Majtényi and Vizi 2004, 333–340). So, ethno-nationalism has been an unambiguous driving force in the formation of these legal systems following the collapse of the Soviet bloc.

Obviously, these and other questions cannot be answered easily and fast. But cultural comparatism, and particularly the concept of legal *mentalité*, if one follows a modest approach, is certainly a great help to deal with those special features of our region which exist under the layer of legal rules. Long-lasting debates are needed, and this forum may be a perfect starting point.

References

Cotterrell, Roger. 2006. The Concept of Legal Culture. In *Law, Culture and Society: Legal Ideas in the Mirror of Social Theory*, 81–96. Burlingon: Ashgate.

David, René. 1964. *Les grands systèmes de droit contemporains*. Paris: Dalloz.

Elison, Larry M. 1961. Kohler's Philosophy of Law. *Journal of Public Law* 10: 409–425.

Frankenberg, Günther. 1985. Critical Comparisons: Re-thinking Comparative Law. *Harvard International Law Journal* 26: 411–456.

Halász, Iván, Majtényi, Balázs, and Vizi, Balázs. 2004. A New Regime of Minority Protection? Preferential Treatment of Kin-Minorities under National and International Law. In *The Hungarian Status Law: Nation Building and/or Mi-*

nority Protection, edited by Zoltán Kántor et al., 328–349. Sapporo: Slavic Research Center, Hokkaido University.

Hoecke, Mark van, and Warrington, Mark. 1998. Legal Cultures, Legal Paradigms and Legal Doctrine: Towards a New Model for Comparative Law. *International and Comparative Law Quarterly* 47: 495–536.

Husa, Jaakko. 2003. Farewell to Functionalism or Methodological Tolerance? *Rabels Zeitschrift für ausländisches und internationales Privatrecht* 67: 419–447.

Husa, Jaakko. 2004. Classification of Legal Families Today: Is It Time for a Memorial Hymn? *Revue Internationale de Droit Comparé* 56: 11–38.

Kuhn, Thomas S. 1996. *The Structure of Scientific Revolutions.* Chicago: The University of Chicago Press.

Legrand, Pierre. 1995. Comparative Legal Studies and Commitment to Theory. *The Modern Law Review* 58: 262–273.

Legrand, Pierre. 1996a. How to Compare Now? *Legal Studies* 16: 232–242.

Legrand, Pierre. 1996b. European Legal Systems are not Converging. *The International and Comparative Law Quaterly* 45: 52–81.

Los, Maria. 1996. Legitimation, State, and Law in the Central European Return to Democracy. In *European Legal Cultures*, edited by Volkmar Gessner, Armin Hoeland and Csaba Varga, 473–481. Aldershot et al.: Dartmouth.

Loss, Sándor. 2005. *Romani Kris* a dél-békési oláhcigányoknál: Elmélet és gyakorlat. [Romani Kris among the Vlach-Gypsies of South-Bekes]. In *Amabilissimus. A legszeretetreméltóbbak egyike. Loss Sándor emlékköny* [*Amabilissimus. One of the Most Loved Persons. A Book Dedicated to the Memory of Sándor Loss*], edited by József Szabadfalvi, 119–134. Debrecen: DE ÁJK.

Nelken, David. 1995. Disclosing/Invoking Legal Culture: An Introduction. *Social and Legal Studies* 4: 435–452.

Nelken, David. 2004. Using the Concept of Legal Culture. *Australian Journal of Legal Philosophy* 29: 1–26.

Palmer, Vernon Valentin. 2004. From Lerotholi to Lando: Some Examples of Comparative Law Methodology. *Global Jurist Frontiers* 4 [http://www.bepress.com/gj/frontiers/vol4/iss2/art1].

Pound, Roscoe. 1912. Scope and Purpose of Sociological Jurisprudence, Part III. *Harvard Law Review* 25: 489–516.

Roth, Stephen J. 1996. The Effect of Ethno-Nationalism on Citizens' Rights in the Former Communist Countries. In *Western Rights? Post-Communist Application*, edited by András Sajó, 273–290. The Hague, London, Boston: Kluwer Law International.

Sajó, András. 2003. Pluralism in Post-communist Law. *Acta Juridica Hungarica* 44: 1–20.

Sajó, András. 2004. The Impacts of EU Accession on Post-communist Constitutionalism. *Acta Juridica Hungarica* 45: 193–212.

Szerb, Antal. 2000. *A világirodalom története* [*History of World Literature*] [1941]. Budapest: Magvető.

Szűcs, Jenő. 1996. The Three Historical Regions of Europe. In *European Legal Cultures* edited by Volkmar Gessner, Armin Hoeland, and Csaba Varga, 14–48. Aldershot et al.: Dartmouth.

Varga, Csaba. 2005. Legal Traditions? In Search for Families and Cultures of Law. *Acta Juridica Hungarica* 46: 177–197.

Varga, Csaba. 2007. Comparative Legal Cultures. Renewal by Transforming into a Genuine Discipline. *Acta Juridica Hungarica* 48: 95–113.

Vinogradoff, Sir Paul. 2000. Methods of Jurisprudence. In *Custom and Right*, 1–20. Union, NJ: The Lawbook Exchange.

Whitman, James Q. 2003. The Neo-Romantic Turn. In *Comparative Legal Studies: Traditions and Transitions*, edited by Pierre Legrand and Roderick Munday, 312–344. Cambridge: Cambridge University Press.

Zweigert, Konrad, and Kötz, Hein. 1998. *An Introduction to Comparative Law*. Oxford: Clarendon Press.

Part II
New Challenges in Ethics and Moral Philosophy

Paternalism and the Virtue of Care

Antal Szerletics

Abstract My paper aims to outline a new and fairly unconventional approach to paternalism based on the ethics of care and virtue ethics. I argue that the main underlying virtue behind paternalistic practices (e.g. parenting, nursing, medical practices) is the virtue of care. If we reinterpret autonomy in a way that focuses on the importance of human relations instead of 'disengaged' rationality, autonomy will develop through the development of caring relations, including paternalism. Moreover, insofar as paternalistic practices are manifestations of the virtue of care, they contribute to the development of human character. In consequence, hard paternalism does not necessarily oppose (relational) autonomy and it might have a more favourable reception in this framework.

1 Introduction

The topic of my paper is the justification of paternalism, examined from the perspective of virtue ethics and the ethics of care. According to the classical definition of Gerald Dworkin, paternalism is '[...] the interference with a person's liberty of action justified by reasons referring exclusively to the welfare, good, happiness, needs, interests or values of the person being coerced' (Dworkin 1972, 62). Typical examples of legal paternalism are the prohibition of euthanasia, the criminalisation of drug use or the obligation to wear seatbelts or crash helmets during driving. It is possible to examine the justifiability of paternalism from three perspectives, corresponding to the three main trends in normative ethics: deontology, consequentialism and virtue ethics.

Deontological theories place personal autonomy in the centre of paternalism and focus on the voluntariness of self-harming decisions. The utilitarian approach determines justifiability by aggregating the positive and negative consequences of paternalistic interventions. Virtue ethics, to put it very simply, requires the paternalistic actor to act out of moral character, as virtuous people would do. Thus, the justifiability of paternalism depends on the question whether paternalism exhibits some form of a virtuous practice or not.

In this paper, I contend that the underlying virtue behind paternalism is the virtue of care. My focus is on virtue ethics which I try to amalgamate with the ethics of care. These ethical theories shift the emphasis from the subject of paternalism to the paternalistic actor and provide a new perspective for approaching paternalism. They clearly do not solve all problems related to paternalism. However, they direct our attention to different issues. Instead of relying on one overarching principle (i.e. the harm principle), they are more case- and context-sensitive.

2 Paternalism and virtue

The central question of virtue ethics is how to identify the virtues of a given society. Aristotle starts from a teleological viewpoint: '[...] every craft and every line of inquiry, and likewise every action and decision, seems to seek some good; that is why some people were right to describe the good as what everything seeks' (Aristotle 1999, 1). Good ends differ in each case: health is the end of medicine, victory of generalship, and wealth of household management. However, there is a universal *telos* (which is 'complete without qualification') that human beings strive for.[1] Aristotle calls this *eudaimonia*, which can be translated as blessedness, happiness or prosperity. *Eudaimonia* is the activity of the soul in accordance with virtue. It is achieved by exercising virtues and by developing a virtuous character. Virtues are human capacities that help us realising the internal goods of practices (health, victory, wealth, etc.) and also *eudaimonia*.

Aristotle differentiates moral and intellectual virtues. While intellectual virtues can be directly taught and learned, virtues of character develop through experience. The virtue of courage, for example, cannot be learned from books, but only through acting courageously. Virtues are embedded in practices and they develop by exercising practices. Virtues of character are always located between the extremes of vices. Courage is a virtuous trait that is midway between the vice of rashness and the vice of cowardice (see Shafer-Landau 2007, 664). But is it not a *petitio principii* to claim that becoming virtuous requires the exercise of virtue? Without knowing the virtue, we would hardly ever start exercising a practice, which is the only way to know the virtue. The answer lies in the 'compulsion' of external circumstances. Someone, for example, may start to practice a virtue because of his upbringing or education. Virtue ethics, thus, receives a perfectionist twist here.

[1] Aristotle gives an account of the good which is at once particular and universal. This tension explains the problem between moral relativism and the existence of objective virtues that modern virtue ethicists have to deal with (see MacIntyre 1981, 148; Nussbaum 2007).

To understand the nature of this external compulsion, I refer to an example suggested by Alasdair MacIntyre. When Aristotle speaks of excellence, he generally refers to some type of human practice: flute-playing, farming, physics, politics and so on. By exercising a practice, there are two kinds of good somebody can achieve. Consider the case of a child whom I wish to teach to play chess (see MacIntyre 1981, 188). Assume that the child has no particular desire to learn the game. Therefore, I offer him candies each time he plays chess with me. It is clear that he will play chess only because of the candies and not because he wants to improve or obtain human capacities that are connected to this particular practice, for instance strategic thinking. There are goods externally and contingently attached to chess playing (in case of the child in our example, candy; in case of adults prestige and money that can be earned by professional chess playing) and there are internal goods. Thus, the compulsion of external circumstances might help developing virtues but moral value is attributed only to those acts that are performed out of a need for internal goods.

Now, how does virtue ethics relate to paternalism? To demonstrate that virtue ethics provides a different rationale for regulating paternalism than deontology or consequentialism, consider the following example. 'Price gouging' is the practice when a seller sets a much higher price than what is considered to be reasonable or fair. In the summer of 2004, Hurricane Charley hit the Gulf of Mexico and swept across Florida to the Atlantic coast (see Sandel 2009, 3). Shopkeepers, exploiting the vulnerable situation of people, raised the price of certain essential products (e.g. bottled water or ice) to unreasonably high levels. We may rightfully ask whether it is wrong for shopkeepers and service providers to take advantage of natural disasters and whether it is permissible for the state to interfere with the prices on a competitive market.[2] Price gouging is very similar to usurious lending. A limitation on these practices can be considered indirect paternalism to protect vulnerable parties from entering into disadvantageous contracts. Consequentialists could defend anti-price gouging laws by arguing that the market does not always lead to economically optimal results. Deontological ethics would refer to the coercive and exploitative character of usury and price gouging and transform the problem into soft paternalism (i.e. that the person accepted the contract under the 'coercion' of external circumstances). The virtue argument, by contrast, would trace back the wrongness of price gauging and usury to the vice of *greed*.

2 Currently, there are thirty-three US states that have laws against price gouging. These laws use three definitional elements: (1) period of emergency (e.g. natural disasters); (2) necessary items (i.e. restrictions only apply to items that are essential to survival); (3) price ceilings (prescribed either by exact percentage or with words such as 'excessive' or 'unconscionable') (see Zwolinski 2008, 347).

> Greed is a vice, a bad way of being, especially when it makes people oblivious to the suffering of others. [...] A society in which people exploit their neighbors for financial gain in times of crisis is not a good society. Excessive greed is therefore a vice that a good society should discourage if it can. (Sandel 2009, 7)

There are two questions that shall be addressed at this point: (1) Is paternalism (i.e. paternalistic character) a virtue in itself? (2) Do paternalistic practices promote the development of (other) virtues? The issue at stake here is not negligible: if paternalism is a virtue or it promotes other virtues, it becomes morally non-objectionable because it develops human character.

(1) I am reluctant to qualify paternalism as a virtue in itself. Firstly, it seems difficult to directly relate paternalism to one specific type of practice. Paternalism appears in various forms, in a multitude of human practices and relations (e.g. medical practice, pedagogy, parent-child relations, politics, legislation, etc.) and, as a consequence, it seems to exhibit other virtues (i.e. other than paternalism) depending on the specific situation (e.g. care, love, family values, devotion, professional commitment). In other words, paternalism is hardly a fundamental character trait: there are other virtues that lie behind it.

(2) The other question to be examined is whether paternalism, even if not a virtue in itself, promotes other virtues or values. Such virtue-promoting paternalism can be affiliated with the idea of moral paternalism which emphasises the long-term effects of paternalism in shaping character and desires (see Scoccia 2000, 56). In contrast to pure legal moralism which attaches moral values to acts, moral paternalism seeks to promote good character. It is mainly determined by perfectionist considerations, and can be also based on the social harm that can be expected from people with deficient characters.

(3) This type of perfectionist paternalism is vulnerable to the 'virtue cannot be coerced' objection (i.e. the 'endorsement constraint' in Dworkin's terminology, see Dworkin 2000, 217–218). However, this argument is not necessarily fatal. It is true that coercion, in the short run, may cause 'immoral' persons to comply with moral requirements for surface reasons (cf. MacIntyre's example on internal/external goals). Virtues, on the other hand, develop by practice: it might be reasonable to expect that in the long run, due to some psychological effect, people will endorse previously rejected moral principles.

Writing thank-you letters seems to be out of fashion nowadays. A lot of people assume that as long as they feel grateful, they do not need to write thank-you letters. Moral perfectionists argue the other way around: it is the writing of thank-you letters that will eventually cause the feeling of gratitude to emerge and build up in people's psyche (see Sandel 2009, 198).

It seems to me that the main underlying virtue behind paternalism is the virtue of care. Care is a fundamental virtue that, in my opinion, remains distinct from other fundamental virtues. Although it has an affective element, care is not merely a feeling but amalgamates a benevolent caring motive with a caring practice. The benevolent caring motive is facilitated by the affective element that can be identified either as a sort of 'love' or 'empathy' towards the Other. Since it is possible to care for someone whom we do not love (and exceptionally also love someone whom we do not care for), the basic affective element behind the virtue of care seems to be the feeling of empathy. Care, very simply put, is the manifestation of empathy. A virtue conceived in this way corresponds very well to our previous 'Aristotelian' definition of virtues. Care develops human nature through developing the capacities of empathy in the individual. To feel empathy and to care about others is a virtue, even in individualistic and alienated modern societies.[3] It is an essential element of human life and has a central role in defining the 'Self' in the light of the 'Other' (see Kultgen 1995, 8). The intrinsic good of *caritas* is that it establishes and strengthens social relations while fostering human character as well. Care, however, must stay in the 'golden middle' in order to qualify as virtue: both an exaggerated form of care (i.e. over-caring that involves excessive violation of autonomy) and the lack of care that culminates in egoism and negligence towards others transform into vice.

Paternalistic practices, if genuinely motivated by benevolence, exhibit – as a common denominator – the virtue of care. From a critical perspective, legal paternalism that lacks the element of care is nothing else than a mask for exploitation. 'The distant and impersonal relations of bureaucracies foster the opposite of sincerely cooperative [i.e. caring] paternalism, that is, conflictful paternalism – exploitative relations in the guise of paternalism' (Douglas 1983, 197). Overall, care seems to be an important element of justifiable paternalism. If paternalistic practices exhibit care and care is a virtue, then paternalism contributes to the development of a virtuous character and to the self-fulfilment of individuality: it helps people to reach completeness (*eudaimonia*). At this point, the bad connotations attached to paternalism in the deontological framework are removed: paternalism becomes not only non-objectionable but even morally valuable.

3 In the Christian tradition, 'charity' or *caritas* (in the sense of *agape* or love) is one of the three fundamental theological virtues. 'Though I speak with the tongues of men and of angels, and have not charity, I am become *as* sounding brass, or a tinkling cymbal. And though I have *the gift of* prophecy, and understand all mysteries, and all knowledge; and though I have all faith, so that I could remove mountains, and have not charity, I am nothing. And though I bestow all my goods to feed *the poor*, and though I give my body to be burned, and have not charity, it profiteth me nothing. [...] And now abideth faith, hope, charity, these three; but the greatest of these is charity.' Paul's First Letter to the Corinthians, 13. Emphases added.

3 Paternalism and the ethics of care

The ethics of care was developed in feminist ethical theories as a response to traditional ethical theories that, according to feminist writers, follow a predominantly male rationale (see Gilligan 1982; Slote 2007, 3; Kymlicka 1992, 263; Kultgen 1995, 26). They claim that women tend to reason in a 'different voice' than men. Carol Gilligan demonstrates this difference through describing a boy's (Jake's) and girl's (Amy's) approach to the moral dilemma of whether a man should steal a drug he cannot afford in order to save the life of his ill wife (Gilligan 1982, 24). The boy's reasoning reflects rationality, logic and abstraction. He concludes a firm moral judgement (i.e. that the man should steal the drug to save his wife). Amy's approach is less black and white. She does not see the dilemma as an abstract and logically approachable problem, independent of human relations. When arguing against stealing the drug, she does not focus on property rights but on the possible effects stealing can have on the relationship of husband and wife. For example, if the husband is arrested, he has to leave his sick wife, what is even worse than having no medications. Similarly, when arguing for stealing the drug, she concentrates on the effects that the wife's death would have on her family. She is disturbed by the lack of information concerning human relations in the particular case. From a 'male' viewpoint, her position seems insecure and immature: she admits that the man should not steal but neither should he let his wife die. Her solution lies in improving interpersonal relations. She is confident that 'if Heinz [i.e. the husband], and the druggist had talked it out long enough, they could reach something besides stealing' (ibid., 28). Thus, Amy understands morality in a framework of relationships and tries to resolve moral dilemmas through communication.

This example is particularly useful for understanding the characteristics of an ethics of care. (1) As opposed to the ethics of justice (especially Kantian ethics), this ethical theory, just as virtue ethics, stands in opposition to the idea of universal principles and focuses on particular human relations and situations (see Kymlicka 1992, 266–269). The ethics of justice takes the standpoint of the 'generalised other', abstracting from the identity of the other and focusing on what is common or universal between people. The ethics of care focuses on the unique and particular features of a situation. (2) The opposition to universal rationality brings along an opposition to impartiality. Impartiality, based on the presupposition of socially detached (i.e. atomistically separated) individuals, overlooks the importance of emotional ties that exist in human relations (see ibid., 268). We have limited resources for caring and we preserve these resources for those to whom we are bound by positive emotional ties. Far from being a sentimental theory, the 'toughness' of care ethics compels us to make priorities in caring and dictates actions that are sometimes opposite to the principles of deontological ethics (e.g. killing a husband who has been brutally abusing his wife and children for years, see Noddings 1995, 25).

Two caveats shall be made before applying this new ethical approach to paternalism. The distinction between the ethics of justice and ethics of care is not necessarily a gender distinction. Though it might be true that men tend to argue along the rationale of justice and women along the rationale of care, it is far from an exclusive categorisation. Similarly, the two 'paradigms' complement, rather than exclude each other (see Pieper 2004, 102). It seems to me that paternalism conceived as care can complement but not replace the traditional deontological approach. The tenderness of caring and the rigour of rules go hand in hand in a 'well-ordered' society. As Kultgen remarks,

> [r]eal societies are not composed of fully developed and completely caring people. People who do care must deal with many who do not. [...] Rules prohibiting wrongful behavior with a certain rigor and strictness are particularly in place in this context. Only by imposing and following them is it possible for people of ordinary good will to clear a space in which they can take care of one another without heroic virtue and undue sacrifice. (Kultgen 1995, 33)

4 An alternative approach to paternalism

The problems associated with the traditional autonomy-based approach of paternalism (cf. Kultgen 1995, 90, 136) call for an alternative model based on virtue ethics and the ethics of care. Although some care-ethicists deny the connection between virtue and care ethics (see Noddings 1995, 23), I tried to show in the previous sections that care actually qualifies as a virtue. Care ethics, conceived as a form of virtue ethics, is based on the dichotomy of two fundamental virtues, care and justice, giving priority to the former over the latter. The domain of justice is characterised by firm and clear moral principles as provided by deontological ethics and (in the case of paternalism) the harm principle. *In opposition to this, a care-based theory provides a less clear-cut, but also less permissive approach to paternalism.* By applying the notion of autonomy reinterpreted in care ethics, it becomes possible to reconcile 'our general repugnance' (Feinberg 1986, 111) towards hard paternalism with its 'apparent necessity' without resorting to a perfectionist rationale. I think it is important to take into account the following four elements when examining the justifiability of a paternalistic intervention in this new framework: (a) The relational concept of autonomy; (b) The virtue of care as the foundation of paternalism; (c) Contextuality and case-based approach; (d) The possibility of care in public relations. In the rest of the paper I discuss these four elements.

4.1 A reinterpreted notion of autonomy

If caring is a central concept of morality, does it imply the abandonment of autonomy? This seems unnecessary and even undesirable if we reinterpret autonomy in a way that focuses on the importance of human relations, instead of individuality and disengaged rationality.

So what does such a 'relational autonomy' mean? At first sight, relational autonomy seems to be an oxymoron, at least as long as one understands autonomy as independence from external influences. However, if we consider autonomy as social in nature, self-authorship depends on how we have interacted with others and with the world in general (see Slote 2007, 67), and it will develop through the development of caring relations. This approach emphasises the external conditions of autonomy. Roughly speaking, the more relations we have, the more choices are open to us and the more autonomous we become. This is certainly true in case of children where caring is central to establishing future autonomy. It is also true in the case of competent adults. Caring social interactions can provide us with additional options by increasing our positive liberty. Realisation of personal preferences and life plans require cooperation with others. But relations also have a role in the creation of identity and in the formation of preferences, which constantly change in response to impulses from the outside world. Thus, autonomy's internal conditions are also affected by human interactions.

Relations constitute autonomy and autonomy affects relations in exchange. Does it matter what kind of relations constitute autonomy? I believe it does. Caring relations essentially improve autonomy. A repressive and debilitating relation, on the other hand, does not contribute to relational autonomy. An oft-cited example is the case of Muslim women in fundamentalist societies who seem to 'willingly' accept their subordinate role but their acceptance is the result of continuing repression and conditioning (see Oshana 2006, 101). It is possible to argue that a 'woman who willingly embraced the strictures imposed on her by the Taliban in Afghanistan should not be considered autonomous, whatever her attitude toward her social role may be' (Westlund 2009, 30). As critics point out, such a substantive view of relational autonomy has built-in moral (egalitarian) presuppositions, consequently it is suspect for 'undue' perfectionism (see ibid., and Holroyd 2009, 324–325). Nevertheless, I agree with the statement that '[...] autonomy calls for independence from other persons and from social roles and traditions of a variety deemed to be inhospitable to autonomy' (Oshana 2006, 72). Care-based paternalism is not inhospitable to autonomy because caring relations increase the subject's relational autonomy.

Shifting the focus from the subject of paternalism to the paternalist, it seems at first sight that care imposes serious obligations on caretakers. We might rightfully ask if these duties do not decrease the caretakers' autonomy. I refer back to virtue ethics at this point: exercising care develops the character of the paternalistic agent, so it is actually beneficial to him as well. Care should not be conceived of as an obligation but as a possibility for mutual help and character formation.

To sum up, it is possible to say that relational autonomy is generally less harsh on paternalism than the 'traditional' account of personal autonomy. There are disagreements about this statement. Slote, for example, writes that 'it is less clear that care ethics will or should want to disagree with liberalism about paternalistic examples' (Slote 2007, 84). Obliging motorcyclists to wear crash helmets against their wishes is not only a violation of personal autonomy in the traditional sense. Such an intervention can be regarded as being inconsistent with 'good relationships', even if the paternalistic actor is fully empathic of the motorcyclists' preferences. Coercion can surely deteriorate relations. Nevertheless, it seems to me that a certain degree of paternalistic coercion is compatible with relational autonomy, because the element of care builds an 'interpersonal bridge' between the actor and the subject that strengthens human relations in the long run.

4.2 The virtue of care

Even if paternalism is not a virtue in itself, I think it is hard to deny that care qualifies as a virtue. As we have seen, it does not only increase the autonomy of the person who is being cared for, but also the autonomy of the one who cares (provided that care is given in moderation). In other words, caring makes people autonomous. Additionally, it improves human character in general. It seems that care has a source in universal human feelings (i.e. empathy) but it develops only by exercising it. In other words, everyone has an innate capacity for care which can be developed by practice (or suppressed if not practised). Kultgen argues that care is an essential element of human life:

> Care is not only an essential structure of the way we exist, it is at the core of the way we should exist. We should care for and take care of ourselves. We should take care of certain others as we do ourselves. [...] To be human, is to be able to care, to want to care, and to care deeply and widely. The companions of care are commitment, obligation, anxiety, and inevitably failure and guilt. [...] When we endure a lifetime of care, we become careworn. But we also become human. The crow's-feet of care are marks of humanity. (Kultgen 1995, 7)

4.3 Contextuality and case-based approach

The ethics of care calls for a contextual decision-making process. We might call this approach '*ad hoc* paternalism' as opposed to paternalism that rests on firm ethical principles.

> To be an *ad hoc* paternalist is to admit that one has no powerful, overarching test that will allow anything more than intuitive confidence (either before or after one acts) that one is on the right side of this line [between justified and unjustified forms of paternalism]. (Kennedy 1982, 638)

So why does an *ad hoc* approach seem more promising than traditional ethical approaches?

First of all, the basis of paternalism is *lived* intersubjectivity (cf. ibid., 639). In most cases, when we have to make paternalistic decisions, we cannot start by 'hypothesising' how the other feels, which ethical rules are 'for' or 'against' the paternalistic intervention, etc. We simply have to act, and we act to protect the other, because if he hurts himself, we are hurt as well. This is due to the 'intersubjective unity' that exists between the paternalistic actor and the subject in the given situation. Thus, paternalism comes from an innate instinct of self-preservation to avoid pain and being hurt. On the other hand, care is also something we need, enjoy and something that provides fulfilment (see ibid., 640).

The feeling of 'intersubjective unity', it seems to me, develops on the basis of certain special relations or emotional ties that exist between the subject and the paternalistic actor. This unity also exists between strangers due to the ontological relatedness of human beings, but 'unity' seems to be a matter of degree. If it is really a matter of degree, it seems normal to make priorities in caring and also in paternalism. Thus, there is no objective test for the justification of paternalism. It is natural that we care more for those whom we love, and this may justify a higher degree of paternalism towards them.

To sum up, if 'intersubjective unity' develops through relations and emotional ties, it is necessary to thoroughly assess the context of paternalism to decide about paternalism's necessity and justifiability. It is necessary to see clearly all relations that are present in the context, even those that might seem irrelevant at first sight. This is exactly what the ethics of care requires. Consider, for instance, the girl's special attention to the relations and circumstances of the case in Gilligan's example. Nel Noddings also remarks that women often ask for more information than man when facing a hypothetical moral dilemma. They want more information in order to form a picture of the situation, and to know more about the reasons that point to feelings, needs and emotional motivations (Noddings 1995, 23).

4.4 The possibility of care in public relations

Most moral philosophers claim that the public and the private sphere should operate according to different moral codes (see Clement 1996, 67). The public sphere should be governed by abstract principles, i.e. by the ethics of justice, which is suitable to handle the morality of the public domain, characterised by self-interest, competition and autonomy. The private sphere, on the other hand, should be the domain of care ethics, which is sensitive to the issues of altruism, interconnectedness and dependence.

This separation seems plausible. However, it is necessary to extend the ethics of care to the public sphere if we want to apply a care-based approach to paternalism in the sphere of legal institutions. Some writers have indeed challenged the public-private dichotomy. Slote argues that the ethics of care does not only complement classical ethical theories but offers an alternative to them (Slote 2007, 2). It is unnecessary to restrict the notion of caring to people with whom we have an actual relationship; 'one can have a caring attitude toward (groups of) people one is never going to be acquainted with' (ibid., 11).

Others claim that there is no need to apply different ethical theories for the public and private spheres, because these are not fundamentally different (see Clement 1996, 69–75). The separation seems artificial, especially when we consider that the 'infrastructure of care' permeates all social relationships, from the private to the public sphere. Care can 'spill over' from the private sphere to the public and *vice versa*. Care that a person experiences at home, for example, makes him more caring and attentive to people at his workplace (see Kultgen 1995, 30).

5 Conclusion

It seems clear that caring paternalism prevails only in direct personal relations. It would be a mistake to 'assume that justified forms of public paternalism exactly parallel those of personal paternalism' (Kultgen 1995, 161).[4] The law presupposes a certain degree of standardisation and treats people in an abstract and impersonal manner. Nevertheless, care can find its way through the barriers of abstraction by the 'infrastructure of care'. If benevolent paternalism is a manifestation of care and care is a virtue, then the state has a perfectionist task to develop the 'infrastructure of care', that is, the institutions, organisations, practices and shared beliefs by which a society nurtures mutual care among its members. It is my impression that the reason why virtue ethics allows for more space to paternalism than the traditional deontological approach is that it is not focused exclusively on the autonomy of the subject. However, the way a virtuous person would act, is a matter of interpretation and it is strongly related to the specific situation. Once again, this is why it seems quite challenging to build a theory of *legal* paternalism on the concept of care.

4 To note, personal is close to private but the two are not exactly synonymous. I suppose that most but not all forms of public paternalism are impersonalised.

References

Annas, Julia. 2007. Being Virtuous and Doing the Right Thing. In *Ethical Theory: An Anthology*, edited by Russ Shafer-Landau, 735–745. Malden (MA): Blackwell.

Aristotle. 1999. *Nicomachean Ethics.* Indianapolis: Hackett.

Clement, Grace. 1996. *Care, Autonomy and Justice: Feminism and the Ethic of Care.* Boulder (CO): Westview Press.

Dworkin, Gerald. 1972. Paternalism. *The Monist* 56: 64–84.

Dworkin, Ronald. 2000. *Sovereign Virtue.* Cambridge (MA): Harvard University Press.

Feinberg, Joel. 1986. *The Moral Limits of the Criminal Law, Vol. 3. – Harm to Self.* New York: Oxford University Press.

Gilligan, Carol. 1982. *In a Different Voice: Psychological Theory and Women's Development.* Cambridge (MA): Harvard University Press.

Holroyd, Jules. 2009. Relational Autonomy and Paternalistic Interventions. *Res Publica* 15: 321–336.

Douglas, Jack. 1983. Cooperative vs. Conflictful Paternalism. In *Paternalism*, edited by Rolf Sartorius, 171–200. Minneapolis: University of Minnesota Press.

Kennedy, Duncan. 1982. Distributive and Paternalist Motives in Contract and Tort Law, with Special Reference to Compulsory Terms and Unequal Bargaining Power. *Maryland Law Review* 41: 563–658.

Kultgen, John. 1995. *Autonomy and Intervention – Parentalism in the Caring Life.* New York: Oxford University Press.

Kymlicka, Will. 1992. *Contemporary Political Philosophy.* Oxford: Oxford University Press.

MacIntyre, Alasdair. 1981. *After Virtue.* London: Duckworth.

Noddings, Nel. 1995. Caring. In *Justice and Care: Essential Readings in Feminist Ethics*, edited by Virginia Held, 7–30. Boulder (CO): Westview Press.

Nussbaum, Martha. 2007. Non-Relative Virtues: An Aristotelian Approach. In *Ethical Theory: An Anthology*, edited by Russ Shafer-Landau, 684–700. Malden (MA): Blackwell.

Oshana, Marina. 2006. *Personal Autonomy in Society.* Aldershot: Ashgate.

Pieper, Annemarie. 2004. *Van-e feminista etika?* [*Does Feminist Ethics Exist?*] Budapest: Áron.

Sandel, Michael. 2009. *Justice: What is the Right Thing to Do?* London: Allen Lane.

Scoccia, Danny. 2000. Moral Paternalism, Virtue and Autonomy. *Australasian Journal of Philosophy* 78: 53–71.

Shafer-Landau, Russ (ed.) 2007. *Ethical Theory: An Anthology.* Malden (MA): Blackwell.

Slote, Michael. 2007. *The Ethics of Care and Empathy.* London: Routledge.

Westlund, Andrea C. 2009. Rethinking Relational Autonomy. *Hypatia* 24: 26–49.

Zwolinski, Matt. 2008. The Ethics of Price Gouging. *Business Ethics Quarterly* 18: 347–378.

Practical Reason and Practical Reasonableness: Raz and Finnis on the Basis of Practical Philosophy

András Zétényi

Abstract Although Joseph Raz is a legal positivist and John Finnis is a proponent of natural law, their practical philosophies are based on strikingly similar concepts. The paper examines whether the two theories are compatible with the requirements of pluralism, an important characteristic of contemporary Western societies. Both theories manage to deal with pluralism, but they do so at different levels. Finnis's meta-ethical objectivism leads him to a moderate version of pluralism, while Raz may rightly be considered a radical pluralist. By way of conclusion, it is argued that Finnis's theory as formulated in his *Natural Law and Natural Rights* meets the requirements just as well as Raz's.

1 Introduction

Without doubt, Herbert Hart was one of the leading legal philosophers of the 20th century. Perhaps his two best known students are Joseph Raz and John Finnis. While Raz followed his professor's footsteps in developing a positivist theory of law, Finnis, influenced by Germain Grisez,[1] became a proponent of natural law. Initially, both scholars focused their research on jurisprudence, but later their theories became general theories of practical philosophy,[2] encompassing ethics and political philosophy as well. Although they developed very different theories, those are based on strikingly similar conceptions of practical reasoning.

1 Especially by his article on the first principle of practical reason (Grisez 1965).

2 Practical philosophy aims to answer the question: 'What is to be done?', or as Finnis puts it: 'What should I decide to do and equivalently, what kind of person should I resolve or allow myself to be?' (Finnis 2003, 115). Answering this question leads to a choice of conduct. But before we make this choice we have to work out what to do. This 'working out' is called practical reasoning (as opposed to theoretical reasoning, which guides thinking) (see O'Neill 1998, 1).

Both scholars claim that practical reasoning is more than instrumental reasoning, since its aim is not just to figure out how to reach certain ends but also to identify the ethically important ones among these ends. This means that both want to show that a proper understanding of practical reasoning is necessary for a proper understanding of morality (see Batnitzky 1995, 167). Quite unsurprisingly, their views on morality are also similar to a certain extent, since they both reject utilitarianism and more generally consequentialism and share the view that co-operation and commitment to one's community are important factors in moral decisions.

The most important difference in their views concerns the relation between practical reasoning and human goods. For Finnis, there are seven basic human goods, all referring to the self-evident basic principles of practical reason. Since practical reasonableness is one of the basic goods itself, this means that the framework of his natural law theory (i.e., practical reason) cannot be separated from (a part of) its content (i.e., practical reasonableness). Consequently, he thinks it impossible to speak about practical reason without also speaking about particular human goods. According to Raz, however, there is no link between practical reason and any particular good(s). For him, social forms are even more important than particular goods, since any human good – basic or not – is only possible if there exists a particular social form which enables it, since 'a person's well-being depends to a large extent on success in socially defined and determined pursuits and activities' (Raz 1986, 309).

One way to judge these theories is by examining whether they are compatible with the pluralism characteristic of most contemporary Western societies. A society is pluralist if different conceptions of good life are present (or would be allowed to be present) and many of these tend to be generally accepted as worthwhile. (In this paper, 'pluralism' will have two different meanings: it will be used to describe the modern state of affairs and will also mean a philosophical answer to this situation.)

Of the two philosophers it is Finnis who needs to be defended here, since proponents of natural law are still treated by many as scholars whose relations to contemporary pluralism looks problematic. This is due to the fact that they ground their theories on necessary conclusions derived from 'strong', unprovable metaphysical assertions. According to Finnis, Joseph Raz is mistaken, for Raz thinks natural lawyers are 'those philosophers who think it a criterion of adequacy for theories of law that they show [...] that it is a necessary truth that every law has moral worth' (Raz 1990, 162; cf. Finnis 1980, 26). My aim is to examine the two theories, arguing that, in the words of Finnis, 'there is more to theories of natural law than superstition and darkness', and to show that Finnis's theory, at least as formulated in his *Natural Law and Natural Rights*, can be interpreted in a way that allows for pluralism. But first, a more detailed examination of the two theories is in order.

2 Finnis

According to Finnis, natural law theory 'claims to be able to identify conditions and principles of practical right-mindedness, of good and proper order among men and individual conduct.' (Finnis 1980: 18) This means that practical reason leads us to intrinsic values which guide our decisions as practical principles. He identifies seven basic goods: life, knowledge, play, aesthetic experience, sociability (friendship), practical reasonableness and 'religion'[3] (ibid., 86–89).[4] These goods are incommensurable, self-evident and universal (ibid., 83–84; Grisez, Boyle and Finnis 1987, 110). Since these values exist independent of those seeking to attain them and are not ends external to the means by which they are pursued, they can only be participated in through innumerable projects, commitments and actions (Finnis 1980, 96 and 94). Finnis claims that basic goods can only be grasped through acts of the intellect, through which one comes to realise the point of doing something for its own sake (see Batnitzky 1995, 162). Of the basic goods only practical reasonableness requires explanation, which is 'the basic good of being able to bring one's own intelligence to bear effectively (in practical reasoning that issues in action) on the problems of choosing one's actions and lifestyle and shaping one's own character' (Finnis 1980, 88).[5]

As we have seen, participation in the good of practical reasonableness means choosing a coherent life plan, which entails the coordination of participation in the basic goods. The requirements of practical reasonableness are the following: a coherent plan of life, no arbitrary preference among values, no arbitrary preference among persons, detachment and commitment, the (limited) relevance of consequences: efficiency within reason, respect for every basic value in every act, the requirements of the common good and following one's conscience (ibid., 103–127).

The requirement of a coherent (or as Rawls formulates it: rational) life plan means that one must have a set of purposes, orientations and effective commitments which are in harmony (see Rawls 1999, 80). Living from moment to moment, drifting or following one's immediate cravings have to be avoided.

If commitment is made to follow a coherent plan of life, it is unavoidable that some basic goods are participated in at the expense of other forms of good. This commitment is rational only if it is based on one's capacities, circumstances, even

3 'Religion' here refers to knowledge about the 'universal order-of-things', not specifically to some institutionalised form of worship (cf. Finnis 1980, 89–90).

4 Finnis later reformulated these basic goods in the following way: knowledge, skilful performance (in work and play), bodily life, friendship, marriage, practical reasonableness and harmony with the ultimate source (Finnis 1993–1994, 691–692).

5 According to a later definition, practical reasonableness is harmony between one's feelings and one's judgements (inner integrity), and between one's judgements and one's behaviour (authenticity) (Finnis 1993–1994, 692).

on one's taste. Since according to Finnis the basic goods are self-evident, it would be unreasonable for any intelligent person to deny that these are good in themselves.

The prohibition of arbitrary preferences among persons means the requirement of fundamental impartiality among those who (might) participate in the basic goods. If we reformulate this in the language of moral philosophy, this means that one's own moral preferences and judgements need to be universalisable. In classical thought this is called the Golden Rule: 'Do to/for others what you would have them do to/for you' (Finnis 1980, 103–108).

It would be unreasonable to adopt an attitude which would lead one to consider his/her own life devoid of sense if one's project failed, so 'in order to be sufficiently open to all the basic forms of good in all the changing circumstances of a lifetime', one must detach himself/herself from one's existing projects. The requirement of commitment on the other hand means the need for fidelity towards one's projects, to persevere instead of dropping out (ibid., 109–110).

'The (limited) relevance of consequences: efficiency within reason' requires that 'one brings about good in the world (in one's own life and the lives of others) by actions that are efficient for their (reasonable) purpose(s).' Although there is ample room in many contexts to take the possible consequences into consideration, 'as a general strategy of moral reasoning, utilitarianism or consequentialism is irrational' (ibid., 111–112). Finnis considers the latter senseless, for it cannot give a good reason to prefer altruism to egoism (ibid., 115–116).

The rejection of consequentialism entails that the requirement of respect of every basic value in every act becomes self-evident. As long as one refrains from choosing directly against a basic value, this requirement is fulfilled.[6]

The requirements of the common good need no explanation: most of the moral duties and obligations stem from this source. The ninth requirement of following one's conscience can be considered either an aspect of the seventh requirement, or as the summary of all the requirements (ibid., 125).

There are other first principles of practical reasoning besides the basic goods. These are presupposed in all practical reasoning. One is the principle of non-contradiction which prohibits incoherence. The other states that 'good is to be done and pursued' which means the prohibition of pointlessness.[7]

Finnis argues that theories of natural law have always accepted the existence of a variety of human opinions and practices, although he acknowledges that classical theorists took it for granted and 'often enough bluntly asserted that human beings

6 Since participation in one of the basic goods necessarily means at least to a certain degree a choice against another basic good, the above requirement only implies the avoidance of causing direct harm (see Finnis 1980, 118–120, 123).

7 The prohibition does not *prevent* pointlessness, it only requires its elimination upon discovery (see Grisez, Boyle and Finnis 1987, 119–120).

are not all equally devoted to the pursuit of knowledge and justice, and are far from united in their conception of what constitutes worthwhile knowledge or demand of justice.' He cites Leo Strauss who regards this as a necessary condition for the quest for natural right to emerge (Finnis 1980, 29), and also refers to Aquinas, who in his *Summa Theologiae* writes about disputes on the ultimate ends of human existence (see *ST* I–II, q. 1., a. 7; I, q. 2. a. 1. ad 1).

If a theory wants to embrace pluralism, more is needed than the acceptance of the variety of human opinions and practices. The theory needs to treat very different ways of life as equally worthwhile. Finnis's reformulation of natural law does just that. He states that there are many admirable forms of human life and there are an infinite number of ways in which one may participate in the basic goods (Finnis 1980, 29–31). In his discussion of basic values he remarks that each of us has a subjective order of priority among them and as long as the requirements of practical reasonableness (such as the 'no arbitrary preference among values' mentioned above) are met, one can participate in the basic values in any way he chooses (ibid., 93).

3 Raz

One of the major goals of Raz's practical philosophy is to give a proper explanation of how projects and relationships are connected to practical reason (see Raz 1986, 284). This project started with his early book *Practical Reason and Norms* which gave a conceptual analysis of norms, reasons for action and their relationship. The book stressed the important role of exclusionary reasons in the understanding of norms and related normative concepts (Raz 1990, 178). In his *Postscript* to the second edition, Raz concludes that the aim of his book was to show that exclusionary reasons are systemically related to central structures of practical reasoning (ibid., 190–191).

In a more recent collection of essays called *Engaging Reason: On the Theory of Value and Action*, Raz 'explores some aspects of the complex interdependence of value, reason, and the will' (Raz 1999, 1). The main theme of the book is the analysis of intentional conduct that is based on values that constitute reasons for action. The essay entitled 'Agency, Reason and Good' aims to defend what Raz (based on G. E. M. Anscombe) calls the classical approach which holds that the central type of action is intentional, that is reason-based; and that 'reasons are facts in virtue of which those actions are good in some respect and to some degree' (ibid., 23). An objection to this approach can be that acts only need to be intelligible objects of choice, they need not be good or of value, since for example many people readily acknowledge having done something that they knew would hurt someone else (ibid., 25).

Raz shows that the objectors fail to offer a coherent account of reasons that would allow properties that are not good-making to be reasons for action, and reasons to have normative force at the same time (ibid., 28). Still, there are 'many cases of people acting for reasons which are morally neutral, contribute to no Value, not even to the well-being of their agents, manifest no virtue, moral or other, and display no skill or accomplishment of any note.' These, according to Raz, are still valuable, although they do not possess a good-making property that links them to 'big' values (like justice, for example) (ibid., 29–30).

Another problem with the critique of the classical approach is that it overlooks 'contexts to which value is central', such as justification and evaluation. These

> allow us to check on any claim that some consideration is a reason because it makes an act an intelligible object of choice: if this is so then the same consideration must also show that the act is justified or at least that there is something to be said in its justification, something that in the absence of contrary considerations makes it justified. (ibid., 31)

Since justification and evaluation do not depend on the agent's reasons for action, the objection cannot be defended.

The essay's final parts deal with anomic reasons and expressive action. The former are the reasons behind actions that are believed to be evil or wrong. Their existence cannot refute the classical approach, since they can only be understood as inversions of real values, which establishes that they are just degenerate cases, exceptions that prove the rule (ibid., 31–35). A similar case is that of actions which at least in part look as if they were intentional because they are expressive, not because of some reasons for action. Since they involve some diminution of control, they are not paradigmatic cases of intentional action and thus their existence does not contradict the classical approach either (ibid., 36–43). To sum up, the essay proves a firm link between intention, reason and the good, which, albeit in a less elaborate way, already formed the basis of Raz's earlier treatise on political philosophy, *The Morality of Freedom*.

In that earlier book, the starting point in the elaboration of his conception of practical reasoning was a critique of utilitarianism and consequentialism. Theories of these types cannot resolve the conflict that arises when the result of the calculation (which shows which action would maximise desirable outcomes) is not in line with 'the agent's own projects which are central to his life.' Citing Bernard Williams and Robert Nozick, Raz concludes that in such conflicts people stick with their projects and life plans instead of choosing according to prior calculations, which means that the decisions that require one to evaluate one's commitments should be viewed as agent-relative (Raz 1986, 284–285).

For Raz the aim of practical reasoning is the success of a person's life from his own point of view, that is his personal well-being (ibid., 288–289). To be able to achieve personal well-being, one needs the ability to choose freely, and this is one of the reasons why personal autonomy is one of the central concepts in *The Morality of Freedom*. It should be noted that personal well-being is not a stand-alone concept, it has to be understood within a social context, since, according to Raz, it is not possible to speak about personal well-being (or personal autonomy) without speaking about social forms (see Batnitzky 1995, 168). This entails that personal well-being has to be clearly distinguished from self-interest. Raz argues that those who hold the view that self-interest is natural while the concern to do what is morally right is not, are mistaken (Raz 1986, 315). He states that 'it is false that we pursue our goals, which define our well being, because they are our goals. We pursue them, because they are, as we believe, worth pursuing' (ibid., 316). This pursuit, however, is dependent on the existence (the 'availability') of appropriate social forms. A complex goal can only be achieved if it is based on a widely practised form of behaviour. While the improvement of existing social forms and the creation of new ones is also possible, one cannot break free from current social forms (ibid., 312–313).

4 Pluralism

Although both scholars deal with pluralism, they do so at different levels. Finnis advocates a 'moderate' version, while Raz embraces a 'radical' form of pluralism. Moderate pluralism means that different choices (different ways of life) can be accepted as rational if and only if they fit into the given framework of practical reason. As noted above, the reason for Finnis to accept pluralism was that it is evident that nobody is capable of living a life that participates in all the basic goods to an equal degree. We have to decide how to live our lives but we should not question the value of each other's choice – as long as they do not contradict the common conception of practical reason. This stems from the incommensurability of the basic goods, which means that there is no hierarchy among them. The radical pluralist regards this conception or framework too limiting, as it does not allow for accepting forms of life that disregard some basic goods, for example 'religion'.

We can test the moderate version of pluralism by evaluating how it deals with same-sex partnership, which is a legally accepted way of life in most Western societies, although with substantially less rights than marriage. If Finnis's theory accepts same-sex partnerships as a worthwhile way of life, that is, if in his view one can participate in all the basic goods while living in a homosexual relationship, we can conclude that it is compatible with the requirements of pluralism.

It is fair to note that even if same-sex partnership can be fitted into Finnis's theoretical framework, it is definitely against his intentions, since he vigorously opposes the legal recognition of same-sex partnerships. In the famous US case *Romer v. Evans* (517 U. S. 620 [1996]), he testified in favour of an amendment of the Colorado state constitution (later found unconstitutional by the Supreme Court) which prohibited all local and county governments in the state to take any action that would recognise homosexuals as a 'protected class' according to US anti-discrimination law. His reformulation of the basic goods cited above makes his position concerning same-sex partnership quite clear:

> [T]he sexual association of a man and a woman which, though it essentially involves both friendship between the partners and the procreation and education of children by them, seems to have a point and benefit that is irreducible either to friendship or to life-in-its-transmission and therefore (as comparative anthropology confirms and Aristotle came particularly close to articulating, not to mention the 'third founder' of Stoicism, Musonius Rufus) should be acknowledged to be a distinct basic human good, call it marriage. (Finnis 1993–1994, 691–692)

This means that those living in homosexual relationships cannot lead a life that is acceptable, since they deliberately choose not to participate at all in marriage, which according to Finnis is *per definitionem* reserved for heterosexuals, and thus will fail to meet all the requirements of practical reasonableness, as this way they cannot have respect for every basic value in every act.

Nevertheless, it is possible to interpret his theory, at least in its initial form we find in *Natural Law and Natural Rights*, in a way that would allow for the acceptance of same-sex partnerships. In his first formulation of basic goods (Finnis 1980, 86–90) only life can be considered problematic, especially if the transmission of life by procreation is considered to be an essential part of this basic good, in which all acceptable ways of life should participate to a certain degree. Finnis explicitly rejects this, since he writes that

> we need not be analytically content with an anthropological convention which treats sexuality, mating, and family life as a single category or unit of investigation; nor with an ethical judgment that treats the family, and the procreation and education of children, as an indistinguishable cluster of moral responsibilities. (Finnis 1980, 86–87)

Homosexuals may participate for example in the 'pursuit of the value of life that is involved in simply keeping the child alive and well until it can fend for itself' (ibid., 87).

5 Conclusion

As a matter of fact, these two scholars do not have a common concept of pluralism. For Raz, pluralism means the plurality of social forms, while Finnis speaks of the plurality of persons pursuing goods (persons pursuing their own way of life). This difference stems from the difference in their meta-ethical views. For Finnis, those rejecting basic goods are mistaken, their conduct has nothing to do with the validity of his thesis, which means that he is a meta-ethical objectivist, Raz rejects this claim, since for him different social forms mean (at least the possibility of) forms of life that are incommensurable. Finnis presumes that the basic goods will stay basic goods whatever changes may take place in the future in different societies, while Raz maintains the possibility of new values, new goals worth pursuing. The aim of this paper was to show that under the current circumstances, Finnis's natural law theory is just as compatible with the requirements of pluralism, as Raz's.

References

Batnitzky, Leora. 1995. A Seamless Web? John Finnis and Joseph Raz on Practical Reason and the Obligation to Obey the Law. *Oxford Journal of Legal Studies* 15.2: 153–175.

Finnis, John. 1980. *Natural Law and Natural Rights.* Oxford: Clarendon Press.

Finnis, John. 1993–1994. Liberalism and Natural Law Theory. *Mercer Law Review* 45: 687–704.

Finnis, John. 2003. Law and What I Truly Should Decide. *American Journal of Jurisprudence* 48: 107–129.

Grisez, Germain. 1965. The First Principle of Practical Reason: A Commentary on the Summa Theologiae, 1-2, Question 94. Article 2. *Natural Law Forum* 10: 168–196.

Grisez, Germain, Boyle, Joseph, and Finnis, John. 1987. Practical Principles, Moral Truth and Ultimate Ends. *American Journal of Jurisprudence* 32: 99–151.

O'Neill, Onora. 1998. *Practical Reason and Ethics* [http://www.phil.cam.ac.uk/u_grads/Tripos/Ethics/course_material/6_practical_reason_05.pdf].

Raz, Joseph. 1986. *The Morality of Freedom.* Oxford: Clarendon Press.

Raz, Joseph. 1990. *Practical Reason and Norms.* 2nd ed. Princeton: Princeton University Press.

Raz, Joseph. 1999. *Engaging Reason: On the Theory of Value and Action.* Oxford: Oxford University Press.

Rawls, John. 1999. *A Theory of Justice.* Rev. ed. Cambridge, Mass.: The Belknap Press of Harvard University Press.

The Legal Challenges to Equality and Freedom in the Age of Genomic Medicine

Marta Soniewicka

Abstract The paper addresses the issue of the necessary scope of legal protection of a person in the age of genomic medicine. More specifically, the paper aims at analysing the problem of genetic discrimination and identifying justified restrictions on the use of genetic test results and genetic information, especially in the areas of employment and insurance. There will be discussed the main controversies that arise when the legal restrictions on the use of genetic information are at stake.[1]

1 Introduction

A great multi-billion dollar international scientific effort called the Human Genome Project (HGP) began in 1990 and was aimed at determining the sequence of chemical base pairs which make up DNA and at identifying and mapping the approximately 20,000–25,000 genes of the human genome. A working draft of the genome was released in 2000 and a complete one in 2003. In 2000 President Bill Clinton and Prime Minister Tony Blair announced to the world that this was the most significant discovery of our times. 'Without a doubt, this is the most important, most wondrous map ever produced by humankind' – said President Clinton in his speech, since thanks to it – 'we are learning the language in which God created life. We are gaining ever more awe for the complexity, the beauty, and the wonder of God's most divine and sacred gift' (see Collins 2006, 2). Francis Collins, who was one of the participants of the HGP, added: 'It's a happy day for the world. It is humbling for me, and awe-inspiring, to realize that we have caught the first glimpse of our own instruction book, previously known only to God' (ibid.).

1 The paper is a revised and shortened version of an essay published previously under the title 'What Is So Unfair About Our Genes? The Problem of Genetic Discrimination' in the volume *Studies in the Philosophy of Law vol. 5: Law and Biology*, edited by J. Stelmach, B. Brożek, and M. Soniewicka, 53–69. Krakow: Jagiellonian University Press 2010.

Human genetic technology, based on the knowledge obtained from the Human Genome Project, has brought about a revolution in health care. The revolution consists in transforming medicine into genomic medicine where treatment is individualised, based on genetic information. Genetic information provides the ability to diagnose or predict genetic conditions for the risks of illness and may bring about significant benefits to health care in the future. However, the use of genetic information poses daunting questions and great challenges to public healthcare and our legal systems. One of the most demanding issues of the integration of new genetic technologies into medicine is the challenge to *equality*. The second biggest issue is the challenge to *freedom*. It means that in the age of genomic medicine we have to reconsider the problem of how to define and guarantee in our societies the basic liberal values of equality and freedom.

2 Unequal access to medical resources

New technologies applied in medicine give people greater opportunities of enhancement than were ever known before but these technologies are not available to a broad segment of the population. Quite to the contrary, access to genetic technology and genetic information is expensive and restricted to the most advantaged individuals in highly developed nations. Thus, exclusive genomic medicine gives rise to new challenges in the fair distribution of health care resources within and among nations. Of course, we do not have to draw any futuristic vision to understand the problem. We are all facing the problem right now in our current world. Over 50% of the causes of mortality in developing countries are completely curable in high-income countries (Human Development Report 2005, 3–25). Sometimes it is only a matter of vaccines that cost 20 cents each or even just a matter of anti-mosquito nets (one of the measures against malaria). One cannot expect neither a similar quantity nor quality of life among all the inhabitants of our world. Genomic medicine is another step in medical advances that can either broaden the gap between the least advantaged and the most advantaged inhabitants of the world or narrow the gap. Since genomic medicine is based on the newest and most expensive technology, it is more probable that it will broaden the gap.[2] This is a problem of national and global distributive justice that occurs in a new challenging perspective and cannot be solved by itself. It requires global and national initiatives in public health policy that will combat new social divisions based on health status and health care opportunities.

2 For current data on the problem of equity in medical services based on genetics see Wertz and Fletcher (2004, 14–18); Krajewska (2008, 206–212). On the problem of justice in the age of genetics see Buchanan et al. (2007, passim). See also Annas (2010, 251–266).

3 Eugenics

Another problem occurs when we consider the issue of eugenic decisions that can bring about changes for the entire human species and could undermine the whole concept of justice.[3] Eugenics is a term invented by Francis Galton, Charles Darwin's cousin. The term comes from ancient Greek where εὐγενής means 'well-born', which is meant as hereditarily endowed with good genetic qualities (see Kevles 1995, IXff.). The main aim of eugenics is the improvement of the human race or more simply the production of the best possible children. Eugenics manifests itself in birth control aimed at 'encouraging' procreation of 'fitter people' and 'discouraging' procreation of 'unfit people'. It may also manifest itself in the improvement of human nature by the manipulation of a genotype, where human abilities are quite restricted so far. Eugenic state policies that were rooted in social Darwinism of the late 19th century were largely discredited in the 20th century (see Glover 1998; Kevles 2008, 205–207; Müller-Hill 2006, 231–236; Buchanan et al. 2007, 27–60). However, the idea of eugenics itself has not been discredited yet. Quite to the contrary, it is deeply rooted in people's minds and it is still present in social practices.

At the beginning of the 21st century, state eugenics is being replaced by private eugenics. It means that procreative decisions based on genetic information can be taken only by individuals, not by the state or doctors who can neither force nor suggest them. As Jürgen Habermas (2003, 26ff.) points out, in contrast to former authoritarian eugenics, we are now faced with liberal eugenics. This liberal eugenics seems justified since it is natural for people to crave the best possible for their children or at least for having healthy children. Nevertheless, there is much concern about the whole idea of producing 'better babies' that may bring about stigmatisation and direct discrimination of 'defective' human beings.[4] What is more, 'improving humans' may create in the future a division between super-humans (improved ones) and sub-humans (not improved) that would be two separate species, called by Lee Silver (1985, 110–111) the 'GenRich' and the 'naturals'.[5] If such a division appeared, the notion of 'justice' would be useless since one of the necessary conditions of justice is approximate equality in natural powers among human beings (see Aristotle 2007, 1134a, 180; Hume 2005, 21; Hart 1998, 263–264). If there were a human race biologically endowed with such power that would enable them to permanently dominate other races, justice would be impossible as David Hume writes (2005, 21). The whole idea of taking control over human evolution poses significant

3 Justice is understood here as a distribution of goods among individuals treated as equals and according to a set of justified criteria.

4 On the problem of genetic discrimination resulting from the use of prenatal and pre-implantation genetic diagnosis see Krajewska (2008, 241ff.).

5 Such a situation was vividly illustrated by the famous science-fiction movie *Gattaca* (1997) directed by Andrew Niccol with Uma Thurman and Ethan Hawke.

questions concerning notions such as 'better' or 'improvement' with regard to a human being.[6] Such normative notions can be understood in different ways and we could never be sure if we are right about what would be better for our descendants or what kind of improvement future generations would require.

4 The use of genetic information in insurance, employment and education

Last but not least, one should consider the use of genetic information in situations in which people can be significantly limited in equality of opportunities and freedom of choice as far as their insurance, employment, education, adoption, social status and private relations are concerned. Especially worthy of attention are situations in which individuals are treated differently with regard to the information about symptoms of a disease that they may develop in the future. This concerns situations in which people who are apparently healthy (asymptomatic) undergo genetic testing that detects their future illness risk. Some insurers deny coverage or raise the premiums of those asymptomatic individuals who are at risk of an illness.[7]

It may also happen that employers use the genetic test results included in an employee's medical record in group health plans as a basis for refusing health coverage as part of their benefits. Employers may also use the results of genetic tests in taking decisions such as promotion, hiring or firing. An employer may want to avoid additional costs that individuals at risk of a disease may produce (health insurance costs, absence in work, lower flexibility, danger of harm, for instance in case of a driver or a pilot) and to guarantee the highest possible efficiency by giving the job to the prospectively most efficient worker.

One can go one step further and imagine situations in other spheres of life where similar discrimination may occur. For instance, the use of genetic information in relation to education may occur when people with inherited genetic predispositions or susceptibility for a disease are refused access to a particular school because of the information about their future illness risk or they are treated differently in school on the basis of their genetic inheritance (see Rothstein 1997, 317–331). Surveys show that while people generally distrust insurance companies or employers, they trust the education system. Most people who took part in a global survey on genetic

6 George Annas (2004, 35 ff.) expresses deep scepticism about genetic engineering and warns that the 'enhancement' of human race can bring about genetic genocide.

7 Of course, analysing the problem of the use of genetic information in the insurance system, we have to take into account all the differences between countries. The health insurance system in Europe and Canada, in contrast to the US, provides universal access to health resources. Thus, if we discuss the problem within European context, the problem of unfair differential treatment may manifest itself only as far as life insurance is concerned.

discrimination would not want to disclose their genetic test results to insurers or employers (if their health insurance depends on their employment) but they would be willing to disclose the results of their children to a school system to guarantee them the most appropriate education and treatment (see Wertz and Fletcher 2004, 63–74). Therefore, it is quite obvious that so far only discrimination in the context of insurance has gained special attention, as reflected in numerous legal acts that responded to the problem or the fear of the problem.

5 The legal prohibition of genetic discrimination

Countries that decided to regulate the use of genetic information in the field of insurance adopted either specific non-discrimination and privacy acts or included new rules within their existing regulations. The former model of regulation can be illustrated by the US Genetic Information Nondiscrimination Act (GINA) passed by the House of Representatives and signed by President George W. Bush on May 21, 2008 (H.R.493 ENR, became Public Law 110-343 on 10/3/2008). According to the Act, group health plans and health insurers are prohibited from denying coverage to a healthy individual or charging that person higher premiums based solely on a genetic predisposition to developing a disease in the future. The legislation also bars employers from using individual genetic information when making hiring, firing, job placement, or promotion decisions. The latter model of adopting special rules within other regulations can be illustrated by the Polish insurance law (Insurance Activity Act of 22 May 2003, Dz.U. 2003 Nr 124 poz. 1151). According to Art. 21 and 22 of the Insurance Activity Act, an insurance company can *require* from an individual medical examination or diagnostic examination, *with the exception of genetic testing*, in order to estimate the insurance risk and specify his rights to service and the level of premium. GINA offers a much broader protection of patient rights since it forbids the use of information about a genetic predisposition to developing a disease, irrespective of how and from whom the insurer obtained it.

Insurers object to the prohibition of the use of genetic information in their procedures for many reasons. They argue that genetic information cannot be distinguished from other medical information about health status or condition of an individual that are the basis of the insurance system. Companies gather personal health information, including age, health care history, and family health care history, in underwriting individual insurance policies. They use statistical correlations of these data with future illness to predict whether they result in claims for payment under an insurance policy. Furthermore, the insurance companies establish their policy terms, as well as their premiums on the basis of such predictions. If the estimated risk is too great or unpredictable, which means that it can bring more costs than benefits, the companies used to refuse coverage. If insurers are allowed to obtain and use other personal medical data, including family health care history, it remains unclear why they are prohibited from using genetic test results, so the argument goes.

What is more, insurers usually invoke the so called 'adverse selection' effect as a crucial argument that the prohibition of the use of genetic information by insurers would be unfair. If applicants for individual insurance coverage have undergone genetic testing and had no obligation to disclose the results to the insurance companies, they would be in a privileged position. People with positive test results would buy the coverage and those with negative would not. Taking into account that all individuals were to be charged the same premium and offered the same coverage irrespective of their personal information, those applicants who were at the lowest risk would desert the insurance companies and there would remain only those at the highest risk who would generate inadequately high costs for the companies (see Berry 2008, 98). This would result in increasing premiums or eventually, the collapse of the insurance system.

6 Genetic exceptionalism

New regulatory regimes that face the problems raised by the use of genetic information by insurance companies demonstrate quite the opposite view. The non-discrimination or privacy laws provide a double standard of protection with regard to genetic information by distinguishing them from other medical or personal information. As George Annas, Leonard Glantz and Patricia Roche write: 'Genetic information is uniquely powerful and uniquely personal, and thus merits unique privacy protection' (Annas, Glantz and Roche 1995, 360). The view that genetic information is unique, exceptionally sensitive and therefore requires wider and separate protection from other health related medical records is called genetic exceptionalism (see Hodge 2003, 1019–1020; Murray 1997, 60–73; Krajewska 2008, 59–66). Genetic exceptionalism is based on a descriptive and a normative assumption. The descriptive one is that genetic information is distinctive and can be distinguished from other medical information. The normative assumption is that genetic information ought to be specially protected.

This view is supported by several arguments. First, genetic information can be seen as highly sensitive and unique because of its special *predictive character*. It does not only describe people's health in the past and present but it may predict people's future health, by detecting a predisposition or susceptibility for illness in healthy asymptomatic individuals. Second, genetic information provides much more personal information than medical data. It does not only include information about the individual's health status but also about many other significant personal characteristics. Third, genetic information is unique and highly sensitive since it reveals information not only about an individual but also about an individual's family (ancestors, siblings as well as current or future offspring). Fourth, genetic information exists beyond our control and cannot be changed by our actions or decisions. Finally, genetic information is very easy to obtain without the consent or even the knowledge of an individual. For instance, one can perform genetic testing on a tiny genetic material included in somebody's saliva left on a cup of coffee or on a licked envelope.

Although all these arguments seem very persuasive, they have been frequently questioned. First, most illnesses can be seen as genetically based, so all such medical information about illnesses can be treated as genetic, irrespective of its source. Second, there are many sorts of information that have a predictive ability, not only genetic information. Third, non-genetic health records can also provide many personal details, as well as some information about the individual's relatives. What is more, information about certain diseases based on non-genetic (e.g. environmental) conditions can be as important for family members (a spouse, offspring or siblings) as any genetic information. It depends on the disease, not on the source of the disease. Fourth, there are many non-genetic factors relevant to the onset of a disease that are absolutely beyond our control, such as pollution, smoking parents or co-workers.

In sum, we have to admit that it is extremely difficult to treat genetic information as something separate from medical data. However, it does not mean that genetic information does not require special protection. We can still argue that genetic information ought to be specially protected *as if it were* distinctive. However, any regulation based on these assumptions may be inefficient in practice because of the difficulties in distinguishing genetic information and the ambiguity of its definition.

7 The concept of genetic discrimination

In my opinion, the debate over genetic non-discrimination acts goes into a blind alley when it focuses on the question as to whether information is genetic or non-genetic. Instead, the debate should focus on the character (what sort of information it is, e.g. about identity, future or current illness of an individual) and the use of the information, especially on its context (whether the use genetic information is aimed at diagnosis, treatment or prevention of a disease or whether it is aimed at limiting people's rights or maximising one's interests).[8] Only by analysing the particular context of the use of genetic information can we consider whether a particular use is wrong (discriminative) and should be restricted.

8 For instance, the use of genetic information which results in denying a job can be aimed at the protection of health of the person when the working conditions would increase the risk of the onset

In order to understand the problem better, let me introduce the concept of discrimination. By discrimination one may understand a situation when individuals who are alike in *every relevant respect* (not in absolutely every respect) are treated differently or when individuals who are different in *some relevant respect* are treated alike (see Feinberg 1973, 99). Direct discrimination takes place when the different treatment is based on unjustified criteria. Indirect discrimination takes place when the different treatment is based on neutral criteria but it brings about the unjustified exclusion of particular individuals or groups that are unable to meet such criteria.

By genetic discrimination one usually understands '[a]ctions taken against or negative attitudes toward a person based on that person's possession of variation on the genome, or variations in the genome of his or her biological relatives' (Epps 2003, 956). To put it differently, genetic discrimination means that one's own genetic characteristics are unjustified criteria of a difference in treatment or are wrongly included in the aim of a distribution or the definition of an institution. One can argue that a number of differential treatments are based on inherited genetic characteristics (e.g. rewarding individual merits and punishing individual vices – taking any decisions based on inherited characteristics such as intelligence, talent, appearance or inclinations). But discrimination occurs only if this differential treatment is unjustified, i.e. the criteria used are irrelevant with regard to the aim of the distribution of rewards and punishments or the aim of the distribution or a definition of an institution are wrong.

Therefore, in considering the problem of genetic discrimination, we have to analyse whether the genetic information is relevant or not as regards the criteria of different treatment of people in a particular case. We cannot say that employers or insurers should be prohibited from using genetic information in general. There can be situations in which health condition is essential for taking a decision concerning denying the job. This is the case when an occupation can be dangerous for people with a particular disease or when a health dysfunction interferes with work performance and causes serious danger for other people. The same problem is at stake when we consider the use of genetic information in insurance. Let me present the decision of an automobile insurance company as an example (cf. Billings 1992, 476–482). Consider a person who has had a driving license for twenty years and has never had any accident or traffic violation is now denied car insurance by the automobile insurance company on the basis of genetic test results that detect a genetic disorder (Charcot–Marie–Tooth disease) of the driver.

However, there can be many situations in which the justification of using genetic information would not be clear but rather controversial. It is, for instance,

of a disease. Reproductive genetic testing can be also aimed at either elimination of a dysfunction of an embryo or the elimination of an embryo. It is difficult to provide a general distinction between the different aims of the use of genetic information. It should be considered case by case.

very difficult to find consensus as far as the use of genetic information by an adoption agency is concerned. An adoption agency may seek to find the best possible parents for children and to reject the application by parents who are at risk of future illnesses. Billings cites a case where a couple wanted to adopt a child because the wife was at risk of developing Huntington disease and they did not want to pass the Huntington genes to the children (ibid.). They were rejected by an adoption agency although the first symptoms of the disease usually occur around the age of 40 or 50. The rejected woman who was a respondent to the US national survey on genetic discrimination, said:

> We understand the right to choose the BEST 50 couples out of some 500 applicants per year for placement. Availability of children is incredibly limited. And yet, should I be judged by a disease that I am only at risk for and that may not develop for some years to come? Does this make me different than anyone with diabetes or cancer, for example, in their ancestry? (Billings 1992, 480)

Considering situations such as this one we can have ambiguous feelings. On the one hand, we understand that the decisions of rejecting insurance or adoption were rational and seemed to be justified. On the other hand, we can feel that the decisions were unfair since people who were genetically disadvantaged were significantly limited in their social opportunities and choices. One can argue that a driver who did not undergo genetic tests can be more dangerous than a driver who knows that she is ill and is under permanent medical control. The same argument can be used in the adoption case. It can also be argued that there are many other aspects which are much more relevant than health condition when we choose the best possible parents.

8 Genetic determinism

I think that the pivotal issue in all such cases lies in the fact that *genetic information cannot solely determine people's life* and health condition, although its predictive value can be very strong. One of the most troubling matters in this respect is the so called genetic determinism. Genetic determinism (essentialism or reductionism) is a belief that genes determine human beings and their life (see Epps 2003, 956). Nobody expressed this belief better than James Watson, one of co-discoverers of the structure of DNA and Nobel Prize Winner who also helped establishing the HGP: 'We used to think our future is in our stars, now we know our future is in our genes' (quoted in Annas 2008, 33).[9]

[9] However, it is much more accurate to say with George Annas that '[t]he truth is that at the beginning of the last millennium we *knew* that our future is in the stars; now, at the beginning of this millennium, we *think* that our future is in our genes' (Annas 2008, 42).

Genetic determinism is a position that neglects all other relevant and important information about human beings such as environmental and social conditions, as well as individual free will and the ability to make reflective judgements, and reduces a human being to her genes only. To challenge this statement, 'we should give genes their due, but no more than that' as Thomas Murray (1997, 70) puts it. Genetic determinism is the main source of public fear of genetic discrimination and stigmatisation.

9 Conclusion

My claim is that the fundamental argument in favour of legal restrictions on the use of genetic information is that they are (or ought to be) aimed at challenging genetic determinism. If one rejects genetic determinism, accepting that nobody should be reduced to her genetic features, then the differentiation in treatment based *solely* on information about genes for the condition of disease is unjustified. Laws protecting genetic privacy and prohibiting genetic discrimination should be based on the fundamental assumption that having a gene for a condition is something different from having the condition. Thus, a healthy individual who has a predisposition or susceptibility for a disease cannot be treated on a par with an already ill individual who has developed the symptoms of a disease. It would be discriminatory since individuals who are different in some relevant respects ought to be treated differently.

Nevertheless, taking into account the aforementioned definition of discrimination, it may be justified to use genetic information as the criteria of distribution of goods (including insurance or employment) when this is *relevant* to the aim of distribution. If we accept that the insurance system is based on probability calculations and the estimation of future risks, we should admit that actuarial methods can provide justified criteria of different treatment of applicants. Therefore, the increased likelihood of using health care services among individuals who are in a group at higher risk of development of a disease could justify their different treatment by insurers. In this regard it should not matter whether the estimation of risk is based on genetic test results or family health care history. Yet if there are no such actuarial justifications, people with a predisposition or susceptibility for a disease should not be treated differently from other asymptomatic healthy individuals. In other words, the analysis of justified and unjustified criteria of distribution of insurance should take into account the distinction between the predictive value of genetic information and its statistical correlation to risk. Laws prohibiting genetic discrimination should be focused on challenging the idea of genetic determinism and on highlighting the significance of the distinction between asymptomatic and symptomatic individuals, as well as between the diagnosis and prognosis of a disease.

Finally, considering the problem of discrimination in the insurance system we have to take into account the aim of the distribution. The main aim of insurance companies is to maximise their profits. The main aim of applicants, on the other hand, is to get access to health services or to guarantee their family members financial support when the main wage earner in the household dies. Legislators and state policies have to weigh the interests of all parties and to pursue the main aim of the health care system which is to promote public health and guarantee appropriate treatment or prediction of diseases among people. To realise this aim, legislators should adopt laws that encourage people to perform genetic testing and screening and ensure the use of genetic information for the improvement of public health conditions. This is one of the greatest challenges to health care policies in the age of genomic medicine.

References

Aristotle. 2007. *Etyka nikomachejska* [*Nicomachean Ethics*]. Translated by D. Gromska. Warszawa: PWN.

Annas, George J. 2004. *American Bioethics: Crossing Human Rights and Health Law Boundaries.* New York: Oxford University Press.

Annas, George J. 2010. *Worst Case Bioethics: Death, Disaster, and Public Health.* New York: Oxford University Press.

Annas, George J., Leonard Glantz, and Patricia Roche. 1995. Drafting the Genetic Privacy Act: Science, Policy and Practical Considerations. *Journal of Law, Medicine and Ethics* 23: 306–366.

Berry, Roberta M. 2008. Health Care and the Human Genome: Regulatory Challenge and Response. In *Legal Perspectives in Bioethics*, edited by Ana S. Iltis, Sandra H. Johnson and Barbara A. Hinze, 95–125. New York, London: Routledge.

Billings, Paul R. et al. 1992. Discrimination as a Consequence of Genetic Testing. *The American Journal for Human Genetics* 50: 476–482.

Buchanan, Allen, et al. 2007. *From Chance to Choice: Genetics and Justice.* Cambridge: Cambridge University Press.

Collins, Francis C. 2006. *The Language of God: A Scientist Presents Evidence for Belief.* New York: Free Press.

Epps, Phyllis Griffin. 2003. Genetic Discrimination. In *Encyclopedia of Bioethics*, vol. 2, edited by Stephen G. Post, 956–959. New York: Macmillan Reference.

Feinberg, Joel, 1973. *Social Philosophy.* Englewood Cliffs (NJ): Prentice-Hall.

Glover, Jonathan. 1998. Eugenics: Some Lessons from the Nazi Experience. In *The Future of Human Reproduction: Ethics, Choice, and Regulation*, edited by John Harris and Soren Holm, 57–65. Oxford: Clarendon Press.

Habermas, Jürgen. 2003. *Przyszłość natury ludzkiej. Czy zmierzamy do eugeniki liberalnej?* [*The Future of Human Nature. Are We Heading Towards Liberal Eugenics?*]. Translated by M. Łukasiewicz. Warsaw: Scholar.

Hart, Herbert L. A. 1998. *Pojęcie prawa* [*A Concept of Law*]. Translated by J. Woleński. Warszawa: PWN.

Hodge, J. G., Jr. 2003. Genetic Testing and Screening: The Public Health Context. In *Encyclopedia of Bioethics*, vol. 2, edited by Stephen G. Post. New York: Macmillan Reference.

Human Development Report. 2005. [http://hdr.undp.org/reports/global/2005/].

Hume, David. 2005. *Badania dotyczące zasad moralności* [*An Enquiry Concerning the Principles of Morals*]. Krakow: Zielona Sowa.

Iltis, Ana S., Johnson, Sandra H., and Hinze, Barbara A. (eds.) 2008. *Legal Perspectives in Bioethics*. New York, London: Routledge.

Kevles, Daniel. 1999. Eugenics and Human Rights. *British Medical Journal* 319: 435–438.

Kevles, Daniel. 1995. *In the Name of Eugenics: Genetics and the Uses of Human Heredity*. Cambridge (MA): Harvard University Press.

Krajewska, Atina. 2008. *Informacja genetyczna a zakres autonomii jednostki w europejskiej przestrzeni prawnej* [*Genetic Information and the Scope of Individual Autonomy in the European Legal Space*]. Wroclaw: Wroclaw University Press.

Murray, Thomas H. 1997. Genetic Exceptionalism and 'Future Diaries': Is Genetic Information Different from Other Medical Information? In *Genetic Secrets: Protecting Privacy and Confidentiality in the Genetic Era*, edited by Mark A. Rothstein, 60–73. New Haven, London: Yale University Press.

Müller-Hill, Benno. 2006. Lessons from a Dark and Distant Past. In *Bioethics: An Antology*, edited by H. Kuhse and P. Singer, 231–236. Malden (MA), Oxford: Blackwell Publishing.

Post, Stephen G. (ed.) 1997. *Encyclopedia of Bioethics*, vol. 2. New York: Macmillan Reference.

Rothstein, Laura F. 1997. Genetic Information in Schools. In *Genetic Secrets: Protecting Privacy and Confidentiality in the Genetic Era*, edited by Mark A. Rothstein, 317–331. New Haven, London: Yale University Press.

Rothstein, Mark A. 1997. *Genetic Secrets: Protecting Privacy and Confidentiality in the Genetic Era*. New Haven, London: Yale University Press.

Silver, Lee M. 1985. *Remaking Eden: Cloning and Beyond in a Brave New World*. New York: Free Press.

Wertz, Dorothy C., and Fletcher, John C. 2004. *Genetics and Ethics in Global Perspective*. Dordrecht: Kluwer Academic Publishers.

Joint Criminal Enterprise: Towards a New Concept of Criminal Participation?

Charis Papacharalambous

Abstract Revived through the case law of the *ad hoc* Tribunal for the former Yugoslavia and the International Criminal Court Statute, 'Joint Criminal Enterprise' (JCE) aims at ascribing responsibility to individuals due to their mere membership in a joint venture. Contrary to the traditional distinction between principals and accessories all agents tend to be equally accused for every act materialising the common purpose. This transforms criminal law doctrine and criminal policy aims. Pre-emptive penal legislation, organised crime laws, and the penalisation of 'aggregates' (instead of defendants' individualised treatment) form the appropriate context. Thus, the responsibility concept undergoes a radical alteration. Naturalism regarding objective imputation is abandoned, the causality nexus between deed and effect is enfeebled and *actus reus* has been 'spiritualised'. Further, *mens rea* requirements are reoriented towards the prerequisites of strict liability. Establishing 'vicarious' responsibility for group conduct, JCE lets progressively a kind of 'collective guilt' resurface.

1 The notion and its recent development

Joint Criminal Enterprise (JCE) presents a qualified form of complicity. It arises when two or more people together embark on the commission of an offence. Emblematic in its use through the case law of the *ad hoc* Tribunal for the former Yugoslavia (ICTY), the construct aims at transferring responsibility to individuals indirectly, i.e. through the fact that they were members of a group having committed international crimes in furtherance of a jointly decided and approved plan or purpose.

JCE was already well known in the common law tradition before its revival through the jurisdiction of the ICTY. This has been more the case in Australian law, whereas JCE remains less accepted in the British one (see Ormerod 2008, 182). Concerted action is the gist of JCE leading to a crucial differentiation from traditional accessorial liability, since every member of the JCE is equally accused for every act materialising the plan or purpose. Thus, the doctrine departs from the demand to accurately prove the uniqueness of each accomplice's conduct and to differentiate his/her behaviour as e.g. instigation, aiding or abetting. Instead, *the accused is always principal offender* due to his/her involvement in the enterprise and irrespective of the form of the specific *actus reus* otherwise attributable to him/her (see Herring 2008, 849–850, 900–901; Ashworth 2009, 422–423, 434; Cassese 2008, 191, 211; see also Hamdorf 2007, 218–224). Thus, what can be imputed is always more than what has been committed, if 'commission' is naturalistically conceived of as 'voluntary act' (cf. critically Powles 2004, 610–611).

2 Differentiations

JCE has been the inspiring feature or theoretical-practical underpinning of several modes in criminal legislation. Far from being just a peculiarity of the ICTY jurisprudence, JCE reveals a deeper transformation of the respective dogmatic features on complicity as well as of the attitudes of modern criminal policy in general. Phenomena like pre-emptive penal legislation, organised crime statutes, or the penalisation of aggregate entities (instead of defendants' individualised treatment), do form the contextual environment for the flourishing of such a holistic notion of criminal liability, for many a rather 'totalising' concept of complicity. Of course, *exceptions* are made in cases of crimes where the offender must have a special capacity or where the crime can be only corporally committed (e.g. rape); then, the accused becomes again secondary participant (e.g. instigator). Also, cases of innocent agency are not counted as JCE cases, as long as the commission through another who is acting as a mere tool, is an independent type of principal's criminal liability (see e.g. Herring 2008, 844; Allen 2009, 48, 124, 221; Cryer 2004, 242). Equally, the specific discussion on the principal's mode of liability when the agent is guilty though erring in some significant part, is of no concern here (see Cryer 2004, 242).[1]

Finally, JCE is principally different from *conspiracy*, in that the latter, in its being an inchoate crime, is mainly a rather subsidiary form of imputation when the commission of the act planned is lacking, notwithstanding the fact that in common law the concurrence with the committed act can be considered as a real one. In cases of JCE a clear part of the agreement has to be materialised, whereas in conspiracy cases no further overt act beyond the agreement is needed, according to the prevailing opinion in academia (see in general on conspiracy e.g. Herring 2008, 797–803, 834–840; Allen 2009, 223–224, 280–299; Ormerod 2008, 182–183, 399–437). On

1 For the respective discussions in the civil law tradition, see representatively: Cramer in Schönke and Schröder (1985, Vorbem. zu §§25ff., Rn. 78; §25, Rnn. 18–24, 33–35, 38); for an overview of the German doctrine on participation in general see Hamdorf (2007, 209–218).

the other hand, however, no substantial contribution to the JCE is required from the part of an accused, when the materialisation of the common design has sufficiently taken place through acts of others; *it thus meets extreme notions of conspiracy*, like the one expressed in *Pinkerton*, holding an inmate liable for acts done by another conspirator acting as a free man (see van der Wilt 2007, 94; Chouliaras, manuscript, 11 and n. 54; Danner and Martinez 2005, 140–141). This perverts though the very notion of conspiracy inasmuch as, as van der Wilt puts it:

> The gist of conspiracy has always been, and should remain, a common understanding that warrants mutual attribution of the conduct of the participants. Losing sight of this basic element will ultimately result in the demise of the concept. (van der Wilt 2007, 100)

3 JCE as formed through the Tribunals' jurisdiction

Resurfaced in the scope of international criminal law, especially through the *ICTY Tadić Appeal Judgment*, JCE appears in *three types*:[2]

(a) JCE I (*basic form*): it means participation at the common design (*ICTY Trial Judgments* in *Krstić, Simić* cases). In *ICTY Trial Judgment* in *Brđanin* case the Tribunal excluded the case where the principal offenders had not participated in the plan; the fact that the planners used on their own behalf the activity of the principals who had not been part of the design's formation became crucial in the respective Appeals Chamber Decision (to which I come back below);

(b) JCE II (*systemic form*): it means participation in the functioning of an institutionalised criminal framework (so-called 'concentration camp cases'). All those not withdrawing from organised ill-treatment are responsible. In the representative *Hadamar* case (1945), tried before a US Military Commission, a hospital director and accomplices were sentenced to death for mass killing of coerced labourers who got ill;

(c) JCE III (*extended form*): this is joint participation in a commonly designed plan in awareness of the risk that a primary offender may commit an incidental act lying beyond the common design. The accused must have foreseen the risk of an unconcerted crime due to circumstances indicating its predictability and this crime must be a typical outgrowth of the design. For foreseeability to establish imputation it suffices that it is the mental outcome of a person of reasonable prudence. Foreseeability is thus simultaneously abstract-concrete and objective; subjective shortcomings in forecasting the incident do not alleviate the *mens rea*: in *ICTY Krstić* case the General was hold guilty in the first instance for atrocities against fugitives from

2 See on the following distinctions mainly Cassese 2008 (191–209); see also Satzger (2009, 61); Ambos (2007, 159–161); on *Krstić Trial Chamber Judgment*, see also van der Wilt (2007, 97).

Srebrenica due to foreseeability measured by this objective yardstick, although according to the Appeals Judgment he was found guilty of having the *mens rea* of a secondary offender in genocide.

The JCE III could theoretically *be limited* only in cases of *dolus specialis* (e.g. genocide; persecution) to those sharing it, as well as wherever a secondary offender can be charged with a lesser degree of culpability, e.g. with manslaughter instead of its qualified form, murder, or with inhuman treatment and not torture, etc. (see Cassese 2008, 205–207).

In the 21st of May 2003 ICTY *Appeal Judgment on JCE* (*Dragoljub Ojdanić*) the latter has been considered as customarily establishing co-perpetration and no form of accessorial liability. Admittedly, this took place without properly and thoroughly deepening in the objection the appeal raised, an objection against JCE as such, which has not been invoked in *Tadić*. The case law which the Tribunal referred to in *Tadić Appeal Judgment* was rather scarce, i.e. mainly the 1947 *D' Ottavio et al.* decision of the Italian Court of Cassation (Powles 2004, 614–617; on *D' Ottavio et al.* case see also Cassese 2008, 204 n. 18).

Following this judgment, however, the ICTY decided accordingly among others in *Krnojelac, Kvočka* and *Brđanin Appeal Judgments*; the Appeals Chamber of the International Criminal Tribunal for Rwanda (henceforth: ICTR), as well, decided so in the *Ntakirutimana* case. Distancing itself from the WW II complicity concept which was rather based on the notion of having control over the crime scene, as well as from the *Tadić Appeal Judgment*, the May 2003 decision of the ICTY made liability, especially as to the JCE III, *extremely subjective*. It allowed, in parallel, an interpretation, according to which the culpability mode of the accused could be reduced to recklessness in the sense not of the '*dolus eventualis*' of the civil law tradition but in that of a kind of grave negligence having nothing to do with intent even in a 'thin' form. In the spirit of such an interpretation the constructive knowledge of the offender (what he/she must have known, which is to be proved via circumstantial evidence) is replaced by a fiction consisting in what he/she should have known, which renders intentional wrongdoing similar to strict liability (see Olasolo 2009, 265ff; Satzger 2009, 64; on the Tribunals' case law see also Chouliaras 2010b, 561–570). As Olasolo summarises:

> [F]or some authors, the extended form of joint criminal enterprise could also be applied in situations in which the defendant is not aware that the commission of the foreseeable crimes is a possible consequence of the implementation of the common criminal plan. *As long as the defendant is, objectively, in a position to foresee that possibility, it is irrelevant whether he actually foresees it.* (Olasolo 2009, 281, my emphasis)

The impact of this theorising is huge whereby the accused has to be considered as co-perpetator of those committing crimes with specific intent or crimes with *mens rea* entailing ulterior intent ('*dolus specialis*'). E.g. the JCE member who should have foreseen the inclinations of some of the principals towards turning an ethnic cleansing into genocidal acts, could be held liable as their accomplice, even if his culpability is not going beyond negligence and there is no *dolus specialis* commonly shared between him and the killers; thus far only policy arguments can theoretically underpin JCE or deliver a legitimacy to it (see Olasolo 2009, 281–285). This occurs in especially acute form where the foresight of the accused refers to 'crimes', which rather shield general modes of liability than depict specific criminal behaviour, as is the case with 'complicity in genocide' of the Genocide Convention, which has been inadvertently repeated in the ICTY and ICTR Statutes.[3] Also aiding and abetting the JCE III is rather unconceivable: if these 'accessories' know about the risk of causing death in implementing a plan for torture, they become JCE-members themselves, i.e. co-perpetrators (cf. Powles 2004, 612–613). *By watering down the mens rea qualifications* the *nullum crimen* principle is fundamentally altered. Thus, the construct meets again what the Nuremberg Trials declared as 'criminal organisations', indirectly referring back to collective responsibility, ramified in indisputably assuming the criminal nature of these organisations and in reversing the burden of proof for their accused members (see Chouliaras, manuscript, 15–19, 34f; Ohlin 2006, 4–6, 8, 11–13, 15f; see also Powles 2004, 618–619).

In the Rwandan tragedy this link has been made obvious in several decisions of the *ICTR Appeals Chambers in the Karemera* case, where the JCE III has been considered as the proper mode in dealing with *'vast scope' joint ventures*, even though at the cost of tentatively violating the '*nulla poena sine culpa*' principle (see Satzger 2009, 62–64, 66–67). Besides, the already mentioned ICTY Appeals jurisdiction rejects any need of *express* or *explicit agreement* for the JCE to be established (as it has been initially argued in the *ICTY Trial Chamber Brđanin* case). In cases of a linkage between *multiple and partly overlapping JCEs* it is anyway not required that every accused principal belonging to, say, JCE1, has agreed upon the commission of the crimes with the planners, belonging to, say, JCE2; it suffices if the accused belongs to a JCE1 some members of which are participating at the plan agreed upon with the 'masterminds' (JCE2), themselves not physically perpetrating the crimes planned. Further, also the plans of the separate JCEs do not need to fully coincide, they need just to be somehow interlinked and one of them be the overwhelming and preponderant (see Gustafson 2007, 143f). Gustafson points out that insofar: '[...] contrary to the implicit conclusion of the *Brđanin* trial Chamber, it does not nec-

3 The connection between JCE and the Genocide Convention liability models has become an issue of itself; see on this Powles (2004, 613–614) and critically Satzger (2009, 65–67).

essarily follow that [...] there must be an explicit agreement' – and that in case of a partial linkage between the groups – 'the two groups have clearly not formulated their respective criminal plans independently of each other. As such, [...], it should be reasonable to attribute JCE liability' (ibid., 148).

In this regard, the elusiveness of the concept increases and the rupture as to the conspiracy tradition is made evident (see the critique to the above mentioned case law of the ICTY and ICTR Appeal Judgments in van der Wilt 2007, 98–102).

4 JCE and the ICC Statute

It is to be stressed that as to art. 25 (3)(d) of the Statute of the ICC, a JCE can be assumed only under the term that this provision may be interpreted so that it establishes an exception from the 'intent' rule laid down in art. 30. This is as such accepted by the Statute due to the 'unless otherwise provided' clause in the beginning of the latter article. Further, as Cassese rightly points out, the provision repeats, historically seen, art. 2 (3) of the 1997 International Terrorist Bombing Convention, more aligned to the Italian criminal law construct of the so called 'external participation in mafia-style organisations' (*concorso esterno in associazione mafiosa*). This is a *peculiar kind* of secondary participation, not a JCE: the 'extraneus' either shares the common purpose – thus being actually a 'non-intraneus' part of JCE (!) – or knowingly aids and abets the association, but not the principal(s) personally, as aiders and abettors usually do (see Cassese 2008, 212–213; cf. Ohlin 2006, 9; Cryer 2004, 241). Powles comments as to the legislative motivation behind art. 25 (3)(d) of the ICC Statute, arguing that art. 25(3)(d) ICC Statute targets conspiracy at the very most:

> [I]f Article 25 (3)(d) was intended as an alternative, compromise basis of liability to conspiracy, it may not have been the intention of the drafters to include a basis of liability that could render an accused guilty even if he did not intend the ultimate outcome of his actions pursuant to the common purpose. (Powles 2004, 617)

If the above is taken under due consideration, then also the reference in *Tadić Appeal Judgment* to art. 25(3)(d) of the ICC Statute does not seem quite accurate; the latter does not necessarily cover JCE, at least not in its entirety.

What, however, one has most probably to expect is that ICC will maintain the doctrine of JCE, even in its expanded form, due to the fact that after *Tadić* JCE forms part of customary international law, i.e. a source of law applicable by the ICC in the framework of its jurisdiction. The court will though probably maintain it rather as a subsidiary form of imputing liability in cases of joint ventures. That means that JCE will probably function as a 'safety net' for avoiding lacunae of penal protection wherever straightforward complicity doctrine will eventually not suffice in this respect (see Chouliaras 2010b, 571–572).

5 Deepening the analysis: collectivity and normativity as cornerstones of JCE

Nevertheless, it is admitted that the systemic and macro-criminal nature of the international core crimes, as they are laid down in the ICC Statute, i.e. the very notion of collective wrongdoing (see e.g. Ohlin 2006, 4–6, 19), implies that liability should be dispatched from naturalistic residues. JCE is first and foremost in accord with the systematic, widespread or generally macro-criminal dimension required for crimes such as genocide or crimes against humanity, showing also resemblances with the structure of command responsibility. This means, especially concerning JCE II, that perpetration has to become a *'functional' notion*, in order for imputation obstacles to be circumvented, like the detached bureaucratic anonymity of a camp, exactly purported to make personal guilt invisible. This means also that in such cases a consequent application of the JCE leaves protection loopholes rather than over-penalises, because conspiratorial agreement presupposes agents and not a cog of the wheel of a death and pain machine (see van der Wilt 2007, 94, 100, 102–103). As van der Wilt writes borrowing from Zygmunt Bauman:

> The poor performance of the JCE doctrine in establishing and justifying the criminal responsibility of participants in larger groups or organizations has a more profound cause. [...] the doctrine does not tally with the reality of modern bureaucracies that engage in systematic mass crime. (van der Wilt 2007, 101)

Insofar, contrary to the *ICTY Appeals Chamber Tadić* case, which considers it as emanation of the JCE I, as well as contrary to voices aligning JCE II to JCE III, e.g. in the case of a camp guard foreseeing the torturing of the inmates he guards (cf. in favour of the latter opinion Powles 2004, 608 n. 8, 609–610), the JCE II is distinct from the other two categories. Criminal liability may be incurred on the mere basis of the purely systemic mode of co-offending, itself defying any attempt of differentiating among complicity gradations. Thus far, JCE II can be conceived of as emanating from the organised crime type of conduct, representing what has been called 'institutionalised membership responsibility', whereas JCE III, more akin to traditional conspiracy, represents a responsibility based on so called 'collateral membership', more prone to presuppose some kind of agreement as externalised common state of mind (see Chouliaras 2010a, 205; 2010b, 550–561, 573; manuscript, 35). Therefore, in cases of JCE II only opportunistic participants must have substantially contributed to the joint venture for being held liable, whereas the rest of the members of JCE II are *ipso facto* co-perpetrators (see Cassese 2008, 196, 198–199). Exactly the opposite is the case regarding JCE III, as interpreted until now in the Tribunals' case law. The lack of a criminal infrastructure in this liability form makes the demand of a 'substantial contribution' of the accused to the enterprise irrelevant instead of rendering it (logically, as it seems) absolutely necessary. This is in accord with a very well-known proposal in the theory focusing on the traditional criminal law principle of individual culpability, which is opposed to a victim-based and symbolically proceeding expansive penal law on JCE (see Danner and Martinez 2005, 102–120, 132–146, 150–151). As these authors conclude:

> In the development of JCE doctrine, concern for symbolic vindication of violations of victims' human rights has proven a more potent influence than worries over potential violations of defendants' rights. More importantly, the victim-oriented, civil law model of human rights has diverted attention from the values vindicated by the criminal law-oriented culpability principle (Danner and Martinez 2005, 146).

Consequently, the philosophy of the JCE construct consists generally in tending to overcome the extreme individualism in imputing responsibility and especially culpability. According to its underpinning common law understanding of co-perpetration, no differentiations are made between error in persona and *aberratio ictus*[4] of the principal regarding respective consequences for the planner or instigator, as is the case in the civil law tradition. Instead, the 'transferred malice' theory burdens these persons with the crime committed in the first place, leaving room for differentiations only at the sentencing stage (analogous is Art. 21 of the Cypriot Penal Code). In defying the conceptual pedantry of the civil law tradition, common law does not avail always of the necessary theoretical cohesion which is capable of guaranteeing some predictability of an inquiry's outcome. What is e.g. the meaning of the fundamental difference of the principal's act from crimes envisaged in the planning stage? Or, what should foresight of the accused cover as to the divergences from the common plan in the execution?[5] *Without a normative-functional frame the naturalistic fallacy is lurking again*: one is steadily forced to assume 'facts' and either refer them to external reality, which concerns the *actus reus*, or to 'internal',

4 The term means in the civil law tradition the unintended causing of harm to a person or an object other than the initially targeted, without error as to the identity of the latter. E.g. A shoots against B but kills C passing in front of B in this very moment. A is to be charged with attempt of murder and negligent manslaughter. See generally Cramer in Schönke and Schröder (1985, §15, Rn. 56).

5 Cf. in this respect also Hamdorf (2007, 221–223, 225–226), pleading for returning to the traditional complicity doctrine instead of JCE. In many cases traditional doctrine features as a solution to the problems the non-coincidence between planning and execution poses, especially in the framework of participation. The meaningfulness of answering the question in this way however, depends primarily on whether JCE is an aggravated or qualified (or whatsoever) form of *traditional* participation, which – as I further try to show – is not very much the case.

i.e. psychic states, which allegedly concern the *mens rea*. 'Nature', observable and distinguishable in its details, as it were, must prevail in judging types of deeds and states of mind. By thus reducing imputation to causation and normative ascriptions to scientist explanations, naturalism is, concerning JCE, totally misplaced. Whereas it could have been useful as to the traditional forms of criminal liability where ideally one (or some more) persons form through their acts 'physical units', commonly sensed as usual offences (like manslaughter, rape or robbery), the picture is fully changed when liability forms like JCE come to the fore. Here, no usual accomplices violate legal prescriptions describing crimes, easily intuited as such and discernible through observation one from another. Rather, collectives are offending basic human rights in massive dimensions, as a whole system of evil absorbing individuals irrespective of their position as wrongdoers or victims. This systemic frame cannot be conceived properly without abandoning naturalistic relics and without instead primarily focusing normatively on exactly these systemic-functional parameters. It becomes thus obvious that JCE has to overcome traditional individual imputation models. One has to derive personal culpability from the *global act represented by the enterprise itself* (towards this direction also Ambos 2007, 167–168, 181f.). According to him,

> the traditional system of individual attribution of responsibility, as applied to ordinary criminality characterised by the individual commission of single crimes, must be adapted to the needs of international criminal law aimed at the development of a *mixed system of individual-collective responsibility* in which the criminal enterprise or organization as a whole serves as the entity upon which attribution of criminal responsibility is based. The doctrine has called this a *Zurechnungsprinzip Gesamttat*. (Ambos 2007, 183, his emphasis)

Also van der Wilt writes straightforwardly:

> Such an approach [i.e. individual guilt] is generally to be applauded as it prevents culprits from shielding behind 'Acts of States' and thus declining any personal responsibilities. However, a one-sided emphasis on personal guilt may obscure the collective dimension of system criminality. In their quest for appropriate modes of criminal responsibility that capture the collective aspect of international crimes, international criminal courts may consider doctrines like JCE to be indispensable. (van der Wilt 2007, 108)

It can be thus conclusively held that, *tentatively, it is the agent as 'instance' of a criminally significant implementation of a role, role implementing figure, not as an irreplaceable, non-interchangeable individual; a normative 'persona', not a psycho-physically distinguishable person, who is the addressee of the norm.*

If this *purely normative stance* is the appropriate point of departure, then the question to be posed is this: can facilitating the police and law enforcement instances be a legitimacy basis for extending criminal law in pre-stages of even purely preparatory acts, if the argument in favour of this expansion only consists in that mass action *psychologically* binds so forcefully that no escape is possible, i.e. if the explanation is based on the alleged dangerousness of concerted illegality? The answer is clearly negative. Disposing over a normative approach renders psychology redundant. But even then questions remain. For instance, what makes JCE different from mere guilt by association, different from '*versari in re illicita*'?[6]

Further and deeper more: does perhaps collective *legal* guilt become through the JCE construct intelligible, contrary to its traditional containment to the moral guilt, as emblematically Jaspers thought about the Germans? (see Ohlin 2006, 5, 19; cf. Jaspers 2000, passim and especially 55f.). Does this deny any possibility of presuming secondary participation in cases of JCE, like merchants' selling clothes to its members or people's renting apartments to them or fuelling their vehicles, due to the fact that they know or must or even should have known the intentions of these JCE members, without intending the crimes and of course without sharing the criminals' intent, in the first place? Regarding this, liability based on art. 25 of the ICC Statute (if it is taken as a legal basis for JCE) turns out to be remarkably wide, since all contributions to a JCE have been equated (see Ohlin 2006, 11–13, 17, 20). Ohlin stresses the opposite intention of the traditional criminal law approach:

> Relative culpability is not simply a matter of serving the appropriate time in a penal facility. It goes deeper to the very heart of the criminal offence. The minor participant and the chief conspirator are not simply deserving of different sentences. Their guilt is different and it is this central truth that the current version of joint criminal enterprise obscures. (Ohlin 2006, 20, his emphasis)

The crux is that through this development the responsibility concept is *radically changed*. It abandons any notion of naturalism through objectively imputing criminal effects to 'enterprise-members' merely on the fact that they are such, namely it enfeebles the causality link between deed and effect and 'spiritualises' the notion of *actus reus*.

Further, the requirements of *mens rea* are reoriented towards the prerequisites of strict liability. JCE cannot be reduced as to the *mens rea* requirements to the criteria used in traditional co-perpetration in order for principals and accessories to be eventually distinguished despite the existence of a joint conduct. These requirements are: the 'fundamental difference' between the planned crime, the respective knowledge of the accused and the actual commission of it by the principal, the

6 This is also a broad discussion; see, justifying JCE, Gustafson (2007, 135–136, 137–139); Cassese (2008, 191, 201–205); see also the comment of Schabas (2004, 126–127); cf. critically Chouliaras (2010a, 206; 2010b, 572–578) and critically on conspiratorial inchoate offending, Herring (2008, 837, 840).

knowledge about the existence of weapons in the possession of the principal, the foresight as to the way of their use, etc. Insofar, the established precedents concerning traditional joint offenders' conduct as they have been laid down in British case law,[7] do not help in grasping JCE in its entirety by merely referring to such criteria (see on this case law also Hamdorf 2007, 222–223). Putting thus the proportionality principle under a real 'ordeal' in as much as modes of dealing mainly with regulatory offences are now transposed to serious crimes par excellence, allowing thus for the severest sanctions to be imposed without the fulfilment of equally 'severe' conditions concerning voluntariness or culpability of the wrongdoer, JCE confuses tentatively the extended liability which is traditionally reserved to *risk-averting inside modern complex societies* (i.e., strict, vicarious or corporate liability) and where the wrongdoing is rather a kind of '*malum prohibitum*', with *crimes indisputably regarded as heinous*, i.e. '*mala per se*'. This 'hollowing' of the *mens rea*, its deprivation of its very content is of course not born *ex nihilo*. It is traceable even in the field of traditional complicity where, for instance, 'procuring', i.e. the exploitation of ignorance of a principal with the purpose of driving him/her to commit a crime, is established despite the fact of an existing (even if 'thin') *mens rea* or, in any case, of the voluntariness of the act on the principal's part (see Herring 2008, 225–226, 762–769, 849).[8]

Be it as it may: is this liability which is based on 'assumption of risk' (like in US tort law) the proper mode for legitimising JCE, especially in international criminal law? If there is no specific legitimacy for JCE, levelling different kinds of guilt and allowing only judicial discretion in sentencing, does not suffice. Practically, JCE is then tantamount to 'Just Convict Everyone' (see Ohlin 2006, 15, 20; Chouliaras, manuscript, 23 n. 132). Especially, confusing liability forms and discretionary options in sentencing seems to be extremely opposite to firm criminal law principles if it takes place at the level of international core crimes. Danner and Martinez note in this respect:

> Furthermore, correcting the overexpansive tendencies of JCE at the sentencing rather than the liability phase frustrates one of the transitional justice goals of international criminal trials: providing an accurate account of an individual's role in the relevant crimes. (Danner and Martinez 2005, 142)

7 See on the 1997 cases *R v Powell and Daniels*, *R v English* and on the 1998 case *R v Uddin* in Herring (2008, 858–871); on the first two see also Cassese (2008, 202–203).

8 On producing vicarious liability through a wide and not differentiated notion of 'foresight', see critically also Ohlin (2006, 15–16); see also Chouliaras (manuscript, 38–39).

6 JCE as a moral intrusion into law?

To be sure: the subject is messy; I think though that the inquietude arising out of the gray areas in the JCE doctrine has less to do with the *hyper-normativity of the incrimination*, the fact, that is, that the physical perpetration is programmatically underestimated. This is not that much peculiar in a context of legal theorising which prioritises the normative at the expense of the naturalistic dimension of wrongdoing (loosening the causality link between conduct and effect; reducing wrongdoing to conduct irrespective of the result; in general 'spiritualising' crime's legal notion; see on this passim Papacharalambous 2003; 2009). Even traditionally it has not been embarrassing that e.g. in so called 'composed' crimes in the civil law tradition, all are perpetrators, despite the fact that some do not commit all constituents of the crime (e.g.: A holds the victim and B commits the theft: all are liable for robbery). Not even the weakening of the terms for establishing criminal *mens rea* is that much strange; modern multicultural and porous legal thinking has long been acquainted with the fecundity of flexible constructs like recklessness and constructive intent.

The problem lies, I presume, rather somewhere else. Firstly, *in the assumptive form of imputation*. Due to the lack of transparency as to how the separate crimes materialising the common plan are in details coupled back to this plan, assumptions replace the missing links in order for an imputation judgment to be formed. It goes, of course, without saying that even this kind of imputation does not preclude eventual *in concreto* justifications or excuses at a posterior stage of the procedure. Secondly, there is *the extremely pre-emptive dimension* of the respective penal provisions. JCE represents a threat, the dangerousness of which is often already there, long before the mass atrocities are attempted. JCE is a cardinal example of the primacy of the endangerment at the expense of a plainly tangible harm. Thirdly (and this is of high importance), this type of dealing with JCE is necessary due to *the network-like feature of JCE*, that is the holistically functioning – somewhere tight, somewhere loose – interconnectedness of its members. Because of this feature JCE becomes remarkably *invisible*. Either as conspiracy, as criminal structure or as crucial knowledge of the others' bad intentions (which objectively renders someone guarantor of the safety of hundreds of possible victims), JCE does exist without being observable, it thus becomes rather an explanatory pattern for the sequence 'agreement–planning–layered distribution of "work"–concerted or not concerted commission' (a sequence which may remain finally partly undisclosed) than a qualified form of classical participation. This is the reason of the fact that JCE, *cunning and uncanny, as it were, in its impersonality and anonymity, effaces the possibility of individualisation of guilt in the same time we all well know it somehow exists, in order to restore it as derivation of collective liability.*

We are thus inclined – through another form of 'aggregates' liability' (cf. Feeley and Simon 1992) – to be reminiscent of the old doctrine of *actio libera in causa*, the so-called 'Dutch-Courage' cases of the common law tradition (see Allen 2009, 167). Their extension may be the adequate way for understanding JCE properly: according to the doctrine of *actio libera in causa* someone is guilty not of what one did but of the fact that one had deliberately prepared the causes of what afterwards happened, knowing in advance what will have happened and that then no withdrawal will have been available. This has the same temporality as the JCE guilt, *a temporality of anticipation, of pluperfect tense*. This is the tense of the primordial nature of *moral guilt*, of the 'infinity' of genuine and proper ethical responsibility. Indeed, JCE seems to contribute from its part to the already wide erosion of penal positivism, liberal permissiveness and individualistic self-referential indifference. Irrespective of the legal side-effects it may produce, for collective guilt, i.e. a trans-individual moral guilt par excellence, the moral demand for a self-ascription of blameworthiness and shame regarding wrongs done remains crucial (see Cooper 2001, 213; Corlett 2001, 264). Such self-ascription can be thought of also as an expression of remorse based either on membership to the criminal group or even on the assumption of a 'body' conceived of as a 'plural subject' (see Gilbert 2001, 220f., especially 229–231). JCE is insofar the effect of an endeavour to respond to the enhanced re-moralisation of social control by obliquely or perversely trying to decode collective guilt through the language of law...

References

Allen, Michael. 2009. *Textbook on Criminal Law.* Oxford: Oxford University Press.

Ambos, Kai. 2007. Joint Criminal Enterprise and Command Responsibility. *Journal of International Criminal Justice* 5: 159–183.

Ashworth, Andrew. 2009. *Principles of Criminal Law.* Oxford: Oxford University Press.

Cassese, Antonio. 2008. *International Criminal Law.* Oxford: Oxford University Press.

Chouliaras, Athanasios. 2010a. State Crime and Individual Criminal Responsibility: Theoretical Inquiries and Practical Consequences. In *The Review Conference and the Future of the International Criminal Court. Proceedings of the First AIDP Symposium for Young Penalists in Tübingen, Germany, co-organized by the AIDP YP Committee*, edited by Christoph Burchard, Otto Triffterer and Joachim Vogel, 191–214. AH Alphen aan den Rijn: Wolters Kluwer, and Köln: Carl Heymanns Verlag.

Chouliaras, Athanasios. 2010b. From 'Conspiracy' to 'Joint Criminal Enterprise': In Search of the Organizational Parameter. In *Future Perspectives on International Criminal Justice*, edited by Carsten Stahn and Larissa Van Den Herik, 545–582. The Hague: T.M.C. Asser Press.

Chouliaras, Athanasios. *Individual Responsibility in International Criminal Law: The Theory of Joint Criminal Enterprise* [unpublished manuscript with the author, in Greek].

Cooper, David. 2001. Collective Responsibility, 'Moral Luck', and Reconciliation. In *War Crimes and Collective Wrongdoing: A Reader*, edited by Aleksandar Jokić, 205–215. Malden (MA), Oxford: Blackwell.

Corlett, J. Angelo. 2001. Reparations to Native Americans? In *War Crimes and Collective Wrongdoing: A Reader*, edited by Aleksandar Jokić, 236–269. Malden (MA), Oxford: Blackwell.

Cryer, Robert. 2004. General Principles of Liability in International Criminal Law. In *The Permanent International Criminal Court: Legal and Policy Issues*, edited by Dominic McGoldrick, Peter Rowe and Eric Donnelly, 233–262. Oxford, Portland (Oregon): Hart.

Danner, Allison Marston, and Martinez, Jenny S. 2005. Guilty Associations: Joint Criminal Enterprise, Command Responsibility, and the Development of International Criminal Law. *California Law Review* 93: 75–169.

Feeley, Malcolm M., and Simon, Jonathan. 1992. The new penology: notes on the emerging strategy of corrections and its implications. *Criminology* 30.4: 449–474.

Gilbert, Margaret. 2001. Collective Remorse. In *War Crimes and Collective Wrongdoing: A Reader*, edited by Aleksandar Jokić, 216–235. Malden (MA), Oxford: Blackwell.

Gustafson, Katrina. 2007. The Requirement of an 'Express Agreement' for Joint Criminal Enterprise. A Critique of Brđanin. *Journal of International Criminal Justice* 5: 134–158.

Hamdorf, Kai. 2007. The Concept of a Joint Criminal Enterprise and Domestic Modes of Liability for Parties to a Crime. A Comparison of German and English Law. *Journal of International Criminal Justice* 5: 208–226.

Herring, Jonathan. 2008. *Criminal Law: Text, Cases, and Materials.* Oxford: Oxford University Press.

Jaspers, Karl. 2000. *The Question of German Guilt.* New York: Fordham University Press.

Ohlin, Jens David. 2006. Three Conceptual Problems with the Doctrine of Joint Criminal Enterprise. *Journal of International Criminal Justice* 6: 1–22.

Olasolo, Hector. 2009. Joint Criminal Enterprise and its Extended Form: A Theory of Co-perpetration Giving Rise to Principal Liability, a Notion of Accessorial Liability, or a Form of Partnership in Crime? *Criminal Law Forum* 20: 263–287.

Ormerod, David. 2008. *Smith and Hogan Criminal Law.* Oxford: Oxford University Press.

Papacharalambous, Charis. 2003. *Naturalism and Normative Approach: Causality and Objective Imputation as Cornerstones of the General Theory of Wrongdoing* [in Greek]. Athens, Thessaloniki: Sakkoulas.

Papacharalambous, Charis. 2009. The Notions of Wrongdoing and Agent in the Greek Criminal Law System from the Viewpoint of Law Theory. *Humanitas Journal of European Studies* 3: 77–84.

Powles, Steven. 2004. Joint Criminal Enterprise. Criminal Liability by Prosecutorial Ingenuity and Judicial Creativity? *Journal of International Criminal Justice* 2: 606–619.

Satzger, Helmut. 2009. Commentary (on Case No. ICTR-98-44-AR 72.7, A. Ch., 14.72006). In *Annotated Leading Cases of International Criminal Tribunals – vol. 24*, edited by André Klip and Göran Sluiter, 61–67. Antwerp, Oxford: Intersentia
[http://www.annotatedleadingcases.com/files/pdf/ALC_24_0061.pdf].

Schabas, William A. 2004. The Unfinished Work of Defining Aggression: How Many Times Must The Cannonballs Fly, Before They Are Forever Banned. In *The Permanent International Criminal Court. Legal and Policy Issues*, edited by Dominic McGoldrick, Peter Rowe and Eric Donnelly, 123–141. Oxford and Portland (Oregon): Hart.

Schönke, Adolf, and Schröder, Horst. 1985. *Strafgesetzbuch. Kommentar.* München: Beck.

Van der Wilt, Harmen. 2007. Joint Criminal Enterprise. Possibilities and Limitations. *Journal of International Criminal Justice* 5: 91–108.

Cases

Brđanin, Radoslav (Trial Judgment), ICTY TC (1.9.2004), Case No. IT-99-36-T

Brđanin, Radoslav (Appeal Judgment), ICTY AC (3.4.2007), Case No. ICTY-99-36-A

D' Ottavio et al., Italian Court of Cassation Court/ Criminal Section 1 (12.3.1947), Case No. 270 [as far as published in English translation retrievable in *Journal of International Criminal Justice* 5 (2007): pp. 232–234; photograph of the Italian handwritten original on file with the Journal]

Hadamar Case [= Klein Alfons et al.], US Military Commission Wiesbaden (8.–15.10.1945), Law Reports of Trials of War Criminals, London: UN War Crimes Commission, 1947 (Vol. I: Case No. 4, pp. 47–54 [also accessible at http://www.ess.uwe.ac.uk/wcc/hadamar.htm])

Karemera et al. (Appeal Judgments), ICTR AC, Decisions on Jurisdictional Appeals: Joint Criminal Enterprise, Case Nos. ICTR-98-44-AR 72.5, ICTR-98-44-AR 72.6 (12.4.2006), ICTR-98-44-AR 72.7 (14.7.2006)

Krnojelac,Milorad (Appeal Judgment), ICTY AC (17. 9.2003), Case No. ICTY-97-25-A

Krstić, Radislav (Trial Judgment), ICTY TC (2.8.2001), Case No. IT-98-33-T

Krstić, Radislav (Appeal Judgment), ICTY AC (19.4.2004), Case No. ICTY-98-33-A

Kvočka et al. (Appeal Judgment), ICTY AC (28.2.2005), Case No. IT-98-30/1-A

Ntakirutimana (Appeal Judgment), ICTR AC (13.12.2004) Case Nos. ICTR-96-10-A & ICTR-96-17-A

Ojdanić Dragoliub [= Milutinović et al.], ICTY AC (21.5.2003), Decision on Dragoliub Ojdanić's Motion Challenging Jurisdiction – Joint Criminal Enterprise, Case No. ICTY-99-37-AR 72

Pinkerton et al. v US (10.6.1946), US Supreme Court, 328 US 640, Case No. 719 (also accessible at http://caselaw.lp.findlaw.com/cgi-bin/getcase.pl?friend=nytimes&court=us&vol=328&page=646)

R v English (30.10.1997), UK House of Lords (also accessible at http://www.publications.parliament.uk/pa/ld199798/ldjudgmt/jd971030/powell01.htm)

R v Powell [and Daniels] and Another (30.10.1997), UK House of Lords (also accessible at http://www.publications.parliament.uk/pa/ld199798/ldjudgmt/jd971030/powell01.htm)

R v Uddin [1999] Queen's Bench 431 (Court of Appeal) = 1999 Criminal Law Review 987

Simić Blagoje et al. (Trial Judgment), ICTY TR (17.10.2003), Case No. IT-95-9-T

Tadić, Dusko (Appeal Judgment), ICTY AC (15. 7. 1999), Case No. IT-94-1-A

Part III
Courts Acting and Interacting

The Theoretical Background of Legal Formalism

Krisztina Ficsor

Abstract My aim in this essay is to clarify some questions about legal formalism. Formalism is a controversial view in legal theory and it generates a real problem in judicial practice. In my opinion we should pay attention to it and take the theoretical background of a formalist judicial decision-making process seriously. In order to understand it, we should make efforts to demystify its conceptual and normative character as well. Once we are able to throw light on the main features and theoretical implications of legal formalism, it may be easier to judge whether it is a normatively appropriate theory of adjudication or we should ignore it with all of its theoretical consequences.

> *Formal law is a part of the drama of governance, the trivial or murderous drama of breaking eggs to make omelettes.* (Kennedy 2001, 8637)

1 Introduction

I think we all agree on the plausibility of Dworkin's often cited phrase: 'It matters how judges decide cases' (Dworkin 1986, 1). It really matters because judicial decisions might seriously affect their addressees' life: they can obligate them to pay compensation, evict starving people, put someone in prison and so on. That is why judicial decisions must fit many requirements, and judges must justify all aspects of their decisions. Legal formalism is a theory of adjudication which offers a judicial decision-making method and aims to be a normatively appropriate theory of the decision-making process. Almost every formalist view of adjudication has been challenged by anti-formalist critics among which 'legal realists' are the best known. The problem of legal formalism entails a great number of theoretical issues and it can be approached from many perspectives. For example, it would be an interesting endeavour to clarify the relationship between formalism, legalism and legal positivism. Another fruitful strategy could be to approach formalism from different anti-formalist points of view, particularly from a 'realist' perspective. But these strategies would go beyond the limits of this essay, so I follow another strategy. In light of the theories of some authors who defend formalism I will seek to clarify the main features of a formalist judicial practice – and to show how this formalist theory of adjudication can make part of a general theory of adjudication. Thus, my main purpose is to describe what we mean by legal formalism and what are the underlying issues one has to face before evaluating formalism as an approach.

Why is it important to pay attention to the problem of legal formalism? The simple answer is that if someone is interested in doing research on the problems of judicial decision-making, she should not neglect questions of formalism because it is a problem in actual judicial practice. Formalism offers a model of legal decision-making which is supported by normative principles. At the same time, formalism is a controversial position in legal theory. If we aim at understanding the main questions of adjudication theories, formalism must be at the centre of our attention. What follows from this is that 'any normative and descriptive theory of adjudication must thus start with formalism, even if the theory does not end there' (Moore 1980–1981, 166).

2 Defining legal formalism

Let me start my examination with the example of a Hungarian judicial decision. In 2002, a man was accused of violating the rules of parliamentary elections. According to the facts of the case the defendant was collecting 'recommendation slips' for his father who was a candidate for the election. That, in itself, is not a crime, but the defendant bought some of the recommendation slips for money, which, according to section 211 (a) of the Hungarian Criminal Code, is a criminal act. Despite this fact, the court acquitted him. It justified its decision with a background legal rule, namely a provision of Act C of 1997 on Election Procedure which defines the term 'recommendation slip'. This provision stipulates that people can validly nominate persons only if the recommendation slip is filled in with the nominator's personal data, signature and if it is delivered to the nominee. The court referred to the fact that the slips bought for money were not filled in with personal data and did not contain signatures – that is, they were blank. The court ruled that receiving blank recommendation slips – according to the meaning of the text of the rule – cannot be qualified as nomination, and therefore, the defendant did not commit a crime. His action would have been a crime only if the slips were not blank. The prosecutor appealed against the decision. She argued that the court did not consider all the relevant circumstances of the case (for example, that buying recommendation slips is in itself dangerous to society or that the main purpose of the relevant section of the Criminal Code was to protect the integrity of democratic elections) but strictly adhered to the words of the background rule and ignored the 'spirit' of the criminal provision. However, the court justified the rejection of the prosecutor's appeal with the argument that the prosecutor's reasoning strains the requirements of the rule of law (see Court of Nógrád County Bf. 47/2003. BH 2004: 219). It seems that this judicial decision is a paradigmatic example of formalist judicial procedure and interpretation, as it contains almost every feature of a formalist procedure that anti-formalists usually criticise in legal formalism. Let us now examine what these features of formalism are supposed to be.

It is not an easy task to define legal formalism. In legal theory the term has been applied to many phenomena. What makes clarifying formalism even more difficult is that in legal theory we often encounter the fact that many authors who *prima facie* would not seem to be formalists are accused of being committed to a formalist theory of adjudication.[1]

As mentioned above, my examination focuses on formalism as a theoretical model of legal decision-making, thus my analysis will concentrate on formalism as it figures in *theories of adjudication*. In a broad sense, theories of adjudication address various problems of legal decision-making. They encompass many questions related to judicial decisions, but in my opinion these various questions can be grouped under two main headings. The main issues of a theory of adjudication are (1) the problems of *legal interpretation* and (2) the problems of *legal reasoning*. The first issue covers theoretical problems of (legal) interpretation, e.g. what interpretation is; what the subjects of interpretation can be; the difference between interpreting a text and interpreting a social practice; whether legal interpretation has special features that distinguish it from other kinds of interpretation, etc. Within this dimension, the task of the theorist is to lay the theoretical foundations for legal interpretation.

In the second dimension of the analysis the main task is to work out the theoretical basis of legal reasoning. This concerns questions such as what reasons can and should judges rely on in justifying their decisions; whether moral or political reasons can figure in legal reasoning; what counts as a relevant legal reason, etc. If it is possible at all, these questions may be answered at the level of a general theory of adjudication where the appropriate theoretical background of legal interpretation and reasoning, and the relationship between them may be established. Consequently, the virtues or vices of legal formalism may be estimated on the basis of what position it takes in the questions of legal interpretation and legal reasoning.

1 Here I think of Michael Moore's assertion that Dworkin is a formalist (Moore 1980–1981, 165–166), or Herbert Hart and Lon Fuller who charged each other of formalism (see Kennedy 2001, 8636).

In other words, we are concerned with the question of what theoretical basis legal formalism offers for the problems of legal interpretation and legal reasoning. On the next pages I will try to indicate the possibility of this analysis in brief.

In contrast, formalism can also be approached from a *conceptual point of view*, i.e. by asking questions like 'what is formalism?' or 'what are the features of a formalist judicial practice?' Furthermore, formalism can be analysed from a *normative point of view* as well. This involves the question whether a formalist method of decision-making is good or appropriate. Within the framework of a normative analysis, we can examine the character of the relevant normative principles that allegedly support formalist adjudication. Yet another perspective of the analysis could be an *empirical* one where the main question would be whether there are judges who always or sometimes opt for the formalist method of decision-making.[2]

3 Formalism as strict rule-based decision-making

It seems worth starting the analysis by defining the term 'formalism' in general. In this sense, formalism may be described as an action-guiding attitude. If someone acts in a formalist manner, it means that she fails to ponder every relevant reason for or against her action, acting on a limited scope of reasons instead. These reasons can be various: including habits, traditions, regularities, and so on. There may be cases where we do not balance all relevant reasons for action, but the action comes off automatically. Various motivations may exist at the background of formalist attitudes of action, like habitual behaviour, or the aim to release ourselves from the psychological burden of always thinking over the reasons for and against our actions and their consequences. For example, I walk to work along Baker Street every day. I could opt for another – e.g. a less noisy or shorter – street with more attractive shops[3] but I do not break my habits. So formalism in general can provide a comfortable method of making decisions: we do not have to balance reasons for action and the purposes behind our actions.

Judicial formalism can be explained, at least in part, in a similar fashion. Just like formalism in the general sense, legal formalism may be conceived of as a decision-making model in which judges are forced to restrict the scope of considerations that can figure in the decision-making process. This means that judges committed to formalism rely on certain legal sources without regarding their background reasons and refuse to base decisions on policy arguments. In other words, formalism has to do with 'rule-based decision-making'. The problem of legal formalism proceeds from the fact that in the domain of law our actions are to a large extent guided by

2 Frederick Schauer calls this the psychological aspect of the question of formalism (cf. Schauer 1988).

3 For the example see Raz (2001, 11).

general rules and we must justify our actions by referring to these rules.[4] The main problem raised by rule-based decision-making concerns the relationship between rules and their background justification and the related problem of over- and under-inclusiveness of legal rules (see Schauer 1991a, 27–31).

In this respect, formalism has two forms, that is, we can distinguish at least two kinds of formalism. One may be called *strict formalism*, and is represented for example by Larry Alexander's theory. The other form which can be termed *modest formalism* is represented by Frederick Schauer's theory (1991b, 677). *Strict formalism* endorses the following main theses: (a) Actions should be guided by posited general rules with a determined and clear content, not by standards or principles. (b) Legal decision-makers must adhere to the text of these posited rules and should not justify their decisions with sources from outside of the text. (c) This method of judicial decision-making surely generates a moral dilemma (see Farber 1999, 599) because the results stemming from a strictly rule-based decision will not be optimal in every case. Sometimes they may be unjust, unreasonable or immoral. Strict formalists argue, however, that we are unable to solve this dilemma: it will be always present in judicial decision-making. At any rate, they emphasise that the moral value of the existence of rules in a plural society overweighs the disadvantages of rule-based decisions.

Modest legal formalism, in turn, makes efforts to solve or at least to soften the moral dilemma of strict rule-based decision-making. Presumptive positivism, for example, as conceived of by Schauer, serves the goal of moderating this dilemma (see Farber 1999, 598). For presumptive positivism, rules have a presumptive force: if there are compelling reasons against applying the rule, the judge is allowed to ignore the content of the rule in favour of its background justification (see Schauer 1991b, 674–679). Strict formalists criticise this theory. According to Alexander, these and similar strategies simply do not work. They are incapable of eliminating 'the gap' between rules and their background justifications (see Alexander 1999, 553).

To sum up, formalism has to do with strict rule-based decision-making, where judges do not take into account justifying reasons from outside of the text of legal rules. Now we are in the position to make an attempt at answering the question of what formalism has to say about the problems of legal interpretation and legal reasoning.

[4] For an extensive analysis of rule-based judicial decision-making see Schauer (1991a, 18–62).

4 Formalism and the theoretical problems of legal reasoning

Let me start with the question of legal reasoning. As we have seen, formalism is committed to the view that judges should decide legal cases on the basis of determined legal sources, and they must not justify their decisions with reasons from outside of the legal text. In this context, formalism represents the so called *autonomy thesis*, more specifically, the *limited domain thesis* in the sense specified by Gerald Postema and Frederick Schauer. According to the autonomy thesis, legal reasoning is a form of practical reasoning, and autonomy means that the content of norms as the main elements of legal reasoning is to be determined by criteria that do not rely on moral or political considerations. Consequently, legal reasoning is independent of and isolated from moral and political reasoning: it does not need to rely on political morality. According to this view, legal reasoning is only able to fulfil its function if it is independent of moral or political reasoning (see Postema 1996, 82–89). The limited domain thesis is an integral part of the autonomy thesis. It revolves around the notion that law provides a limited domain or scope of practical reasons for decision-makers in law:

> By that we mean that legal decisions are based on legal considerations, reasons and facts, but that the domain of legal considerations, reasons and facts make up only a subset of the entire universe of considerations, reasons and facts and only a subset of even the universe of considerations, reasons and facts accepted within a given society. (Alexander and Schauer 2007, 222)

The basis of these considerations is that the various conceptions of good life and the diversity of individual conceptions of morality demand that there be general legal rules which provide the coordination of behaviours in a democratic society.

An important premise of the autonomy thesis is that the function of law is to mediate between the citizens' reasons for their actions and their decisions made in the public social context. In order to fulfil this coordinative function, law and legal reasoning must be isolated from moral and political reasoning. This isolation can be achieved if legal reasons stem from a limited domain of reasons and if these reasons are determined by criteria independent of moral or political considerations. Simply put, the autonomy thesis says that 'while the considerations which justify a rule exist independently of the rule, they do not constitute the same reason for action that the rule constitutes' (Raz 2001, 13). Thus, to live up to the coordinative function of law, judicial decisions must be the matter of determined legal reasons isolated from reasons of political morality. In other words, judges should not base their decisions on justifications underlying the legal rules, even if the outcome of the decisions will not be optimal. These considerations are at the centre of Larry Alexander's arguments for formalism:

> The function of practical authority is precisely to settle the question of what ought to be done. And settlement requires that those for whom the answer is supposed to settle the question treat the answer as authoritative – that is, as if it is correct. Once the question is settled, those who want to know what to do need only consult the terms of settlement. They no longer need to debate the reasons behind those terms. Moreover, not only are they no longer required to consult the reasons behind the settlement in determining how to act, they are also required not to heed those reasons even if, from their perspective, those reasons conflict with the terms of the settlement. (Alexander 1999, 533)

Consequently, we can characterise formalism as a decision-making method in which judges set aside the balancing of relevant reasons or circumstances of the case and solve legal disputes exclusively according to legal reasons stemming from determined legal sources. Legal reasoning proceeds from the relevant legal reasons.

This claim raises the question of what counts as a recognised legal source, that is, what counts as a relevant legal reason. Schauer's main thesis, for example, is that legal reasons can be isolated from other practical reasons (e. g. moral or political reasons) with the help of a rule of recognition. The relevant legal reasons within the limited domain are determined by a rule of recognition. In this respect, the virtues or vices of formalism can be assessed in a broader framework of theoretical analysis which includes the problems associated with the nature and the normativity of law, and it seems that this kind of analysis will require inquiries into questions of political philosophy.

More recently, Cass Sunstein advocated the view that the value of formalism cannot be defended or questioned by analysing abstract concepts such as the nature of law, democracy, authority or the rule of law. Instead, he claims, formalism should be argued for in terms of empirical claims about judicial and legislative activities. This is to say that formalism can be assessed by examining empirical questions such as whether formalist or non-formalist judges make more mistakes or whether a formalist or a non-formalist judicial practice generates more uncertainty in judicial decision-making (Sunstein 1999, 641). Yet, it seems that the problems of formalism are not merely empirical questions and, consequently, one cannot spare the analysis of normative justifications underlying legal formalism. On the one hand, the concept of 'making a mistake in a judicial decision' is a normative question as well. On the other hand, the value of legal formalism depends on how strong a normative justification can be established in its support, for example, whether there are tenable conceptions of legitimacy, normativity, democracy or the rule of law which can be aligned behind formalism. Most formalists do, in fact, offer certain conceptions of democracy or the rule of law in order to defend legal formalism. Thus, the appropriateness of formalism depends, at least partly, on normative issues.

5 Formalism and legal interpretation

The next question to consider is the relation of legal formalism to legal interpretation. Apparently, we are facing another difficult question here, since '[n]o sensible formalist claims to have offered a complete theory of legal interpretation' (Sunstein 1999, 640).

Michael S. Moore associates formalism with certain *theories of meaning* which may serve as the basis of its interpretive strategy. Indeed, some authors defend formalism in terms of a certain theory of meaning. Accordingly, Moore develops his criticism against formalism at the level of *philosophical semantics*. The starting point of his criticism is that formalism can be related to objective and subjective theories of meaning. Objective theories involve the referential and the criterial theory of meaning.[5] The alternative to objective theories is intentionalism as a subjective account of meaning.[6] I shall come back to Moore's theoretical strategy below.

Frederick Schauer stands for the claim that formalism, in the sense of constraining judges in choosing among various justifying reasons, is possible because the nature of language allows it. According to Schauer (1988, 522), formalism can be understood as a linguistic limitation on judicial decisions. He adds, however, that language and its rules are human creations, contingent and changeable at that. This does not imply that words have no acontextual meaning. It only means that there are many rules and conventions of meaning which are shared by all who have linguistic competence in the same language. It is due to this competence and the shared rules and conventions that we are able to convey meaning without the constraint to reveal the speakers' intentions or the whole context of the given situation (ibid., 522–528). This account of linguistic constraint is called semantic autonomy (see Schauer 1991a, 53–62). In Schauer's view, it is the very nature of language that enables judges to follow a formalist judicial practice, where they can ignore justifying reasons from outside of the relevant legal sources and adhere to the text of the rule.

Another author whose theory of interpretation includes some considerations stemming from a certain theory of meaning is Larry Alexander. Alexander is committed to intentionalism: his main assertion about interpretation (legal and otherwise) is that it 'is a search for speaker's meaning' (Alexander and Sherwin 2008, 133). In law, this means the rule-maker's intentions. To seek the meaning of the words elsewhere is not interpretation but construction. He seems to advocate an interpretive strategy that is the exact opposite of Schauer's semantic autonomy:

5 A referential theory of meaning includes the claim that meaning is identical with the things words refer to or name. A criterial theory 'asserts that the meaning of any word is the criteria, the necessary and sufficient conditions, which govern that word's correct application' (Moore 1980–1981, 169, 173).

6 Intentionalism embraces the claim that the meaning of the words of rules is more or less determined by certain intentions of the rule-maker (see ibid., 180).

> The only meaning that should count and that should guide legal interpretation is the meaning the lawmaker intended to convey through his rule. [...] One cannot attribute meaning to marks on a page or to sounds without reference to an author, actual or idealized, who is intending to communicate a meaning through the marks or sounds. (Alexander and Sherwin 2008, 141, 195)

These claims deny the possibility of semantic autonomy. In Alexander's opinion there is no meaning without knowing the particular context of the text (be it a legal or any kind of text).

It is not our task here to decide in favour of either the one or the other theory of interpretation. It has to be emphasised that there are several strategies of interpretation which can be attributed to legal formalism. Moreover, one has to agree with Cass Sunstein that formalism is rather a matter of degree, which means that there are no formalists who think that literal meaning should be followed at all costs, no matter how absurd or unfair the outcome is.

> Every formalist knows that in many cases it will be necessary to look beyond the text to interpret a statutory term, and to do so self-consciously. The formalist's goal, in such cases, is to develop approaches to interpretation that will push the law in rule-like directions, denying much discretion to judges who will subsequently act on the spot. (Sunstein 1999, 640)

In order to give an acceptable answer to the question of the relationship between legal interpretation and legal formalism, one has to evaluate the possible theories underlying to theories of (legal) interpretation in general. The same applies to the relationship between legal reasoning and legal formalism. In other words, one cannot understand formalism unless one considers the question of which theoretical background supports the formalist type of legal reasoning and interpretation. As we said above, the autonomy thesis and the limited domain thesis can be attributed to formalism as its background theories of legal reasoning. Thus, the appropriateness of formalism as a theory of legal reasoning depends on the plausibility of the autonomy thesis as a characterisation of the nature of legal reasoning.

The feasibility of formalist interpretive strategies also depends on there being a proper justifying theory behind them. Perhaps we can assess formalism within the framework of linguistic philosophy as Michael Moore did. Is this the case, then we may reasonably make efforts to find the correct theory of meaning to justify legal formalist interpretive methods. But this enterprise succeeds only if theories of meaning are the appropriate background considerations for supporting theories of interpretation. If this is not the case (and there are some efforts to show that theories of meaning are unsuitable as background theories for a normative theory of interpretation), then we have to find another kind of theory on which a normative theory of interpretation can be based. This other kind of theory, which is often named as the one providing the correct set of considerations for a theory of legal interpretation, is political philosophy. If this is so, then formalist theories of legal interpretation cannot avoid analysing political philosophical questions, related to legitimacy or the conceptual problems of legal authority (see Bódig 2007, 131–133).

6 Conclusion

A lot of problems surrounding legal formalism remained unanswered here, but I think the essence of legal formalism as a theory of adjudication can be grasped more easily if we find its place within a coherent theory of legal reasoning and interpretation. This task includes the in-depth examination of the question of whether a 'general' theory of adjudication is possible, and whether we are able to reveal the relationship between legal theory and the theory of adjudication and solve the debate over the relationship between the theory of the nature of law and the theory of legal decision-making. These problems, however, might be the subject of another essay.

References

Alexander, Larry. 1999. 'With Me It's All er Nuthin': Formalism in Law and Morality. *University of Chicago Law Review* 66: 530–565.

Alexander, Larry, and Schauer, Frederick. 2007. Is Policy Within the Limited Domain? *Queensland Law Journal* 26: 221–235.

Alexander, Larry, and Sherwin, Emily. 2008. *Demystifying Legal Reasoning.* Cambridge: Cambridge University Press.

Bódig, Mátyás. 2007. Legal Interpretation, Intentionalism, and the Authority of Law. *Acta Juridica Hungarica* 48: 125–142.

Dworkin, Ronald. 1986. *Law's Empire.* London: Fontana.

Farber, Daniel A. 1999. Legal Formalism and the Red-Hot Knife. *University of Chicago Law Review* 66: 597–606.

Kennedy, Duncan. 2001. Legal Formalism. *International Encyclopedia of the Social & Behavioral Sciences*, edited by Neil J. Smelser and Paul B. Baltes, 13: 8634–8638. Amsterdam, etc.: Elsevier

Moore, Michael S. 1980–1981. The Semantics of Judging. *Southern California Law Review* 54: 151–294.

Postema, Gerald J. 1996. Law's Autonomy and Public Practical Reason. In *The Autonomy of Law: Essays on Legal Positivism*, edited by Robert P. George, 79–118. Oxford: Clarendon Press.

Raz, Joseph. 2001. Reasoning with Rules. *Current Legal Problems* 54: 1–18.

Schauer, Frederick. 1988. Formalism. *Yale Law Journal* 97: 509–548.

Schauer, Frederick. 1991a. *Playing by the Rules: A Philosophical Examination of Rule-Based Decision-Making in Law and in Life.* Oxford: Clarendon Press.

Schauer, Frederick. 1991b. Rules and the Rule of Law. *Harvard Journal of Law and Public Policy* 14: 645–694.

Sunstein, Cass. 1999. Must Formalism Be Defended Empirically? *University of Chicago Law Review* 66: 636–670.

The Road from Common Law to East-Central Europe: The Case of the Dissenting Opinion

Katalin Kelemen

Abstract The paper has the purpose of telling the story of dissenting opinions and discusses the use of this instrument by constitutional courts in a comparative perspective. The gradual spreading of dissenting opinions all over Europe illustrates that the countries of East-Central Europe emerging from Communism, in many respects, followed the German model of constitutional justice as a full package, without seeing it first in the details, but only enriching it with new competencies. The paper examines the 'migration' of this legal instrument that left England for the United States in the baggage of common law, then moved to Germany in order to take part in the reconstruction of a country destroyed by war and an extremist ideology, that subsequently traveled to Spain, where it served to uphold and renew judicial traditions, and finally arrived in East-Central Europe to help in the building of constitutional democracy.

1 Introduction

After the breakdown of the socialist regimes, Eastern Europe had to face a significant scarcity of legal rules in many fields of law. The democratic transition required several new norms and institutions. In this specific historical context, turning to solutions already elaborated in other countries can be explained both with the international political and economic pressure, and with the practicality of such a choice that saved time and effort. The gradual spreading of dissenting opinions all over Europe is a perfect example for illustrating this point. At the same time, it shows the gradual convergence[1] between common law and civil law systems.

[1] The expression 'gradual convergence' was coined by Basil Markesinis (1994).

Eastern Europe consists of twenty-three sovereign states and is characterised by a high degree of linguistic heterogeneity, which makes a comprehensive study of this area extremely difficult. Consequently, my research has been limited to East-Central Europe, i.e. that part of Eastern Europe which was not part of the Soviet Union as initially created. Therefore, for the purposes of this paper, East-Central Europe also includes the three Baltic states.

My hypothesis is that the countries of East-Central Europe emerging from Communism, in many aspects, followed the German model of constitutional justice as a full package, without seeing it first in details, but only enriching it with new competencies. The introduction of dissenting opinion in particular was not preceded by specific discussions or objections.

By dissenting opinion we mean a separate opinion that diverges from the opinion of the majority of a group, which means that in a court it can exist only if there is a collegial body to decide the case. Dissent in courts always existed. It is natural and also healthy that judges do not agree on legal issues of a certain importance and difficulty. The question is if it is reasonable to conceal dissent. Judges undoubtedly discuss all cases among themselves and influence one another's opinion. These discussions are fundamental for reaching the right solution (if one right solution exists). Even so, not every legal system allows judges to explain their disaccord to the public in a dissenting opinion attached to the judgment of the court.

This paper aims to show how the use of dissenting opinion has spread through the Western Legal Tradition,[2] starting in a common law system, and arrived in the new democracies of East-Central Europe. However, it is important to observe that in civil law countries it is used almost exclusively in the field of constitutional justice. It is very rare that a legal system of the civil law tradition allows its ordinary judges to publish dissent. This point is especially thought-provoking and raises several questions regarding the very essence of judicial decision-making in the Western Legal Tradition. This essay attempts to explain the reasons for the limitation of the publication of dissent to constitutional justice, by using an historical approach. Therefore, it examines the 'migration' of this legal phenomenon that left England for the United States in the baggage of common law, then moved to Germany in order to take part in the reconstruction of a country destroyed by a war and an extremist ideology, that subsequently traveled to Spain, where it served to uphold and renew judicial traditions, and finally arrived in East-Central Europe to help in the building of constitutional democracy.

2 I use the term 'Western Legal Tradition' as covering both the civil law and the common law legal families, following the approach adopted by Gianmaria Ajani who argues that in the Western Legal Tradition 'the geographic and cultural limits that have traditionally been used in order to classify national legal systems into "legal families" no longer matter' (Ajani 1995, 95).

2 The origins of dissent

2.1 The English roots

Comparison involves history. This is a well-known maxim among comparatists. Getting to its roots, revealing the reasons behind its existence, leads us to better understand each norm and legal phenomenon. A historical approach is especially eye-opening as regards the dissenting opinion. It brings us back to Medieval England where legal disputes, if argued before a panel, were decided separately by each judge of the panel. This practice of the so-called *seriatim* opinions (that is 'opinions given separately') was common in the whole system of justice, with the sole exception of the Appellate Committee of the House of Lords, where the rule of secrecy of parliamentary debates was in force.[3] In the English legal system the practice of delivering separate judgments is a natural consequence of the principle of orality, still in force today, concerning both the trial and the delivery of the decision. It means that there is no judgment representing the opinion of the entire court but every member of the panel expresses his or her own opinion in a separate judgment. However, nowadays it is quite common for English judges to limit themselves to a formal concurrence in the opinion of another member of the court. Even so, a so-called *laissez-faire ethos* prevails, and judges are not obliged to publish a single majority judgment (see Paterson 1982, 108).

2.2 The institutionalisation of dissent in the United States

At the time of the establishment of the American court system, at the end of the 18th century, the House of Lords did not publish separate opinions of the Law Lords, but it was a common practice in all the other English courts. Indeed, the Supreme Court of the United States in the beginning followed the practice of the King's Bench, the court exercising supervisory jurisdiction over lower courts. It is a well-known fact that the common law tradition remained the foundation of the legal system also after the United States gained its independence from England. But two absolutely new features made American law more and more autonomous from English law and, in its turn, a source of imitation for many other countries: the adoption of a Constitution and federalism. The system resulting from the principle of checks and balances, an ingenious innovation of American law, was in practice incomplete, since the Constitution did not specifically mention the power of the judiciary to declare a legislative act unconstitutional. The classic case of *Marbury v. Madison*, 5

3 Publication of the opinions of the Law Lords was permitted the first time in 1848 (see ZoBell 1959, 189).

U.S. 137 (1803), is the U.S. Supreme Court's judgment in which the doctrinal origin of judicial review can be found.

The majority decision in *Marbury v. Madison* was written by John Marshall, appointed Chief Justice by President John Adams in 1801. It is not a coincidence that it was the same Marshall who revolutionised the practice of sentencing in the Supreme Court and asserted the so-called 'opinion of the court' style that is a single judgment which represents the opinion of the entire court. It means that in the first decade of the 19th century the U.S. Supreme Court abandoned the English practice of delivering opinions *seriatim*. This piece of history makes us understand that judicial review and the apparent unanimity of the decision are two faces of the same coin: two important elements of the effort to increase the Court's authority and to raise it to the same level of prestige of the two other branches. The 'opinion of the court' delivered by a single Justice was speaking for the entire court or the majority of its members and showed a united body able to speak with one voice.

However, in this new practice promoted by the Chief Justice expression of separate opinions was not allowed, and almost all the opinions were delivered by Marshall himself. This new custom was bitterly opposed by Thomas Jefferson, the first Republican President of the United States, who considered it 'convenient for the lazy, the modest and the incompetent' (quoted in Morgan 1953, 355–356) and wanted a rule requiring judges to announce their opinions *seriatim*, abandoning the compulsory delivery of a majority judgment. But this was only one of the many points of criticism against Marshall (a declared Federalist and ex-Secretary of State) voiced by Jefferson, whose appointee Justice William Johnson became known as the 'First Dissenter' (see Morgan 1944). In fact, Johnson was able to weaken the dominance of Marshall in the Court, and even though he did not succeed in the reintroduction of the practice of *seriatim* judgments, the publication of dissenting and concurring opinions became more and more common with the passing of years.

So we can see that what we call the 'institutionalisation of dissent' in the United States, is actually a compromise between two opposing tendencies: *seriatim* opinions, that is part of the English tradition, and (apparently) unanimous opinions, the aim of Chief Justice Marshall. It was a half-way solution. While in the English system a judgment (or opinion, in this context it is the same thing) cannot be labeled as dissenting or assenting (using the British terminology) at the moment of its delivery, but only after a thorough analysis of all the opinions, in the American system the judge defines his or her opinion at the moment of writing it. It will be a dissenting opinion if he or she disagrees with the decision of the majority, and a concurring one if he or she agrees with the outcome of the decision in a case but disagrees with the reasoning for it.

3 The emergence of dissent in Europe

3.1 The style of judicial decision-making: common law vs. civil law

It is a well-known fact among jurists and immediately catches the eye of a comparatist that judicial decisions in the civil law tradition differ fundamentally from common law decisions both in form and style and in content. The difference arises from the basic approach that civil law systems take towards judges and their role. The theory of judicial decision prevailing in a legal system affects both the entire judicial process and the product of it, i.e. the judgment. Thus, the extremely abstract style of the *Cour de Cassation* decisions is a natural consequence of French legal mentality that disapproves judicial activism and restricts the role of judges in law-making. Although impersonality of the decision is a basic principle of the German legal tradition as well, the handling of the facts and the law in German decisions is fuller than in French decisions but less extensive than that often given by American courts (see Von Mehren 1956, 208). Decisions are unsigned and apparently unanimous both in France and Germany, and all the other countries that founded their legal systems on one of these two models, i.e. in the whole continental Europe.

The personal nature of common law judgments, instead, opens the door for dissenting opinions. While in the common law tradition a 'judge takes responsibility for what he says, and that responsibility is openly attributed to him by the judgments and published Reports' (Atiyah 1988, 141), in the civil law tradition judges are only 'the mouth that pronounces the words of the law, inanimate beings who can moderate neither its force nor its rigour', using the expression of Montesquieu (1989, 163). The personal character of decisions is somewhat mitigated in the United States by the practice of delivering an opinion of the court, but anyhow it is still assured by the publicity of votes. In this way, we can know which judges voted against and which ones in favor of the majority decision.

Some scholars who argue against the introduction of dissenting opinion in European countries, explain their position by saying that disclosing the opinion of each judge would be a practice alien to the civil law tradition. In fact, in continental Europe dissenting opinions are introduced only in the decision-making process of constitutional courts, they are an exception in the ordinary court systems (Spain and Estonia), and constitutional courts themselves are alien to the civil law tradition. They were born from the brain of Hans Kelsen in the period following the First World War, and spread on the Continent after the Second World War. Publication of dissenting opinions did not diffuse at the same extension but now it is a common practice in German, Spanish and Portuguese constitutional justice and for the constitutional courts of East-Central Europe.

3.2 The myth of the civil law tradition of secrecy of deliberation

It is important to underline that the tradition of secrecy of deliberation in continental Europe is something like a myth, because as a matter of fact there are several historical examples of a contrary practice. In the Spanish legal tradition the origins of dissent date back to the 15th century, to an ordinance of Medina. Even though separate opinions were not published, they were registered in a secret book, hence their name *voto reservado*. This rule was preserved by the statutes on civil and criminal procedure from 1881 and 1882, and remained in force until 1985, when the use of dissent was extended to the whole justice system (see Luatti 1995, 163–169). In Italy, before the unification of the country and the adoption of the French model, some local laws were inspired by Spanish law, so dissenting opinions were filed in the Kingdom of Naples, the Este States, and Tuscany (see Denti 1964, 3–6). Also in Germany, in the State of Baden dissents were published up to the middle of the 19th century (see Nadelmann 1964, 272), while in the State of Württemberg the practice of public voting was maintained until the Second World War (see Oneto 1976–77, 1087).

The first European country where dissenting opinion was introduced by the legislator was Germany (precisely West Germany) in 1970. But this legislative reform was not without precedents. The Federal Constitutional Court, which took up office in September 1951, made the proportion between yes and no votes known to the public the first time in a decision of 8 December 1952, and ten days later Judge Willi Geiger published a dissenting opinion.[4] The Court changed its practice quite gradually, and the next step consisted in the publication of the two opposing opinions that emerged in a case in 1966, though without the names of the judges who took part on the two opposing sides (Decision of 5 August 1966, in *BVerfGE* 20, 162). Beginning from 1967, the Second Section of the Court established the practice of revealing the number of yes and no votes. The bill for the modification of the statute on the *Bundesverfassungsgericht* was proposed by the Federal Government in December 1969, passed by the *Bundestag* a year later, and regulated in detail by the Rules of the Court, modified in December 1971.[5] Under the new rules the Court has the possibility of publishing dissenting and concurring opinions (*Sondervotum*), and of revealing the number of yes and no votes in anonymous way.

4 The subject of the decision was of primary importance for the German legal system. It dealt with the compatibility of the European Defense Community Treaties with the Bonn Constitution.

5 Dissenting opinion was introduced first by the Rules of the Constitutional Court of the Land of Bayern (in 1948), but here dissents are published without the name of the dissenter judge. Afterwards, it was introduced also by the Rules of the Staatsgerichtshof (the Supreme Court) of the Land of Bremen in 1956, but published only on request of the dissenter and is not applied anymore from 1968 (see Luther 1994, 242–243).

3.3 Some examples of current practice in Western Europe

Based on statistics, in Spain, where separate opinions were introduced in the practice of the Constitutional Court in 1978, judges make use of it more frequently than their German colleagues do (see Luther 1994, 250–251). The fact that the example of Germany was followed by Spain and Portugal is not accidental. According to a saying of Roman Herzog, former president of the German Federal Constitutional Court, Spanish and Portuguese courts were the daughters of Karlsruhe, and the Polish and Hungarian courts the granddaughters (see Sólyom 2003, 153). In Spain, the practice of the *voto reservado* registered in a secret book, as mentioned above, remained in force until 1985, and concerned the whole ordinary justice system. As regards constitutional justice, the *Tribunal de Garantías Constitucionales* that can be considered the forerunner of the *Tribunal Constitucional*, in its brief lifetime (1933–1936) during the Second Republic had the possibility of publishing *votos particulares*[6] (public separate opinions) and made abundant use of it. A proper constitutional court was established by the Constitution of 1978, after the breakdown of the Franco regime, and openly followed the European model of constitutional justice. The positive experience acquired in the use of separate opinions led the Spanish legislator to extend, in 1985, the *votos particulares* to the ordinary justice as well, according to a provision of the Organic Law on the Judicial Power.[7] So now dissenting opinions can be published both by constitutional and by ordinary judges and the Spanish legal system is the only one in Western Europe that extends the use of dissent to the whole judiciary.

In Portuguese legal tradition judges could express their dissent in a more limited way, by writing the term *vencido* next to the signature of the decision. At the moment of the establishment of the Portuguese Constitutional Court, in 1982, dissenting opinion was introduced in the practice of this court.

Greece represents a very particular situation, having a common law-type judicial review system, in which all judges can declare the unconstitutionality of a law, but a civil law-type justice system, with three branches of judiciary (ordinary, administrative and auditorial). The rule that prescribes the compulsory publication of dissenting opinions is contained in the Greek Constitution (Art. 93, par. 3). In the Greek practice, however, dissents are anonymous and are delivered by the reporting judge (see Panizza 1998, 115–116).

6 Art. 41 of the *Ley Orgánica del Tribunal de Garantías Constitucionales* de 14 junio de 1933.

7 *Ley Orgánica* 6/1985, de 1 de julio, *del Poder Judicial.*

4 Final destination: Eastern Europe

4.1 A preliminary remark

I state in advance that my research, as the title of this paper suggests, has been limited to East-Central Europe, mainly because of the broad size of Eastern Europe. Currently it consists of 23 countries, so a comprehensive study could be done by a research group, not by a single researcher. I limited my field of research to East-Central Europe which (for the purposes of this essay) includes those former socialist countries that are now members of the European Union and concluded democratic transition already.

4.2 Judicial opinion writing in East-Central Europe

Why were dissenting opinions immediately accepted or soon introduced by the newly established democracies of East-Central Europe? Quoting the words of Julia Laffranque, the only scholar in Eastern Europe who has ever published an essay in English on the topic of dissenting opinions,[8] writing about the practice of her country, Estonia:

> [I]t is an instructive commentary which is especially important for a legal culture that is not yet fully developed, as is the case in Estonia where sometimes a clear and precise provision of a law is lacking, or established interpretation and legal theories in certain issues have still not emerged. The dissenting opinion prepares the ground for changing the court practice. (Laffranque 2003, 172)

Her observation can be extended to all countries of East-Central Europe that experienced transition to democracy in the last two decades. In fact, it can be a possible explanation for the introduction of dissenting opinions in the area. But, in all likelihood, it is due to the simple fact that these countries adopted the German model which at the time of the institution of these new constitutional courts already included the use of separate opinions. The example of Romania can confirm this hypothesis. The Romanian Constitutional Court is a curious cross-breeding of the Italian and the traditional French models, and exercises both abstract *a priori* and concrete *a posteriori* control (in practice, however, the later competence is used in the majority of the cases). Neither Italian nor French constitutional justice allows the publication of dissent. And, indeed, the Romanian Constitutional Courts at the

8 Now she is a member of the Estonian Supreme Court and kindly gave me the opportunity to make a brief interview to her in Rome (Italy) on 26 March 2007.

moment of its establishment could not publish dissenting opinions. It was recognised only subsequently by a legislative reform in 2004.[9]

A curious exception to the rule is Lithuania, which although followed the German model, initially did not allow the publication of dissenting opinions. The reasons probably can be found in the same considerations made in Germany at the moment of the establishment of the Federal Constitutional Court: the court must first achieve authority before it can resist public pressure that can be brought about by the dissenting opinion (see Laffranque 2003, 165). Indeed, one and a half decades later the Lithuanian legislator considered that such authority had been achieved, and in 2008 modified the Constitutional Court Act[10] in order to allow the members of the Court 'to set forth in writing [their] reasoned dissenting opinion within three working days of the announcement of the corresponding act in the courtroom.'[11]

4.3 The Baltic states: three degrees of openness

Examining the rules concerning dissenting opinions in the three Baltic states leads us to an interesting conclusion: until recent times (until the Lithuanian reform of 2008), these three legal systems differed considerably as regards this specific aspect and represented three degrees of openness. First, Lithuania did not authorise the publication of separate opinions at all. Second, in Latvia only constitutional court judges can express a dissenting opinion, and it is not published together with the opinion of the court, but once a year in the collection of judgments.[12] Finally, Estonia, the most open of the three countries from this point of view, allows public expression of dissent in almost the whole judiciary. In this country there is no constitutional court, but there is a special section of the Supreme Court (the Constitu-

9 Act n. 47/1992 on the Constitutional Court was modified and renumbered by Act n. 232/2004 of 3 June 2004. The text of the Act (in Romanian) is available on the site of the Romanian Parliament: http://www.cdep.ro/proiecte/2004/100/30/3/leg_pl133_04.pdf.

10 Article 55. For the text of the Act see the website of the Court: http://www.lrkt.lt/Documents3_e.html.

11 No. X-1806, 11.11.2008, Valstybės žinios (Official Gazette), 2008, No. 134-5179 (22.11.2008). Consequently, the Constitutional Court modified its Rules of Procedure inserting a Section VII entitled 'Dissenting opinion of a Justice of the Constitutional Court' (Decision of 26 November 2008). For the text of the Rules of the Constitutional Court see the website of the Court: http://www.lrkt.lt/Documents4_e.html.

12 See Art. 225 of the Rules of Procedure of the Constitutional Court providing that dissenting opinions shall be kept attached to the case file for three months and after that shall be published; and Art. 33 par. 2 of the Constitutional Court Law providing that once a year the Constitutional Court shall publish a collection of judgments of the Constitutional Court, including all judgments in full and individual opinions of justices attached to cases. The English text of the Rules of Procedure and of the Constitutional Court Law is available on the site of the Court: http://www.satv.tiesa.gov.lv/.

tional Review Chamber)[13] that decides on the constitutionality of laws. The publication of separate opinions is not limited to this Chamber but it is used more frequently by this than by the other three Chambers (Civil, Criminal and Administrative Law Chambers) (see Laffranque 2004, 22). This statistical fact confirms that the publication of dissent is more required by judges when they discuss about constitutional issues than in ordinary civil or criminal law matters in which the judgment has a much smaller impact on the legal system. However, we cannot make similar analyses in other East-Central European countries, the use of dissenting opinions being limited to constitutional justice and not allowed for ordinary courts.

Estonia is the only country in East-Central Europe which allows the publication of dissent (in Estonian called *eriarvamus* that includes both dissenting and concurring opinions) in ordinary courts and extends this possibility to every collegial court of the judiciary. However, lower courts do not use it so often as the Supreme Court. According to Julia Laffranque, this is related to the heavy caseload of judges in the circuit courts and to the fact that the issues of principle, where the likelihood of expressing a dissenting opinion is higher, are in the last instance decided by the Supreme Court (Laffranque 2003, 167).

4.4 The Slovak story: a precedent becomes law

In Czechoslovakia, after the downfall of the socialist regime, but before the separation of the Czech and Slovak Republics, the federal law on the Constitutional Court stated that a judge who did not agree with the decision of the plenum had the right to have his or her separate opinion briefly cited in the voting record.[14] However, the voting record had to be sealed in an envelope and it was not published.

This rule was kept also after the separation of the Slovak Republic and the publication of dissenting opinions has been allowed only beginning from 1st August 2000.[15] This opening towards the publication of dissents can be partly explained by an important precedent, a case decided by the Slovak Constitutional Court on a constitutional complaint. The facts can be summarised as follows: the govern-

13 There are 19 justices in the Supreme Court, appointed to office by the Parliament (*Riigikogu*) on the proposal of the Chief Justice of the Supreme Court. Every justice is a member of one of the Administrative, Civil or Criminal Law Chambers. The Constitutional Review Chamber is comprised of nine justices. The Chief Justice of the Supreme Court is the chairman of the Constitutional Review Chamber. Other eight members of the Chamber are appointed by the Supreme Court *en banc*. See the *Booklet about the Supreme Court of Estonia*, 2004, available on the site of the Court: http://www.nc.ee/vfs/22/RK_2004.pdf.

14 Article 9 par. 5 of Act No. 491/1991. Article 10 par. 5 provided the same right when the decision is made by a Senate and not the Plenum.

15 Slovak law No. 83/1993 on the Constitutional Court originally provided the same kind of not public separate opinion until 2000. I am thankful for these information to Jan Stiavnicky, law clerk at the Slovak Constitutional Court.

ment elected in 1998 abolished the amnesty granted by former Prime Minister Vladimír Mečiar[16] for criminal offenses related to the abduction of the son of President Michal Kovač. A former high-ranking member of the secret service, subjected to criminal persecution after the annulment of the amnesty, lodged a petition to the Constitutional Court, which agreed with the petitioner and annulled the investigator's decision, despite six years of constant refusal to annul any decision contested by means of a petition, and despite the obvious self-serving nature of the amnesty.[17] As Radoslav Procházka writes, '[t]he ruling was so out of line with the Court's case law and so lacking in persuasive legal argumentation that it prompted some of the best legal minds of the country to label it as a direct attack on the rule of law' (Procházka 2002, 196–197). Justice Ján Klučka[18] was disappointed with the decision, and wrote a dissenting opinion which was cited in the voting record. Since the voting record was not public, and the plenum of the Court rejected to publish his opinion in the official Collection, he published an article in a law review criticising the judgment. It was following to this episode that the Slovak legislator decided to introduce public dissenting opinion in the practice of the Court.

4.5 Former Yugoslavia: a separate way

Another interesting case is that of the successor states of Yugoslavia. Publication of dissenting opinion was allowed at all levels of constitutional review also in the socialist era, but the Federal Constitutional Court did not consider dissenting opinions as an important part of its constitutional review activity. Therefore, step by step separate opinions acquired some kind of a 'private character' and they were announced at the Court's session by the dissenting judge, but the text was kept under special separate cover as a non public part of the file of the case. So from 1974 to 1990 the separate opinions were not published anymore simply because no judge requested the publication of his dissent.[19]

4.6 Instances of secrecy of deliberation

Even in countries where dissenting opinions can be published by the judges of the constitutional court, there are some instances in which secret deliberation is pre-

16 Vladimír Mečiar granted amnesty as interim President of the Republic, position vacated after the end of the term of Kovač. According to Article 105 of the Slovak Constitution, until a new President is elected most of the powers pass to the Government.

17 Decision No. 43/99 of 20 December 1999.

18 Professor of International Law and Politics and from 2004 judge at the European Court of Justice in Luxembourg.

19 For this information I express my gratitude to Arne Mavčić, former Head of the Analysis and International Cooperation Department of the Slovenian Constitutional Court.

scribed by the law. In Bulgaria, the secrecy of deliberation concerns two kinds of cases: decision on the lift of a justice's immunity or establishment of his actual incapacity to perform his duties,[20] and decision on impeachments by the National Assembly against the President or the Vice President.[21] The Slovak Constitutional Court renders its decision by secret vote in the case of consent to the criminal prosecution and pre-trial detention of a member of the Court and of disciplinary proceedings regarding the Chief Justice, the Deputy Chief Justice of the Slovak Republic and the General Prosecutor.[22]

These two examples are sufficient to notice that secret deliberation is provided for cases in which the decision concerns the criminal or disciplinary responsibility of a Justice or another high official of the state. So it seems that in these cases the publication of dissent is considered to be inappropriate. The same approach applies in English criminal appeals, where it has been long regarded as imperative that 'the discomfiture of the unsuccessful appellant should not be aggravated by an overt division of opinion among the judges' (Blom-Cooper and Drewry 1972, 81). As to the criminal or disciplinary responsibility of high public officials and judges, the question is even more delicate and has also political implications. In these cases the overt expression of disagreement in the court could lead to friction between the judiciary and the other two branches of power.

4.7 The publication of dissenting opinions

Observing the rules of East-Central European countries we can see that dissenting opinions, where they exist, are part of the judgment, though not binding as the opinion of the court. Proof of this assertion is the fact that separate opinions, with the sole exception of Latvia, are published together with the majority opinion. There is a curious situation in Slovenia, where dissenting opinions are not published in the Official Gazette, but on the website of the Court, in the Digest and in a special law journal. The explanation is simple: it is too expensive, since the Court must pay for publication in the Official Gazette.[23] Also in the Czech Republic dissents and concurrences are published in the Court's own reporter, but not in the Collection

20 See Article 148 par. 2 of the Bulgarian Constitution.

21 See Article 149 par. 1.8 of the Bulgarian Constitution and Article 32 par. 4 of Act no. 106/20 of 6 December 1991 (Rules on the Organisation of the Activities of the Constitutional Court). The English text of the Act is available on *Legislationline.org* at http://legislationline.org/documents/action/popup/id/6197.

22 See Article 136 par. 2-3 of the Slovak Constitution and Article 32 par. 3 of the Act on the organisation of and the proceedings before the Constitutional Court of 20 January 1993. The English version of the Act is available on the site of the Court: http://www.concourt.sk/en/A_ustava/ustava_a.pdf.

23 I thank Arne Mavčič for this information.

of Laws, where there is only a note at the bottom of the judgment that states the existence of a separate opinion.[24]

However, the precedential value of a separate opinion has been a highly debated issue, especially in common law, where the doctrine of binding precedent permeates the legal system and judges need to identify the *ratio decidendi* of judicial decisions. The problem emerges in relation to the so called plurality opinions, or no-clear-majority decisions, in which only the ruling is supported by the majority of judges but not the reasoning. In these judgments more than half of the judges express a separate opinion (dissent or concurrence), and examples are not limited to the common law countries. Also the Hungarian Constitutional Court delivered some plurality opinions which drew the attention of legal scholars, who assert that in these cases it is easier for the Court to change its mind and to deliver a different decision on the same issue in a subsequent case (see D. Tóth 2004, 98).

4.8 The use of dissenting opinions in East-Central European constitutional justice

As to the role of dissenting opinions in the evolution of constitutional law in East-Central Europe, we can observe that there are very few examples of dissents that later became the opinion of the majority. On the other hand, it is not so rare that a dissenting or concurring opinion could influence a later decision and contribute to the argumentation of the court in another case. In Polish constitutional justice an example is judgment no. K 31/04 of 26 October 2005 on restricting access to documents of Communist security agencies, which contains an implicit reference to a 1998 dissenting opinion in the lustration procedure case.[25]

In Slovenian constitutional case law sometimes it happened that a legal principle or institution was first referred to by a particular judge in his or her separate opinion – e.g. the principle of proportionality –, and such principle was later 'officially' introduced as part of the reasoning of a majority opinion.[26]

In Hungary, a dissenting opinion of Justice Imre Vörös, expressed in 1993,[27] six years later became shared by the majority,[28] but there was no explicit reference

24 The judgments, together with the separate opinions, are included in the main computer database of the Czech Republic (called ASPI), but the names of dissenting Justices are redacted out, and only their initials appear. I thank Mark Gillis for this information.

25 I thank Prof. Marek Safjan for this example. The English summary of this decision is available on the site of the Tribunal: http://www.trybunal.gov.pl/eng/summaries/documents/K_31_04_GB.pdf.

26 I thank Arne Mavčić for this information.

27 Dissenting opinion attached to Decision n. 4/1993 (II.12.) AB of 8 February 1993.

28 Decision n. 1/1999 (II.24.) AB of 23 February 1999. Indeed, at the time of this later decision, Justice László Sólyom who wrote the opinion of the court in the 1993 case was not on the Court anymore. The rapporteur of this judgment was Justice Árpád Erdei, and also the former dissenter, Justice

to it in the decision, even though some sentences written by Justice Vörös were repeated literally in the later judgment (see Udvary 2003, 6). In fact, there are no dissenting opinions explicitly cited in the opinion of the court. So we have to study thoroughly the single decisions to be able to deduce a possible influence of a former separate opinion. In some cases this influence is evident and easily traceable, as in the aforementioned case in which a particular legal principle was pronounced the first time in a separate opinion.

The first President of the Hungarian Constitutional Court, László Sólyom wrote some especially influential individual opinions. The necessity test that has later become one of the basic pillars of Hungarian constitutional jurisprudence concerning fundamental rights, was first defined by him in a dissenting opinion enclosed to Decision n. 2/1990 (II.18.) AB of 12 February 1990 (the first separate opinion in the history of the Hungarian Constitutional Court). Another example is his concurring opinion in the death penalty case issued in the same year,[29] in which he expressed his idea of the 'invisible constitution', severely criticised by many legal scholars. He was able to assert this idea in many subsequent majority opinions. In general we can say, using the words of Marek Safjan, former President of the Polish Constitutional Tribunal, that dissenting opinions can stimulate constitutional thinking.[30]

5 Instead of a conclusion: The possible impact of dissenting opinions on a legal system

The impact of dissenting and concurring opinions on the legal system is a widely debated issue in American legal literature, while in Europe scholarly material is limited to general reflections which often lack a thorough analysis involving statistical data. Relevant academic debate is practically non-existing in East-Central Europe.

It is worth considering the words of Justice Robert H. Jackson, member of the U.S. Supreme Court in the mid-20th century: 'We are not final because we are infallible, but we are infallible only because we are final.'[31] These words reveal humility and a modest attitude towards the legal system, recognising its complexity and inability to find an unmistakable solution to each legal question arising in everyday life. Even if this attitude has not been typical of every American judge, a reflection

Vörös took part in the decision of the case. However, there was a dissenting opinion (by Justice Tamás Lábady) attached to this decision as well, joined by two other judges.

29 Decision n. 23/1990 (X.31.) AB of 24 October 1990. In this case the length of the concurring opinion of Justice Sólyom (12 pages) was the double of the length of the majority decision (6 pages). There were five separate opinions in all, expressed by six judges (one dissent and four concurring opinions). The Court was composed of ten judges in that period.

30 Interview with Prof. Marek Safjan made on 18 April 2007 in Fiesole (Italy).

31 Concurring opinion in *Brown v. Allen*, 344 U.S. 443, 540 (1953).

of this kind would be hard to find in a majority judgment. Reflections like this are expressions of a personal opinion.

On the other hand, with a few exceptions, supreme courts in Europe are still dominated by secrecy, and the publication of dissent has been allowed only in constitutional justice. As early as in the 1930s, the eminent Italian scholar of civil procedure, Piero Calamandrei, expressed harsh criticism on the secrecy of judicial decision-making, calling it the 'institutional consecration of conformism' and a 'typical example of unanimity of the State that saves the appearances at the cost of conscience'[32] (Calamandrei 1989, 274). Calamandrei is only one of the several Italian scholars who advocated the introduction of dissenting opinions, and Italian legal scholarship has been traditionally in favour of it. However, Italy remains one of the few European countries that have not accepted it so far (see Panizza 1998, 176). This fact shows the complexity of the debate in civil law systems.

One of the main arguments in favour of the publication of dissent is that the exposure of different opinions is a useful vehicle for the evolution of law. In this way judicial decisions offer a wider range of arguments and courts take the leading role in legal science. Using the words of a well-known member of the U.S. Supreme Court, Justice Antonin Scalia, the result of this practice is that 'the Court itself is not just the central organ of legal *judgment*; it is center stage for significant legal *debate*' (Scalia 1995, 419). Furthermore, a dissenting opinion can be the precursor of a future change in the orientation of the court and it can help to change the law, even if this is rare (see the case of the dissent of Judge Vörös in Hungary, explained above).

On the other side, one of the strongest arguments against the publication of dissent is, indeed, the damage that it would cause to the authoritativeness of the decision and, accordingly, to the authority of the court. Yet, supporters of dissenting opinions reply that the authoritativeness can be even strengthened, if there is a real unanimity. It explains the reason why Chief Justice Warren worked so hard to reach unanimity in the *Brown v. Board of Education* case. He knew that in such an important issue that regards such a delicate social problem the decision of the Supreme Court should show unity to be authoritative. If dissent is permitted, then the public is not deceived by the secrecy of deliberation and can acknowledge that the highest court, in a certain sense, is the mirror of society.

Separate opinions are distinguished by a clearer language and a more linear argumentation, being written by a single judge instead of the expression of a group of judges. Indeed, the opinion of the court has to express the opinion of the majority, and even if the result was agreed to by all the judges voting in favor of that decision, it is not sure at all that all of them arrived to that solution following the same line of reasoning. Separate opinions often reveal facts that help the outsider to better

[32] Translation from Italian by the author.

understand how the court reached that given solution and to better understand the whole case and the decision itself. Especially concurring opinions frequently aim to explain better the opinion of the court or to shed light on some peculiar aspects of it. Thus, also legal doctrine is a beneficiary of separate opinions, and actually legal scholars pay much attention to these opinions which often look like academic writing.

At last, the disclosure of votes also serves to hold the individual judge accountable, even in the face of himself or herself. According to Justice Ginsburg:

> The process of writing signed opinions is a testing venture. [...] The prospect of a dissent or separate concurring opinion statement pointing out an opinion's inaccuracies and inadequacies strengthens the test; it heightens the opinion writer's incentive to 'get it right'. (Ginsburg 1990, 139)

References

Ajani, Gianmaria. 1995. By Chance and Prestige: Legal Transplants in Russia and Eastern Europe. *American Journal of Comparative Law* 43: 93–117.

Atiyah, Patrick S. 1988. Judgments in England. In *La sentenza in Europa. Metodo, tecnica e stile: atti del Convegno internazionale per l'inaugurazione della Facoltà, Ferrara 10-12 ottobre, 1985*, 140–158. Padova: Cedam.

Blom-Cooper, Louis, and Drewry, Gavin. 1972. *Final Appeal. A Study of the House of Lords in its Judicial Capacity.* Oxford: Clarendon Press.

Calamandrei, Piero. 1989 [1935]. *Elogio dei giudici scritto da un avvocato.* Firenze: Ponte alle Grazie Editori.

Denti, Vittorio. 1964. Per il ritorno al "voto di scissura" nelle decisioni giudiziarie. In *Le opinioni dissenzienti dei giudici costituzionali ed internazionali*, edited by Costantino Mortati, 1–20. Milano: Giuffrè.

D. Tóth, Balázs. 2004. Kisebbségi felülbírálat – tanácsadói szerepben? [Minority reasoning: A way of giving advice?] *Fundamentum* 3: 97–110.

Ginsburg, Ruth Bader. 1990. Remarks on Writing Separately. *Washington Law Review* 65: 133–150.

Laffranque, Julia. 2003. Dissenting Opinion and Judicial Independence. *Juridica International* 8: 162–172.

Laffranque, Julia. 2004. Dissenting Opinion in the European Court of Justice – Estonia's Possible Contribution to the Democratisation of the European Union Juridical System. *Juridica International* 9: 14–23.

Luatti, Lorenzo. 1995. *Profili costituzionali del voto particolare. L'esperienza del tribunale costituzionale spagnolo.* Milano: Giuffrè.

Luther, Jörg. 1994. L'esperienza del voto dissenziente nei paesi di lingua tedesca. *Politica del diritto* 2: 241–265.

Markesinis, Basil. 1994. *The Gradual Convergence: Foreign Ideas, Foreign Influences, and English Law on the Eve of the 21th Century.* Oxford, New York: Clarendon Press.

Mehren, Arthur von. 1956. The Judicial Process: A Comparative Analysis. *American Journal of Comparative Law* 5: 197–228.

Montesquieu, Charles de. 1989. *The Spirit of the Laws* [*De l'esprit de lois*, 1748]. Cambridge: Cambridge University Press.

Morgan, Donald G. 1944. Mr. Justice William Johnson and the Constitution. *Harvard Law Review* 57: 328–361.

Morgan, Donald G. 1953. The Origin of Supreme Court Dissent. *The William and Mary Quarterly* 10: 353–377.

Nadelmann, Kurt H. 1964. Non-Disclosure of Dissents in Constitutional Courts: Italy and West Germany. *American Journal of Comparative Law* 13: 268–276.

Oneto, Luisa Paola. 1976–77. Le opinioni dissenzienti dei giudici della Corte costituzionale tedesca. *Annali della Facoltà di Scienze Politiche di Genova*: 1083–1112.

Panizza, Saulle. 1998. *L'introduzione dell'opinione dissenziente nel sistema di giustizia costituzionale.* Torino: Giappichelli.

Paterson, Alan. 1982. *The Law Lords.* London, Basingstoke: Macmillan.

Procházka, Radoslav. 2002. *Mission Accomplished. On Founding Constitutional Adjudication in Central Europe.* Budapest: Central European University Press.

Scalia, Antonin. 1995. Remarks on Dissenting Opinions. In *L'opinione dissenziente*, edited by Adele Anzon, 411–426. Milano: Giuffrè.

Sólyom, László. 2003. The role of constitutional courts in the transition to democracy – with special reference to Hungary. *International Sociology* 18: 133–161.

Udvary, Sándor. 2003. *A médiatörvény alkotmánybírósági múltja és jelene* [*Past and present of the media law in front of the constitutional court*]. Budapest: Alkalmazott Kommunikációtudományi Intézet. [http://archiv.akti.hu/tanulmany/dok/udvary_01.rtf]

ZoBell, Karl M. 1959. Division of Opinion in the Supreme Court: A History of Judicial Disintegration. *Cornell Law Quarterly* 44: 186–214.

Complex Laws and Self-Referential Rules: The European Legal System between Hierarchy and Transnational Network

Mariusz Jerzy Golecki

Abstract Many hopes of the adherents of the constitutional reform in the EU remained in vain after the enactment of the Lisbon Treaty. Meanwhile, the creeping constitutionalisation of EU law led to the empowerment of the EU's quasi constitutional court, the European Court of Justice. This kind of constitutionalism is still firmly grounded in cross-border judicial cooperation. The main purpose of this paper is to address the question as to whether and how the concept of judicial control could effectively supplement if not substitute the notion of constitutional democratic legitimacy. In order to demonstrate that it is logically possible and institutionally feasible to build a system based on circularity and self-reference, the paper analyses recent developments in EU case law which at least partially take this direction.

1 Introduction

It could seem that there is hardly anything more abstract than the contemplation of the features and composition of legal systems *qua* legal systems. The difference between a complex (Hartian) and a simple (Kelsenian) model of a legal system seems, however, to play an important role in the description and explanation of the operations of some actual legal systems. This pertains especially to the existence and character of EU law.

A simple legal system is a normative system based on a stable hierarchy of rules in a Kelsenian sense (see Hart 1983a). As Neil Duxbury recently pointed out, the Kelsenian concept of a legal system validated by the basic norm is affected by some contradictions (Duxbury 2008, 55–60). According to Kelsen's assumption, every legal norm encapsulates an act of will, expressed by some authority that is empowered by another norm to create the given legal norm (ibid., 56). If this is true, however, then the basic norm cannot be regarded as a valid legal norm, for the basic norm could not be created by any authority. Otherwise it could not preserve its exceptional status as the pre-supposition of any legal system (see Alexy 2002, 111). As a result, Kelsen himself changed his attitude towards the concept of the basic norm when he observed that it is a fiction in a special sense, a fiction that not only contradicts reality but is also self-contradictory. As he stated,

> a basic norm [...] not only contradicts reality, since no such norm exists as the meaning of an actual act of will, but also contains contradiction within itself, since it represents the authorization of a supreme moral or legal authority, and hence it issues from an authority lying beyond that authority (Kelsen 1967, 117).

These contradictions have already been revealed by Joseph Raz's careful analysis of the Kelsenian concept of a legal system. Raz contended that the Kelsenian basic norm is obsolete and asked the question about the potential substitute for it (Raz 1980, 134–138).

2 The concept of a complex legal system

Certainly the first possible alternative to the basic norm could possibly be the concept of the rule of recognition as proposed by Hart. Unfortunately, the rule of recognition falls short in confrontation with close scrutiny of its merits. As Matthew Kramer (1988) observed, the rule of recognition presupposes either infinite regress or circularity. It could well be true that it is not possible for the rule of recognition to provide a justification of the origin of a legal order. However, the alleged circularity of it could be explained and justified by Hart himself. When he analysed the concept of so-called self-referring rules, he finally reached the conclusion that the phenomenon of self-referentiality could rightly be deployed as a vehicle apt for the validation of a legal system (Hart 1983b).

A complex legal system is a system whose rules are validated by two apparently different rules of recognition, which means that the practice of judges and officials in a subsystem X is notoriously different from that of subsystem Y. The relationships between the rules of X and the rules of Y may take two forms. First, X and Y could operate as complementary. This would happen if rules X complemented rules Y. Second, X and Y may be regarded as substitutes and thus competing with one another (see Zasu 2007, 379–396).

Moreover, such a system could also comply with the Razian description of a legal system (cf. Raz 1980, 139–140). Raz analyses the structure of a self-validating system as follows: A→B→C→D→A. The symbol → means that rule A validates rule B and so on. Such a system could rightly be characterised as self-referential. The hierarchy of rules is illusive or at most provisional (defeasible). The system is based on a set of self-referring rules, as it was rightly observed by Hart (1983b, 173).

The character of the link between D and A raises the question: How is it possible for the hierarchically inferior rule D to validate a supposedly superior rule A? The solution given to the problem may be supported by the observation that rule D could be a specific and concrete rule, such as encapsulated in the verdict of a court (see Hart 1961, 106–142). The set of such rules creates a proper ground for the reconstruction of the existing rule of recognition, underpinning the existence of the legal system (see ibid., 149–150). If this is so, then the rule of recognition is a sum of practices of the judges and officials and the ultimate source of criteria of validity of the same legal system at the same time (see Dickson 2007, 373–381). As a conventional reason for rule following, the rule of recognition reveals itself as the rule A, whereas as a set of single operations of the legal institutions the same rule consists of rules of the type D (see Marmor 2001, 2–33). Within the context of actual legal systems, a simpler case could be imagined, in which there is only one court issuing verdicts comprising norms of type D.

3 The institutional character of a complex legal system

The theory of complex legal systems offers a peculiar description of the structure and functions of contemporary public institutions. The main characteristics of the systemic nature of law include a coexistence of various judicial bodies and institutional structures of adjudication within a given jurisdiction. Quite often, this kind of coexistence of adjudicating institutions leads to an evolution of their adjudicative functions and expansion of their jurisdiction due to a creative interpretation of existing constitutional and statutory law. Since some courts of last instance gained autonomous positions within their legal systems as institutions responsible for constitutional review of the lawmaking process and for the judicial control of administration, the problem of interpretation and validity of existing legal rules becomes a crucial issue. In other words, the institutional practice of judicial bodies leads to the creation of new legal concepts, principles and rules. This process of the expansion of judicial power seems, however, to be diverse. Generally, the transformation from simple to complex legal systems is discernible at two levels, internal and external.

Let us start with internal complexity. It seems that a process of constitutionalisation of the legal order, accompanied by the emancipation of judicial institutions inevitably leads to competition and conflicts between higher courts. The tensions between judges of the constitutional court and those of the Supreme Administrative Court and the Supreme Court in Poland may serve as a good illustration for the evolution from a relatively simple hierarchical legal system to a complex system based on self-referring rules rather than on the hierarchical order.

According to Art. 8 para. 2 of the Polish Constitution, '[t]he provisions of the Constitution shall apply directly, unless the Constitution provides otherwise.' The question raised by this provision is how to understand the scope and meaning of the so called 'direct' application of the constitution. According to the judges at the Polish Constitutional Tribunal, other courts and even the Supreme Court are not authorised to decide on the constitutionality of specific statutory rules. In case of doubt, courts should rather initiate a preliminary reference procedure and refer to the Constitutional Tribunal, since the authority to determine constitutionality is granted exclusively to the Constitutional Tribunal. Other high courts such as the Supreme Court and Supreme Administrative Court have questioned this interpretation of the Constitution, claiming that in some special cases the unconstitutionality could lead to an automatic invalidation of a given unconstitutional provision by the adjudicating court. In particular, the Supreme Administrative Court invented the doctrine of 'ostensible unconstitutionality', according to which in some obvious cases the question of unconstitutionality could be decided by the Supreme Administrative Court. Additionally, the court claimed an exclusive power to review regulations enacted by the government.

A similar conflict between constitutional and supreme courts took place in 1980 in France where the Constitutional Council initiated the constitutional review, whereas other courts sometimes ignored its verdicts. As Alec Stone Sweet (2007) observed, the French Supreme Court (*Cour de Cassation*) gradually developed a rule that required judges to interpret statutory provisions in a way coherent with constitutional law. Additionally, the Council of State has begun adjusting some general principles of administrative law such as 'individual liberty', 'equality before the law', and 'freedom of conscience' to equivalent constitutional rights.

It seems that this kind of proliferation of judicial centres and 'constitutional reviewers' had already been predicted by Kelsen who warned against the process of constitutionalisation. According to Kelsen, the process of converting constitutional courts from negative to positive lawmakers would lead to the multiplication of conflicting interpretations as to the substance and scope of constitutional rights. Kelsen even suggested that

> different law-applying organs may have different opinions with regard to the constitutionality of a statute, and [...] one organ may apply the statute whereas the other organ will refuse the application on the ground of its alleged unconstitutionality. The lack of a uniform decision [...] is a great danger to the authority of constitution. (Kelsen 1942, 185)

Moreover, the alteration of judicial practice leading to the transformation of courts from negative to positive lawmakers, adjudicating not only on the content of the constitution but also on criteria of validity and legality, leads to a substantial change in the legal system which could only be compared to a revolution. Kelsen argues that

> [t]he principle that a norm of a legal order is valid until its validity is terminated in a way determined by this legal order or replaced by the validity of another norm of this order, is called the principle of legitimacy. The principle is applicable to a legal order with one important limitation only: It does not apply in case of a revolution. […] From the point of view of legal science, it is irrelevant whether this change of the legal situation has been brought about by the application of force against the legitimate government, or by members of the government themselves. (Kelsen 1992, 208–209)

Thus, it seems that the internal complexity of a legal system does not only change the character of the legal order from simple to complex. In addition, it also means that a political change occurs and that the institutional practice of judges and officials may lead to an evolutionary or even revolutionary change of the legal and political order. This change may also concern the external complexity of a given legal system.

As far as political and legal developments in Europe are concerned, the process of integration could be perceived as a state of transition where dogmatic concepts can no longer be adequate to the changing reality of legal and political institutions. The idea of 'stateless law' requires the acceptance of the condition that the authorities which are external to national authorities may take binding decisions concerning the application and interpretation of law. Moreover, the civic sovereignty of people within a state has been directed towards both institutionalised legal proceedings and informal processes.

These instruments enable opinion and will formation in a discursive fashion. There exists a network of communication in the form of anonymously linked discourses that should be organised in such a way that the actions of governmental authorities could regulate the economic system within the social and ecological sphere, while respecting its internal logic. The advocates of stateless law underline that the linear relations among rules have been replaced by a circular or looped hierarchy of laws. A looped hierarchy is defined as an interaction among various levels within the hierarchical order where the highest level directs the lowest level and influences it, while at the same time the highest level is itself determined by the lowest one (see Raz 1980, 139–140).

The concept of stateless law is thus understood as a pluralist concept of law, referring to various systems of law which co-exist simultaneously. At the same time, the concept of the state becomes redundant, since the traditional nation state is not able to unify legal rules and transform them into a single national legal system. Legal systems of member states lose the attribute of sovereignty and homogeneity, being transformed into normative networks.

These phenomena influence the process of application of law by courts in a particular way. It seems that within this sphere the most serious problems are linked to the obligation of a national judge to apply not only legal rules of national, Community and international origin, but also standards, rules and principles of supranational and international character. Hence, the judge should be able to identify the required standard according to which it is necessary to decide a given case. Moreover, he or she should be able to solve a conflict among the conflicting rules or standards, which might be perceived as a form of discretional 'meta-regulation'. If the dynamics of the integration process leads to the acceptance of the 'stateless law' hypothesis, then traditional concepts such as sovereignty and national citizenship begin to lose their traditional meanings.

Complexity pertaining to the application of international or regional law within a particular jurisdiction seems to be external from the perspective of that jurisdiction. This kind of interrelations between legal rules enacted by external actors, operating outside a given jurisdiction, could be associated with the operational features of interrelations and mutual impact of national courts of a given country and supranational authorities. Such complexity could easily be identified in the interaction of the European Court for Human Rights and the Court of Justice of the European Union. The mutual impact of the two leading regional European judicial bodies has been regulated by judicial rulings.[1] Since the establishment of the principle of superiority by the ECJ, the EU legal system may be perceived as an autonomous legal system superior to any national legal order of its members. In addition, the claim for autonomy and integrity of EU law in relation to international law has been recently emphasised in judgments of the European Court of Justice.[2]

The question arises whether the efficacy of EU law in Member States leads to the creation of a single complex legal system or to the interactions of national legal systems. This problem can be analysed accurately following Joseph Raz's ideas. Raz distinguishes between two different situations: on the one hand, the integration of legal orders leading to a single complex legal system; on the other, an exceptional operation of one system within the jurisdiction of another system which does not lead to a single complex system. In discussing the criteria of membership of a legal system, Raz (1980, 102) takes the view that a legal system contains those norms which should be applied by norm-applying institutions such as courts. His focus on law-applying rather than on lawmaking institutions results from the fact that it is the judicial organs that ultimately decide on the criteria of validity they adopt.

1 Cf. case 13258/87 *M vs. GER 'Melchers'*, case 24833/94 *Matthews vs. UK*, case 60350/00 Canela *Santiago vs. ESP*, 56672/00 *Senator Lines vs. Austria, Belgium, Denmark, Finland, France, Germany, Greece, Ireland, Italy, Luxembourg, the Netherlands, Portugal, Spain, Sweden and the United Kingdom*, case 45036/98 *Bosphorus Hava Yollari Turizm Ve Ticaret Anonim Şirketi vs. Ireland.*

2 Joined Cases C-402/05P & C-415/05 *P Kadi and Al Barakaat vs. Council*, Judgment of the Court (Grand Chamber) of 3rd September 2008, par. 282.

The institutionalised practice of law-application could be reconstructed in terms of the rule of recognition of a given legal system. Additionally, Raz distinguishes two different situations or reasons for application of some legal rules within a legal system (Raz 1979, 87–88; 1980, 189–197). First, rules may belong to a given legal system as parts of it. Second, some legal rules may operate within a legal system but do not belong to that given system. This latter case is based on the permission of a legal system in which those rules operate as effective but external norms. If rules can operate either as a part of a legal system or without becoming part of the system, just due to the permission to operate as an external norm, then a question arises about the criteria or conditions for distinguishing between internal and external efficacy of rules. This difference can be explained in the following way:

> Ultimately the problem turns on an accumulation of evidence justifying a judgement whether a norm is enforced on the grounds that it is part of the law's function to support other social systems or because it is part of the law itself. (Raz 1979, 102)

Certainly, the evidence justifying external or internal operation of a given legal rule should be referred to the practice of adjudicating bodies and the justifications provided by them. In other words, whether the EU creates one complex legal system or a set of independent legal systems, depends on the practice of EU courts, the courts of the Member States and on the justification of these practices. What, however, if the practice of courts in different Member States is not coherent?

It seems that this is actually the case with EU law. On the one hand, the European Court of Justice recognises the independent, autonomous and superior character of EU law in relation to national legal systems of Member States.[3] On the other, the highest judicial authorities of some of these national legal orders deny the superiority of EU law. For instance, this is the position of the Polish Constitutional Tribunal, according to which the relation between EU law and the Polish legal system should be understood as the 'coexistence of different legal rules produced by different lawmaking bodies and applied by various court structures'. However, such a coexistence '[i]n no event may lead to results contradicting the explicit wording of constitutional norms' (Polish CT K18/04, 11.05.2005).

In striking opposition to this view, the Spanish Constitutional Tribunal held that the principle of superiority of the EU law includes even constitutional law, since: 'primacy and supremacy [...] operate in different areas of law' (Spanish CT [2005] 1 CMLR 981). Additionally, the Spanish Constitutional Tribunal held that Art. 93 of the Spanish Constitution enabled the transfer of constitutional powers to external institutions.

3 Cf. the ECJ judgments in *Costa vs. ENEL* [1964], ECR 585, *Simenthal* [1978] ECR 629.

The divergence between these two rulings on the superiority of EU law in Poland and Spain means that the operation of EU law in these systems as reflected in the judgments of relevant judicial bodies are of a different character. The divergence in application of the principle of superiority in different Member States leads to the conclusion that the legal system as a whole could rightly be perceived as a complex one.

Certainly, in theory such a legal system could remain a simple one since the practice of the Court of Justice of the European Union (CJEU) would constitute a single and sufficiently coherent rule of recognition. This, however, is not the case, at least not at the present stage of European integration. The question remains as to how a complex legal system of this kind would evolve in the long run if there were many courts which were formally independent from CJEU and belonged to different judicial structures. Certainly, without proper legal instruments it would be impossible for the CJEU to coordinate the operation of the system. In consequence, some heterodox practices of other courts would possibly create other rules of recognition. Therefore, it is crucial to emphasise that the efficacy of the CJEU's coordinating instruments would directly influence the homogeneity of the given complex system, where the CJEU has to coordinate not only its own operations but also the operations of other legal institutions, thus mediating between the rule of recognition which ultimately characterises EU law (and the other components of EU law) and the rules of recognition shaping the ultimate criteria of validity of Member States.

4 EU law as a complex legal system

The relationship between the concept of a simple legal system founded on a single hierarchy of courts and a complex legal system composed of different horizontal levels of judicial institutions and imbued with the operation of different, randomly overlapping rules of recognition has been exposed by the CJEU's decision in *Köbler v. Republic of Austria* (Case C-224/01, [2003] E.C.R. I-10239). The CJEU has endorsed the view that a Member State may be liable in damages for a national court's serious misapplication of EU law. The approach presented in *Köbler* has been repeated and reinforced in case C-173/03 *Traghetti del Mediterraneo SpA v. Italy*, [2006] where the CJEU stated that any limitation of State liability on the part of the court is contrary to Community law if such limitations were to lead to the exclusion of liability of the Member State 'in other cases where a manifest infringement of the applicable law was committed.'[4] Many commentators emphasise the

[4] The CJEU held that 'Community law precludes national legislation which excludes State liability, in a general manner, for damage caused to individuals by an infringement of Community law attributable to a court adjudicating at last instance by reason of the fact that the infringement in

threat of uncertainty and instability of legal positions resulting from these rulings.[5] Some of them express doubts concerning potential distortions resulting from these rulings and the application of the doctrine of state liability to judicial errors (see Somek 2007). It is commonly agreed that the EU legal system after *Köbler* might be characterised as being transformed from a hierarchical structure into three levels or layers of judiciary composed of (1) constitutional courts, (2) highest courts,[6] and (3) lower courts.[7] The fact that national rules of legal procedure enable parties to ask a first instance court to sit in judgment on a verdict of the court of last instance could weaken and in the long run even destroy the traditional linear hierarchy of courts.

Accordingly, if the traditional, hierarchical structure of national courts within Member States is being weakened by the judicature of the CJEU, the question arises about the meaning of such a process and its impact upon the relevant rule of recognition reflecting the actual behaviour of judges in national courts. Imposition of state liability for judicial acts would be likely to lead to the CJEU being called upon to decide whether a national supreme court had acted manifestly wrongly. Lower level national courts may be unwilling to find that superior national courts have acted manifestly wrongly. They might therefore look to the CJEU to make the final judgment. This may lead to the conclusion that the idea of the objectivity of law in Community law cases, whilst not only intellectually attractive but undoubtedly derived from the concept of the Rule of Law, faces serious practical problems.

Within a hierarchical judicial system the coherence of adjudication is preserved by appeals and by the same token by the control of cases exerted by higher courts such as courts of appeal or the Supreme Court. Since every judge tends to avoid being overruled, the judicial system usually sustains cohesion and diminishes the number of judicial errors. Nevertheless, the question arises what would happen if within some jurisdiction the Supreme Court had no authority to review cases from lower instances. Alternatively, what would happen if instead of one court on the top of the centralised hierarchical structure, there were many different courts and each of them had the power to review lower instance cases, and all of them were

---

question results from an interpretation of provisions of law or an assessment of facts or evidence carried out by that court. Community law also precludes national legislation which limits such liability solely to cases of intentional fault and serious misconduct on the part of the court, if such a limitation were to lead to exclusion of the liability of the Member State concerned in other cases where a manifest infringement of the applicable law was committed, as set out in [...] the judgment in Case C-224/01 *Köbler* [2003] EUR I-10239.'

5 The strategy adopted by the CJEU in *Köbler* and *Traghetti* provoked a serious debate in the literature, see Albors-Llorens (2007), Bertolino (2008), Breuer (2004), Ruffert (2007).

6 The second level consists of courts of last instance which end legal procedures. As they vary from case to case, this level of the structure is fluid.

7 This has been emphasised in the literature, see Breuer (2004, 252–254), Chalmers et al. (2006, 498–502), Golecki and Wojciechowski (2009, 173–174; 2007, 9–17).

allowed to rely on the preliminary reference to a specialised court responsible for the efficacy and coherence of the whole adjudicative practice. Such is the situation that currently takes place in EU law.

The relationship between the CJEU and national courts, especially with regard to the courts of last instance cannot be described as a hierarchical structure. The CJEU does not revise or control verdicts of national courts. Concurringly, the European courts do not have power to overrule judgments given by national courts. This situation is somehow puzzling for many commentators as it requires a completely new approach to standardisation and unification of judicial activity.

It seems that the application of liability rules could enhance the coherence of the application of EU law, since national courts would adjudicate under the shadow of the appropriate liability rule. Nevertheless, this outcome is not obvious and it would be attained only in case of a coherent application of the liability rule (proposed in *Köbler*) in different Member States. The result depends heavily on the level of administrative costs, and on the accuracy of verdicts of the courts.

5 Conclusions

At this stage of our argument, a haphazard conclusion could be reached, according to which virtually all legal systems are complex. It is not my intention to contemplate this claim, which would inevitably lead to questions about the nature of law. I must admit, however, that I can see nothing *prima facie* wrong in the conjecture that all legal systems are complex in the sense that their legitimacy is based on circularity. In this, I simply follow Joseph Raz's suggestion that if we compare it to Kelsen's mysterious foundationalism, circularity might be a better option. Kelsen was looking for the ultimate source of validity of a legal system outside that system in order to find that the basic norm may provide such a solid ground. In contrast, does such a complexity not lead to chaos? The answer is negative, at least if we adopt a different conception of the legal system where *ad hoc* rules can modify the rule of recognition. Courts act as a kind of interstitial legislator, providing what is necessary, i.e. closing the connection between all relevant rules of a given system (the A–D connection).

In order to prove that this conclusion is sound, one could address three fundamental and practical questions, especially taking into account the complexity of EU law. Why do lawyers engage in a close and careful scrutiny of the jurisprudence of relevant courts both in common and civil law countries? Why do we await, with hope or anxiety, the forthcoming verdicts of CJEU in Europe? Finally, why does the European Commission carefully and sensitively monitor the jurisprudence of national courts, especially supreme courts within Member States? The importance of the courts' activity seems to be unquestionable. But the soundness of the so-called 'judicial dialogue and cooperation' should be subdued to judicial control exerted by the potential victims of judicial fantasy.

For these reasons, although the liability of Member States for breach of EU law contradicts some assumptions about a monistic and hierarchical legal order, within a complex legal system it seems to be a feasible alternative to traditional judicial hierarchy. Moreover, this kind of liability operates in a direction opposite to traditional judicial hierarchy as it provides a necessary remedy, transforming the 'lack of democratic control' and the alleged deficit of democracy in the EU into a form of 'judiciocracy'. This may be characterised as the control by courts exercised on behalf of the citizenry whose rights have been infringed by misapplication of the law by other courts.

Acknowledgement The article has been prepared within the framework of the *Supporting Grant* (KOLUMB Programme) of the Foundation for Polish Science.

References

Albors-Llorens, Albertina. 2007. The Principle of State Liability in EU Law and the Supreme Courts of the Member States. *The Cambridge Law Journal* 66: 270–273.

Alexy, Robert. 2002. *The Argument from Injustice. A Reply to Legal Positivism*. Oxford: Oxford University Press.

Bertolino, Giulia. 2008. The *Traghetti* Case: A New CJEU Decision on State Liability for Judicial Acts – National Legislation under Examination. *Civil Justice Quarterly* 27: 448–453.

Breuer, Marten. 2004. State Liability for Judicial Wrongs and Community Law: the Case of *Gerhard Köbler v. Austria*. *European Law Review* 29: 243–254.

Chalmers, Damian et al. 2006. *European Union Law*. Cambridge: Cambridge University Press.

Dickson, Julie. 2007. Is the Rule of Recognition Really a Conventional Rule? *Oxford Journal of Legal Studies* 27: 373–402.

Duxbury, Neil. 2008. Kelsen's Endgame. *Cambridge Law Journal* 67: 51–61.

Golecki, Mariusz, and Wojciechowski, Bartosz. 2007. Cyberspace as a Precondition of Application of Law within a Multicentric Legal Area. *Masaryk University Journal of Law and Technology* 1: 9–17.

Golecki, Mariusz, and Wojciechowski, Bartosz. 2009. The Application of Law within a Multicentric Legal System. Economic Analysis of *Köbler* and *Traghetti*. In *Multicentrism as an Emerging Paradigm in Legal Theory*, edited by Marek

Zirk-Sadowski, Mariusz J. Golecki, and Bartosz Wojciechowski, 173–196. Frankfurt: Peter Lang.

Hart, Herbert. 1961. *The Concept of Law.* Oxford: Clarendon Press.

Hart, Herbert. 1983a. Kelsen's Doctrine of the Unity of Law. In *Essays in Jurisprudence and Philosophy*, 309–342. Oxford: Oxford University Press.

Hart, Herbert. 1983b. Self-Referring Laws. In *Essays in Jurisprudence and Philosophy*, 170–178. Oxford: Oxford University Press.

Kelsen, Hans. 1942. Judicial Review in Legislation. A Comparative Study of the Austrian and the American Constitution. *The Journal of Politics* 4.2: 183–200.

Kelsen, Hans. 1967. *Pure Theory of Law.* 2nd edition. Berkeley: University of California Press.

Kelsen, Hans. 1992 [1934]. *Introduction to the Problems of Legal Theory.* Oxford: Clarendon Press.

Kramer, Matthew. 1988. The Rule of Misrecognition in the Hart of Jurisprudence. *Oxford Journal of Legal Studies* 8: 401–433.

Marmor, Andrei. 2001. *Positive Law and Objective Values.* Oxford: Oxford University Press.

Raz, Joseph. 1979. *The Authority of Law.* Oxford: Clarendon Press.

Raz, Joseph. 1980. *The Concept of a Legal System: An Introduction to the Theory of Legal System.* 2nd edition. Oxford: Clarendon Press.

Ruffert, Matthias. 2007. Case C-173/03 Traghetti del Mediterraneo SpA in Liquidation v. Italian Republic, Judgment of The Court (Great Chamber) of 13 June 2006. *Common Market Law Review* 44: 479–500.

Somek, Alexander. 2007. Inexplicable Law. Legality's Adventure in Europe. *University of Iowa Legal Studies Research Papers* 11 [http://ssrn.com/abstract=887149].

Stone Sweet, Alec. 2007. The Juridical Coup d'État and the Problem of Authority. *German Law Journal* 8: 915–928.

Zasu, Yoshinobu. 2007. Sanctions by Social Norms and the Law: Substitutes or Complements? *Journal of Legal Studies* 36: 379–396.

The General Clause: A Measure of Universalising the Content of Law or An Expression of its Diversity? On 'Public Interest' and 'Public Moral' Clauses

Anna Kalisz and Adam Szot

Abstract A general clause can be described as a legislative construct that allows the application of various legally undefined criteria and values in a legal decision. These criteria and values are determined axiologically and come from outside the legal system, though they are often contained in statutory provisions. In cases involving general clauses the role of the court is to take into account such values and to apply them in an individual and concrete process of law-application. The main aim of this paper is to answer the question whether general clauses are a tool for universalising the content of case law in the times of European integration and globalisation or rather an expression of local (regional) values. The paper argues that for supra- and international courts the case is and should be the latter. The argument is illustrated by judgments and decisions of the Polish, European and international courts concerning general clauses of 'public morals' and 'public interest'.

1 Introduction

In the era of globalisation and European integration, among many other theoretical issues there arises the question whether in a process of law application general clauses tend to be measures of introducing uniform interpretation or rather expressions of local or regional systems of values.

In every legal order, there are great many different – sometimes even conflicting – examples of such clauses but this very research focuses on the 'public interest' and 'public morals' clauses. These are examples of clauses that are present in domestic, supranational and international legal orders. At the same time, these clauses often serve as the limitations of constitutional freedoms and human rights.

This paper is an attempt to answer the following questions. What exactly is the content that fills general clauses and at the same time co-creates legal norms? Is it possible and necessary at all to distinguish them *in abstracto*? In other words, to what extent does the content of a certain general clause depend upon the subjective decision of a court (or administrative authority) and to what extent is it determined by an objective 'between-the-lines' meaning, common to the European legal and axiological system (if there is any)? Finally, can we say that in today's world a reference to general clauses is a reference to a kind of universal system of values?

In order to answer these questions it is necessary to analyse decisions taken in processes of application of law at different levels – international, supranational and national –, and their mutual influence. This paper focuses on Poland as an example of a domestic legal system within the European legal order. In comparison to the Polish legal system, judgments and jurisprudence, the paper analyses the decision of the European Court of Human Rights in Strasbourg (ECHR) and the Court of Justice of the European Union in Luxembourg (CJEU).

As for the final question, the intuitive answer would be that the general role of the international (supranational) judiciary is to determine the 'meaning' of general clauses by introducing a uniform interpretation. The paper will argue that this intuition is misleading.

2 General clauses

A 'general clause' (*clausula generalis, Generalklausel*) is a legal rule, term or concept which is not precisely formulated and in fact does not even have a clear core meaning (see Grundmann 2005, 1–4). Thus, the issue of general clauses can be located between the axiological and the legal sphere.

As there is no official legal definition of the term (and it is not a provisional term), one is compelled to rely on doctrinal attempts of creating such a definition. In Polish legal theory, the most significant attempts are those by Józef Nowacki (1998; 1992) and Leszek Leszczyński (2000). According to these authors, general clauses are addressed to various subjects such as individuals or the entire society, but mainly and typically to judicial or administrative bodies that are going to pass legally binding decisions. Thus, while there is no *in abstracto* definition of particular general clauses, there are many attempts at defining them *in concreto* in the process of law application and decision-making, when the legal provisions contain such clauses. Applying a general clause forces decisional bodies to fill it with concrete substantive content. This makes them responsible or rather jointly responsible for the content of binding law. At the same time, it also gives them a wide area of discretion on the matter.

According to the principle of Rule of Law, the body that has power to decide is expected to justify why it exercises that power as it does. The idea that we live under a government of law, not men, seems to be based on the assumption that there is 'one right answer' (see Dworkin 1985) in the sense of a correct legal result that exists quite independent of human knowledge. This supports the importance of certainty (see Carter and Burke 2002). Thereby, the main role of a general clause is to ensure and bring to law application processes two very important values: flexibility and fairness. The obligation to specify the content of a general clause with reference to facts of a specific case makes the individual legal decision even more 'individual'.

3 The decisional process

General clauses appear in various branches of law. They are also applied in different types and paradigms of decisional processes, most importantly by courts and by administrative authorities. The judicial and the administrative paradigms differ in their way of applying values contained in general clauses. This paper focuses solely on the judicial paradigm of the decisional process. This choice was made for an easier comparison of legal processes at national, supranational and international levels. In this way, we avoid difficulties with translating and explaining not only legal terms but also the structure and powers of administrative authorities that vary from state to state much more than in the judiciary.

The most important characteristic of the judicial paradigm of law application is its *independence* from other branches of state power, a feature that hierarchically linked and politically dependent administrative bodies are deprived of (see Russell and O'Brien 2001).

Here arises the theoretical question as to which phases of the judicial paradigm of law application are affected by the fact that the court is applying a general clause. The phase of fact finding has to answer the question whether the situation needs a general clause being involved. Then comes a phase of evaluative reasoning, since the normative basis of the decision lays both inside and outside the legal system. More precisely, as the idea of the hermeneutic circle suggests, in the first place the court has to interpret the meaning of a general clause. Then the process goes back to the fact-finding and evaluation phases.

In a civil law culture legal reasoning and decision making are based mainly on legal provisions (texts). That is why it is called a 'statutory law culture'. Since a general clause is the result of legislation, it is also part of the statutory text, i.e., it is not solely an axiological or social criterion anymore. Thus, a court that passes a decision bases it on a legal criterion.

The starting point for the interpretation is, of course, the literal meaning of a provision containing a general clause. But taking into consideration that these phrases are often unclear, interpretation has to involve the use of extra-linguistic arguments. These additional arguments are mainly axiological in nature.

Usually, at least for lower level national courts the established case law of the domestic Supreme Court (SC) and Constitutional Tribunal (CT), as well as the decisions of the ECHR and CJEU are important 'interpretative aids'. Their judgments are very significant especially in situations where the legal or doctrinal 'definitions' of general clauses are lacking.

Therefore, the decisions of these courts can be considered as the creation of complementary legal sources of a quasi-precedential nature, even if it can be perceived as a 'side-effect' of the judicial decision-making process. This is a relatively recent effect of convergence in the civil law culture.

Nowadays, legal regulation can be located either at domestic (national), supranational or international (either global or regional) level. For instance, Member States of the Council of Europe or the European Union voluntarily conferred some of their power to supra- and international bodies (see, e.g., art. 90.1 of the Polish Constitution). 'Divided sovereignty' (cf. MacCormick 1999, 126) can be noticed not only in legislative or executive but also in judicial activity. One of the most characteristic features of the European legal order is its multicentrism (see ibid.; Ossowski 1967, 116; Łętowska 2005, 3; Mayer 2003; Pernice 1999).

4 'Public morals' and 'public interest' clauses in Polish, European and international law

In contemporary democratic society and a state governed by the Rule of Law, individual rights and freedoms (termed also as 'liberties', 'constitutional freedoms', 'human and citizen rights' or 'fundamental rights', depending on the legal system) are provided and guaranteed by law but also limited by law at the same time. This limitation must, however, be based on strong legal and axiological justification. A limitation of such rights may be imposed by statute only and solely when it is necessary in a democratic state. One of such axiological necessities is the protection of 'public morality'.

At the domestic (Polish) level, these limitations are regulated by art. 31.3 of the Constitution, as well as in several statutory enactments. Art. 31.3 of the Polish Constitution reads as follows:

> Any limitation upon the exercise of constitutional freedoms and rights may be imposed only by statute, and only when necessary in a democratic state for the protection of its security or public order, or to protect the natural environment, health or public morals, or the freedoms and rights of other persons. Such limitations shall not violate the essence of freedoms and rights.

As for international and European law, 'public morals' clauses are phrased differently, as morality, public morality, or public morals. Such a clause is included in art. 8 (right to respect for private and family life), 9 (freedom of thought), 10 (freedom of expression), and 11 (freedom of assembly and association) of The European Convention for Protection of Human Rights and Fundamental Freedoms (the European Convention) which use the phrase 'protection of [health and] morals'. Art. 36 of the Treaty on the Functioning of the European Union (TFEU) provides that '[t]he provisions of Articles 34 and 35 [free movement of goods – A.K., A.S.] shall not preclude prohibitions or restrictions on imports, exports or goods in transit justified on grounds of public morality.' The Polish declaration no. 62 concerning the Protocol 30 ('opt-out') to the Lisbon Treaty (TL) refers to it as follows: 'The Charter does not affect in any way the right of Member States to legislate in the sphere of public morality'. In sum, the 'public morals' clause is a general clause that at the supra- and international levels often serves as a limitation to the aforementioned constitutional freedoms, human rights and European Union freedom of movement of goods.

Another general clause conflicting with individual rights and freedoms is the 'public interest' clause. Unlike 'public morals', it is rather an issue at the national level due to its connection to the state as such. In Polish domestic law the 'public interest' clause appears a few times in the Constitution (e.g. in art. 17, 22, 213) and in over 540 other legal acts (see Wilczyńska 2009). As distinguished from interests of a special nature like 'financial interest', 'common economic interest' or 'strategic interest' that display other values, EU law refers to public interests with the term 'Union interests', e.g. in art. 3.5 ('In its relation with the wider World the Union shall uphold and promote its values and interests'), art. 20.2; 21.2; 24.3; 32; 34; 42.5 ('protection of its [Union – A.K, A.S.] interest') of the Treaty on European Union (TEU) and in art. 106.2 and 309 TFEU, with the clause 'common interest' (art. 881 TEU; art. 107.3, 206 TFEU) or as the 'general interest of the Union' (art. 17.1 TEU and art. 285, 300 TFEU).

The European Convention in its substantive part includes 'interests of morals, public order or national security in a democratic society' (art. 6.1); 'interests of national security, public safety or the economic well-being of the country' (art. 8.2 and 9.2) and 'interests of national security, territorial integrity or public safety' (art. 10.2. and 11.2).

All these are usually balanced with the interest of citizens and member states, see e.g. art. 13 TEU. In this balancing context 'public interest' is also mentioned in art. 15.3 TFEU and in several acts of secondary Union law (e.g. Council Regulation (EC) No 40/94 on the Community trademark).

The common ground for both of these general clauses is made clear by the keyword 'public'. The term public relates to something that concerns or affects a nation, a state, or a community and implies that they serve a value that may be called 'common well-being' or 'general welfare'. Considering the lack of a legal definition, as well as the lack of a well-defined social value system and a common doctrinal approach, their content can only be determined by national, European and international courts.

It is worth emphasising that in the case law of CJEU or ECHR these terms are not as strictly separated as in Polish case law. Public interest and public morals happen to be interpreted as expressions of a 'general interest' that requires protection (CJEU judgment C-65/05) or the two are even treated equally ('Protection of morals is undoubtedly of public interest and the conditions set out [by statutory and case law – A.K., A.S.]') (ECJR 5493/72).

5 Case studies

As mentioned, the meaning given to general clauses depends on a decisional body which takes part of the 'responsibility' for the final shape of a legal norm or, to go ever further, for the legal system and law itself.

The cases presented below illustrate how 'public morals' and 'public interest' are examined in the judgments of Polish, European and international courts.

In Polish law, 'public interest' is not defined in legal provisions and has been the subject of judicial interpretation since Poland regained its independence in 1918. However, the first and last serious attempt to define it was in the 1930s when the term 'interest' was described as 'an existing or future good, possibly of both material or personal nature, that is related to the organisation of social life and its proper functioning'. The adjective 'public' was interpreted as a collective interest of a social group, state or self-government, or social life generally (judgment of Polish Supreme Court, II K 285/33). The 'public morals' clause has never been defined *expressis verbis*, not even for *in concreto* purposes. Going further, Polish national courts in numerous judgments refer to both clauses in general without making any attempt to define them (see, e.g., Polish Supreme Court I CKN 134/98; Polish Supreme Court V CSK 377/06; Polish Constitutional Court K 46/07; Polish Constitutional Court K 11/94).

As mentioned, 'public interest' and 'public morals' are usually in conflict with individual rights and interests (Polish Supreme Court I CKN 134/98; ECHR 33583/96; ECHR 34049/96). Some judicial decisions explicitly point out this conflict in a democratic state ruled by law (Polish Constitutional Tribunal W8/93). Even if the two general clauses hardly have been defined, there is a visible tendency in Polish judiciary to unify their meaning. The judgments refer to each other and suggest that there is such a thing as the 'objective' public interest or morals. It is also worth emphasising that all limitations of liberty due to 'public morals' or 'public interest' are to be interpreted strictly (*interpretatio restrictiva*) (Polish Supreme Court I PK 27/08). Also, as mentioned, both the ECHR and CJEU notice that such limitations shall be prescribed by law and they can be introduced only if they are necessary in a democratic society.

Regarding the judgments of ECHR and CJEU, the first thought coming to the reader's mind is the unifying role of these courts: their activity creates common standards that can or should be followed by national legislation and legal practice. Since the provisions of supra- and international legal acts (namely, the European Convention and the EU treaties) are often phrased not quite precisely, these courts pass decisions that not only specify the legal consequences but also determine the scope and the contents of substantive provisions of the convention and treaties.

Another issue of great importance that makes the idea of the clauses' unifying role even stronger is that in both cases the interpretative phase is actually 'removed' from the decisional process of national courts. According to art. 267 TFEU, national courts may or must request the CJEU for preliminary judgment, which means that the interpretative power is generally given to CJEU (except for cases that bear no relation to the subject matter of the main action, as well as *acte clair* or *acte éclairé* situations). As for the ECHR, despite the fact that there is no similarly hard legal provision for a preliminary reference to the ECHR, over six decades of its activity made the court's case law a complementary substantive legal source for the European Convention (see Garlicki 2008, 4).

Even though these considerations appear to justify the thought of a unifying role of CJEU and ECHR, a more detailed analysis of their decisions shows different results. The CJEU has not created any kind of 'judicial general definition' of 'public interest' or 'public morals'. On the contrary, the court has emphasised flexibility as a value that accent should be put on ('Each of the grounds [...] calls for separate examination. [...] The public interest taken into account in the examination of each of those grounds [...] may, or even must, reflect different considerations, depending upon which ground [...] is at issue', CJEU C-456/01). As a result, it tends to point out that public interest is a factor spreading out of the national law of the member states (CJEU C-51/94; CJEU C-222/02) that conflicts with individual interest and shall be treated as a legal issue of 'delicate nature' (CJEU C-266/05 P). In consequence, it should be rather the national court that 'determines whether those conditions are fulfilled in the case pending before it, taking account of the factors [set out in provisions, also the general clause of public interest – A.K., A.S.]' (CJEU C-234/03; ECHR 43278/98).

In all cases of limitation of fundamental rights, the court must be aware of and follow the proportionality principle, which means that

> [the final decision] must strike a 'fair balance' between the demands of the general interest and the requirements of the protection of the individual's fun-

> damental rights. There must be a reasonable relationship of proportionality between the means employed and the aim pursued. In determining whether this requirement is met, the Court recognizes that the State enjoys a wide margin of appreciation with regard both to choosing the means of enforcement and to ascertaining whether the consequences of enforcement are justified in the general interest for the purpose of achieving the object of the law in question. (ECHR 28272/95, 22774/93, 25088/94)

In case of general clauses, the 'balancing of principles' (cf. Dworkin 1963; 1973) is a 'two-dimensional' phenomenon. First, the use of general clauses leads to balancing between 'public' and 'individual' interests and values that shall lead to a 'fair balance'. Second, at a meta-level the nature of supra- and international law creates a need for balancing between the principles of unity and subsidiarity. In spite of the 'divided sovereignty', the axiological diversity cannot be – and is not – ignored.

A not very recent but enormously important (a 'milestone') 'public morals' case could provide a good illustration. In *Handyside* (ECJR 5493/72) the court argued as follows:

> [I]t is not possible to find in the domestic law of the various Contracting States a uniform European conception of morals. The view taken by their respective laws of the requirements of morals varies from time to time and from place to place, especially in our era which is characterised by a rapid and far-reaching evolution of opinions on the subject. By reason of their direct and continuous contact with the vital forces of their countries, State authorities are in principle in a better position than the international judge to give an opinion on the exact content of these requirements as well as on the 'necessity' of a 'restriction' or 'penalty' intended to meet them. [...] the qualification of what is moral in a democratic society remained within the framework of the State's margin of appreciation.

And in a Strasbourg case, the court argued that it is not possible and necessary to define such a term *in abstracto*: the state's margin of appreciation takes into consideration not only the cultural and moral context in which particular rights operate within the society but also the regional 'moral climate' (ECHR 13470/87, 7525/76).

In other words, both ECHR and CJEU case law leave a certain 'margin of appreciation' to national legislators and courts.[1] They refrain from extending their jurisdiction on such 'delicate matters'. Rather, in order to control the framework and the proportions they focus on the principle of proportionality and the question whether exceptions, bans or limitations as 'prescribed by law [...] are necessary in a democratic society' (Yourow 1996, 112–113).

1 To note, the term 'margin of appreciation' comes from administrative law and its construct of administrative appreciation (discretion).

6 Conclusions

The initial view of the unifying role of CJEU and ECHR case law in the interpretation of 'public interest' and 'public morals' turned out to be misleading. Actually, even though one of the general roles of the judiciary is to introduce uniformity into the content of law, in case of general clauses, especially those that limit, rather than increase, individual liberty, there is a noticeable discrepancy between domestic and supra- or international practice.

While stressing that general clauses enable passing a legitimate but also flexible, appropriate and right decision in individual situations, in numerous decisions the Polish Supreme Court seems to make an attempt to stabilise interpretations (Polish Supreme Court II CZ 178/99; V CSK 5/05; III CZ 78/06; II UK 246/07).

Such a policy of uniformity, however, would be undesirable at the supra- and international levels. There are three reasons for this. First, the dynamic nature of EU law and the European Convention systems imply that supranational organisations and their legal norms arise from the sovereignty of the Member States and not reciprocally. The European legal order is still a system *in statu nascendi*.

Second, the subsidiarity and proportionality principles that are common to both systems mean that decisions must be taken at a level as close as possible to the citizens. Supranational institutions take actions only when it is more effective than actions taken at the national, regional or local level and such actions are limited to what is necessary to achieve the supranational objectives.

Third, many legal provisions in European Union law and in the European Convention only provide a framework. The open-textured character of supra-national legal provisions allows for divergent national interpretations.

This multicentrism – as emphasised *inter alia* in numerous decision of the Polish Contitutional Tribunal – is based on the respect for local traditions and values,[2] so that both CJEU and ECHR put efforts to avoid answering the key questions and leave a wide area of discretion to domestic courts on such matters – 'the acceptable margin of appreciation'. Axiological convergence is an issue of delicate nature. Courts like CJEU and ECHR are aware of this and try not to affect it artificially.

To sum up, the main purpose of general clauses is to ensure flexibility in processes of law application and give a decisional body the possibility to revise *stricti iuris* criteria. This also seems to be the way how CJEU and ECHR understand the role of general clauses. Thus, they leave a wide margin of discretion for national decisional bodies to interpret them.

2 Cf. art. 6.3. of TFUE that refers to 'constitutional traditions', even if to those that are common to all of the Member States.

References

Carter, Lief, and Burke, Thomas. 2010. *Reason in Law.* 8th edition. New York: Longman.

Dworkin, Ronald. 1963. Judicial Discretion. *The Journal of Philosophy* 60: 624–638.

Dworkin, Ronald. 1973. The Original Position. *University of Chicago Law Review* 40: 500–533.

Dworkin, Ronald. 1985. *A Matter of Principle.* Cambridge (MA): Harvard University Press.

Garlicki, Leszek. 2008. Wartości lokalne a orzecznictwo ponadnarodowe – „kulturowy margines oceny" w orzecznictwie strasburskim? [Local Values and Supranational Adjudication: Is There a 'Cultural Margin of Appreciation' in Strasbourg Case Law?] *Europejski Przegląd Sądowy* [*European Judiciary Review*] 4: 4–13.

Grundmann, Stefan. 2005. General Standards and Principles, Clauses Generales, and Generalklauseln in European Contract Law – A Survey. In *General Clauses and Standards in European Contract Law: Comparative Law, EC Law and Contract Law Codification*, edited by Stefan Grundmann and Denis Mazeaud, 1–19. The Hague: Kluwer Law.

Leszczyński, Leszek. 2000. *Tworzenie generalnych klauzul odsyłających* [*Creating General Clauses*]. Lublin: Wydawnictwo UMCS.

Łętowska, Ewa. 2005. Multicentryczność współczesnego systemu prawa i jej konsekwencje [Multicentrism of the Modern Legal System and its Consequences]. *Państwo i Prawo* [*Law and Politics*] 4: 3–10.

Mayer, Franz. 2003. The European Constitution and the Courts. Adjudicating European Constitutional Law in a Multilevel System. *Jean Monnet Working Paper* 9/03 [http://centers.law.nyu.edu/jeanmonnet/papers/03/030901-03.pdf].

McCormick, Neil. 1999. *Questioning Sovereignty.* Oxford: Oxford University Press.

Nowacki, Józef. 1988. O przepisach zawierających klauzule generalne [On Provisions Containing General Clauses]. In *Prawo i polityka. Księga pamiątkowa ofiarowana Profesorowi Kazimierzowi Opałkowi z okazji siedemdziesiątej rocznicy urodzin* [*Law and Politics. Festschrift for Professor Kazimierz Opalek on his Seventieth Birthday*], edited by Artur Bodnar, Jerzy Wiatr, and Jerzy Wróblewski, 78–101. Warszawa: PWN.

Nowacki, Józef. 1992. Problem blankietowości przepisów zawierających klauzule generalne [The Problem of Provisions Containing Blanket General Clauses]. In *Prawo w zmieniającym się społeczeństwie. Księga jubileuszowa Profesor*

Marii Boruckiej-Arctowej [*Law in the Changing Society. Festschrift for Professor Maria Borucka-Arctowa*], edited by Grażyna Skąpska et al., 127–142. Kraków: Wydawnictwo Adam Marszałek.

Ossowski, Stanisław. 1967. *Dzieła IV* [*Works IV*]. Warszawa: PWN.

Pernice, Indolf. 1999. Multilevel Constitutionalism and the Treaty of Amsterdam. European Constitution-Making Revisited? *Common Market Law Review* 36: 703–750.

Russell, Peter, and O'Brien, David (eds.) 2001. *Judicial Independence in the Age of Democracy. Critical Perspective from Around the Word.* Charlottesville: University Press of Virginia.

Wilczyńska, Aleksandra. 2009. 'Interes publiczny w prawie stanowionym i orzecznictwie Trybunału Konstytucyjnego' [Public Interest in Statutory Law and Case Law of the Constitutional Tribunal] *Przegląd Prawa Handlowego* [*Commercial Law Review*] 6.6: 48–55.

Yourow, Howard Charles. 1996. *The Margin of Appreciation Doctrine in the Dynamics of European Human Rights Jurisprudence.* Dordrecht: Martinus Nijhoff, Kluwer Academic.

Cases

Court of Justice of the European Union in Luxembourg

C-65/05 – judgment of 26.10.2006, *Commission v. Greece*, ECR 2006, p.I-10341.

C-456/01 P – judgment of 29.04.2004, *Henkel v. OHIM*, ECR 2004, p.I-5089.

C-51/94 – judgment of 26.10.1995, *Commission v. Germany*, ECR 1995, p.I-3599.

C-222/02 – judgment of 12.10.2004, *Paul and others*, ECR 2004, p.I-9425.

C-266/05 P – judgment of 01.02.2007, *Sison v. Council*, ECR 2007, p.I-1233.

C-234/03 – judgment of 27.10.2005, *Contse and others*, ECR 2005, p.I-9315.

European Court of Human Rights in Strasbourg

5493/72 – judgment of 07.12.1976, *Handyside v. UK.*

33583/96 – decision of 14.09.2002.

34049/96 – judgment 19.06.2001, *Zwierzyński v. Poland.*

43278/98 – judgment of 15.03.2007, *Velikovi and Others v. Bulgaria.*

28272/95 – judgment of 21.02.2002, *Ghidotti v. Italy.*

22774/93 – judgment of 28.07.1999, *Immobiliare Saffi v. Italy.*

25088/94 – judgment of 29.04.1999, *Chassagnou and Others v. France.*

13470/87 – judgment of 20.09.1994, *Otto Preminger Institute v. Austria.*

7525/76 – judgment of 22.10.1981, *Dudgeon v. UK.*

Polish Supreme Court

II K 285/33 – judgment of 31.05.1933, OSN(K) 1933/8/157.

I CKN 134/98 – decision of 29.09.1999, LEX nr 142535.

V CSK 377/06 – judgment of 4.01.2007, OSP 2008/1/8.

I PK 27/08 – judgment of 12.09.2008, OSNP 2010/5-6/69.

II CZ 178/99 – decision of 04.02.2000, OSNC 2000/7-8/147.

III CZ 78/06 – decision of 21.11.2006, OSNC 2007/5/78.

V CSK 5/05 – decision of 29.06.2005, LEX nr 180935.

II UK 246/07 – decision of 31.01.2008, LEX nr 449007.

I CKN 134/98 – decision of 29.09.1999, LEX nr 142535.

Polish Constitutional Court

K 46/07 – judgment of 8.07.2008, Dz.U. 2008.123.803.

K 11/94 – judgment of 26.04.1995, OTK 1995/1/12.

W8/93 – resolution of 16.3.1994, Dz.U. 94.39.148.

Part IV
Law and Politics in International Relations

'Peace Through Law': Kelsen's (and His School's) Struggle for Universal Peace

Jürgen Busch, Judith von Schmädel,
and Kamila Staudigl-Ciechowicz

Abstract The crisis of the League of Nations on the eve of World War II provoked an increased scholarly debate on new structures in international law appropriate to replace the current dysfunctional system. Kelsen, between 1933 and 1940 professor at the seat of the League of Nations in Geneva, devoted a considerable part of his work to this question at that time. His related writings show that there is more to Kelsen and his view on the role of legal structures as means to the end of (world) peace than the alleged 'emptiness' of his legal theory would suggest. In this paper, his conception of reforming the international legal system is compared to other, sometimes conflicting, examples from within the Kelsenian school: those of Verdross and Campagnolo.

1 Introduction

Hans Kelsen who is mostly known for his *Pure Theory of Law* also worked on theories concerning the perseverance of peace and issues of collective security since as early as the end of World War I (WWI). However, it was not before 1944, during the final stages of World War II (WWII) and on the eve of the birth of the United Nations, that he completed his major work on peace and security. His views, which he published in his 1944 book *Peace through Law* (Kelsen 1944a), were widely discussed but also strongly opposed both for epistemological and ideological reasons by many of his contemporaries, including his own students.

Little is known about the biographical context of Kelsen's work on international peace and security through law and its evolution that started with his personal experiences during WWI and led to his first reflections on the topic. Major lines and epistemological grounds of his later arguments on 'peace through law' were published in a famous 1920 book on sovereignty.[1] In that book he argues for a correlation between the general and specific basic epistemological choices available for theorising the relation of state law and international law on the one hand and the ethical-political choice between imperialism and pacifism in international relations on the other. Firstly, he juxtaposes the basic epistemological principles of subjectivism and objectivism; secondly, the basic legal hypotheses of the primacy of state law and the primacy of international law; and thirdly, the political and ideological principles of imperialism and pacifism. In his view, the choice between primacy of state law (correlating with subjectivism and imperialism) and primacy of international law (correlating with objectivism and pacifism) turns out to be an ethical choice leading to ethical conflicts between related epistemological, legal, and political principles (see Kelsen 1920, 317ff., especially 319). The consequences of this basic insight for the use of the social technique of law to obtain security, stability, and through these peace in international relations were further elaborated and specified during his years at the Postgraduate Institute of International Studies in Geneva (IUHEI).[2]

The book published in 1944 with the programmatic title was the result of the combination of these old theoretical insights with new practical challenges generated by the collapse of the League of Nations. It was closely witnessed by Kelsen, who was staying in Geneva and participated in the scholarly attempts of the IUHEI to describe this development and its consequences for international stability and world peace. It also formed the theoretical basis of Kelsen's analysis and critique of UN law after WWII. Consequently, the genealogy of *Peace through Law* provides a key for a better understanding of Kelsen's focus on structures, means and ends of international law, and of his critique of its central organ, the United Nations Organisation, at the end of his career. In his view, both the League of Nations in the interwar period and its successor after WWII, the UNO, lacked an international court with binding jurisdiction, which he regarded as the only way to ensure the uniform and sustainable implementation of a centralised legal order. According to Kelsen's standards, the UNO did not succeed in transforming institutionalised international relations from a political community (with a political body in its centre, as in the case of the League of Nations) into a 'judicial' one (with a court with binding jurisdiction in its centre).

1 See Kelsen (1920, concluding sections 9 [§§ 52, 53] and 11 [§§ 63, 64, 65]). This book is also regarded as the first elaborated manifestation on the pure theory of law (as expressed in its subtitle: *Beitrag zu einer Reinen Rechtslehre* ['Contribution to a Pure Theory of Law']). See Kelsen's own personal review of this book as a milestone in the formulation of his pure theory in Kelsen (2007, 22f.).

2 Institut universitaire de hautes études internationales (IUHEI), where Kelsen worked between 1933 and 1940, and again in 1952/53. (Now: L'Institut de hautes études internationales et du développement [http://graduateinstitute.ch/, 07 03 2011]). See Bersier Ladavac (1996; 2004; 2009).

What may be even less known is that two prominent students of Kelsen from different periods of his career, Alfred Verdross and Umberto Campagnolo also developed theories related to Kelsen's ideas on the perseverance of peace in international law and international relations. This paper discusses the evolution of Kelsen's *Peace through Law* (section 2), points out some of the core aspects of his arguments (section 3), and compares them to Verdross's and Campagnolo's theories (section 4). In a last section, we address the question of whether today, some sixty years later, these arguments are still relevant, especially when it comes to the experience of more than fifty years of integration through law within the European Union. Unlike other papers on Kelsen's writings on *Peace through Law*,[3] we merely attempt to offer an evolutionary view of the development of his ideas and to contextualise his views within his biography and in relation to debates with other authors belonging to his circle.

2 The evolution of *Peace through Law*

2.1 Where law ends and politics start

In a famous quote from 1927, Kelsen expressed his concern about the fact that the law and the constitutionalisation of society (by means of centralised organs like courts with binding jurisdiction) can only moderate but not abolish power and coercion (see Zeleny 2009, 74):

> The question on which natural law focuses is the eternal question of what stands behind the positive law. And whoever seeks the answer will find, I fear, neither an absolute metaphysical truth nor the absolute justice of natural law. Who lifts the veil and does not shut his eyes will find staring at him the Gorgon head of power. (Kelsen 1927, 55; English translation in Dyzenhaus 2000, 20 n. 1)

A consequence of this insight is the necessity to supplement the pure theory of law – an anatomy of positive law – by a political theory reducing the elements of force in society to their unavoidable minimum: to involve everyone and to provide a system of checks and balances and the possibility to vote against those in power. In this light, Kelsen's writings on *Peace through Law* and his political theory, particularly his theory of democracy, have to be understood as two sides of the same coin. A democratically organised (and educated) society is the political precondition of the possibility to use the social technique of law to achieve peace. Those who

[3] Major contributions to the debate on Kelsen and law as a means to the end of peace (in international relations) have been made by Bersier Ladavac (2009), see also the bibliography there; Jabloner (1997), Pfersmann (1993), Rub (1995), von Bernstorff (2001), Zeleny (2009), Zolo (1998). See further several articles in Ehs (2008), and Brunkhorst and Voigt (2008).

are (unavoidably) subject to legal coercion have to share in the power which is in control of the means of law and decides on its content.[4]

2.2 Where biography comes in: Kelsen as eyewitness of WWI

His involvement in the legal service of the war ministry of the Austro-Hungarian Empire during WWI[5] offered Kelsen plenty of opportunities to get a first hand insight into the sheer abuse of law (especially when it came to the punishment of 'deserters'). With support from influential mentors,[6] Kelsen climbed the career ladder in the legal service of the Ministry of War.[7] After dealing with all kinds of questions of international law, of war in general, and legal questions concerning war prisoners and cases of desertion, the legitimacy of children of unmarried soldiers, mercy pleas of so called war criminals and the establishment of a central archive for the military field tribunals and army courts (*Feldgerichtsarchiv*) in particular, he became legal advisor to the last minister of war of the Habsburg Empire, Rudolf Stöger-Steiner. In this capacity, Kelsen had to deal with questions of constitutional reform of the Empire for the time after WWI and especially the future status of the joint army in a more decentralised federal structure. It was this position and the related personal network throughout the declining Empire that made Kelsen known as one of the leading experts on constitutional reform in Austria and resulted in his involvement in drafting the constitution for the first Austrian republic. His conception of constitutional review, which appeared in the Austrian Constitution, was later shifted to the level of international relations.[8] At the same time, Kelsen's position during WWI and the political influence of the war minister opened for him the door of the Faculty of Law at the University of Vienna[9] as a tenured professor of public law.[10]

4 Recent publications stressing the complementarity of Kelsen's legal and political writings are Brunhorst (2008), Ehs (2008; 2009), Vinx (2007).

5 See Oberkofler and Rabofsky (1988). For a recent reconsideration of Kelsen's involvement in the legal service of the Austro-Hungarian Ministry of War during WWI see Busch (2009).

6 Among them Ernst Seidler, his former academic supervisor at the *Exportakademie* in Vienna (a college for foreign trade relations where Kelsen taught until 1918) and prime minister in one of the last governments of the collapsing Empire, and Ignaz Verdross, a highly decorated general (*Generalmajor*) who commanded Tyrolian elite troops, the father of his early student Alfred Verdross.

7 See Busch (2009, 63–64). At the outbreak of WWI a severe lung disease saved him from the front and allowed him to take positions in military administration.

8 See below in sections 2.3 to 3.

9 Kelsen was appointed associate professor in 1918, then full professor at a constitutional law chair after the death of one of his academic mentors at the faculty, Edmund Bernatzik, in 1919.

10 A position otherwise almost impossible to achieve under the political conditions of the late Habsburg Empire (that was also one of the reasons why Kelsen converted to the Catholic faith in 1905, and, related to his marriage, again in 1912 to Protestantism). See Olechowski (2008a).

2.3 The Geneva years: Witness of WWII and the insufficiency of the League of Nations

After a whole range of big personal disappointments related to the increase of public manifestations of anti-Semitism in Austrian interwar society and politics, personal conflicts at the law faculty in Vienna (see Olechowski 2008b, Busch and Staudigl-Ciechowicz 2009), and the politically motivated removal from the post of a judge at 'his' constitutional court in 1929 (see Neschwara 2009, Walter 2005), Kelsen decided to leave Austria and accept an appointment at the University of Cologne, this time as professor of international law. When Hitler came to power in Germany in 1933, Kelsen was Dean of the law faculty and among the first professors of Jewish origin to be immediately removed from their positions by the new leaders (see Lepsius 2009). Already in 1930, the Geneva IUHEI and its director William Rappard tried to appoint Kelsen. Now as he literally had to save his life from the Nazis, he gladly accepted the offer of the HEI and continued his research and teaching in the international atmosphere of Geneva.[11]

In his inaugural lecture at the HEI in Geneva in 1933, Kelsen addressed the problem of the 'technique of international law and the organisation of peace' for the first time (Kelsen 1934).[12] He identified the problem of the perpetual maintenance of peace merely as a question of social technique rather than one of political disagreement. Regarding the paralysis of the League of Nations, he argued that the core problem consists in the denial of its legal character and its being a central part of the international legal community. According to Kelsen, the problem of the arms race cannot be solved by abolishing coercion and replacing the League (which, as a legal community, could apply sanctions upon those violating international law) with a moral community guided by the nebulous idea of justice. On the contrary, the solution has to lie in the acceptance of the order of international relations as a proper positive legal order. Consequently, war and all forms of reprisals fulfil a clearly defined function within the international legal order: they are acts of coercion following the violation of international law. Thus, war can only be justified as a sanction imposed by law upon its violation (see Kelsen 1934, 241ff).

The core of the problem is now seen in the fact that international law lacks crucial characteristics of well-developed centralised legal systems of nation states: there

11 In 1936 Kelsen for a last time tried to return to a position at a German speaking university and took up a position for international law at the Charles University in Prague (1936–38, alternating with his position in Geneva, which he kept). From Prague he fled the direct threat of fascism and racism for a last time, this time back to Geneva (see Olechowski and Busch 2011).

12 For earlier and other writings related to peace in international law see the selection in Bersier Ladavac (2009, 293, in this case n. 13), and for a complete list compare the Kelsen-publications marked 'VöR' (for international law publications) at http://www.bunken.tamacc.chuo-u.ac.jp/scholar/morisue/datei.htm (07. 03. 2011).

are no centralised organs functioning on the basis of a division of labour and empowered to create and execute law. The stability of peace in any society depends on the success of replacing the social technique of self-defence by another, more sophisticated and developed technique of social steering: a centralised legal order (see Kelsen 1934, 245). Looking into the centralisation process of law in single states, the first fruits of centralisation of legal systems are not so much the legislative organs, but those of adjudication: first came the courts, then the parliaments. And it is the courts that not only apply the law but develop it further and also adapt it to new social situations (see Kelsen 1934, 246). The next logical step for a progress of international law thus has to be seen in the establishment of a centralised court. Consequently, the first step to be taken towards the centralisation of the international legal order is described as the development of the international legal community into a judicial community (*Gerichtsgemeinschaft*).

These ideas were elaborated on in two research proposals submitted by Kelsen to the director of the IUHEI in 1938 and 1939 (see IUHEI 1967, 21ff.). Stimulated by requests of the American Rockefeller Foundation, the main sponsor of the IUHEI, director William Rappard called for research proposals by his colleagues on two occasions. The first call was intended to encourage joint research by groups of HEI members; the second one addressed questions of the future maintenance of peace.

Kelsen answered the former in a letter on February 19th, 1938,[13] entitled 'Les différentes possibilités d'une organisation juridique de la communauté internationale': Research shall be oriented according to the experience gained from the League of Nations. Which of its aims has it achieved and which of them could it achieve? In which areas has it failed and for what reasons? He further proposes to join forces with other research institutions devoted to the intellectual shaping of an international organisation with a more efficient structure than the present system.

In answering the latter call, entitled 'Questions concernant la future paix européenne' from November 1939, Kelsen, together with his colleague Paul Guggenheim (see Rub 2004, with biographical details on Guggenheim at 192ff.), further elaborates on the future shape of a new international organisation, which should be better structured and equipped than the League of Nations for securing peace in Europe.[14] They distinguish ten core domains to be addressed by different researchers (for the full list of topics see Appendix 1). Kelsen himself opted for dealing with point III ('Fundamental character of the organisation: community of jurisdiction

13 Archives of the IUHEI Geneva, folder 'Echange de correspondence entre W. Rappard et des professeurs de l'Institut concernant une étude sur la paix 1939–1940'.

14 Archives of the IUHEI Geneva, folder 'Echange de correspondence entre W. Rappard et des professeurs de l'Institut concernant une étude sur la paix 1939–1940'. This part of Kelsen's project proposals in 1938/39 was reprinted in IUHEI (1967, 50ff). The only author who took notice of (the 1967 reprints of parts of) this project proposals belonging to the 'peace through law' complex in Kelsen's work before Bersier Ladavac (2009) and this article is Goněc (2007, 146ff).

or political community?'),[15] Guggenheim for point II ('The territorial and personal scope of the community'). The others were put on offer to other colleagues at the institute. One month later, some refinements took place and Rappard sent back to Kelsen an English translation of a new proposal by the latter entitled 'An International Court or an International Government?'. Obviously this is Kelsen's further elaboration on point III of the original proposal and a reaction to comments made by colleagues on the first draft (for the full list of topics see Appendix 2).[16] The step from the proposal in French of November 1939 to the revised proposal in English of December 1939 marks Kelsen's shift from a regional conception of Europe in the direction of a world state. Moreover, it clearly inspired his works and discussions with some of his students at that time, like Umberto Campagnolo (as further discussed below).

2.4 The Holmes lectures

In 1940, Kelsen left Geneva for the US. It was the threat of Hitler invading the neutral Switzerland, the collapse of the League of Nations, and the resulting insecurity of the HEI that made him decide to emigrate from a devastated Europe. After two years at Harvard, he found his last intellectual and personal home in the Bay Area of San Francisco, at the University of California in Berkeley.[17] Kelsen's central points on 'Peace through Law', such as the distinction between a political and a legal community, the necessity of a court with binding jurisdiction and the question of the world state reappear in the Oliver Wendell Holmes lecture series[18] he held at Harvard in 1940/41. Here he extensively discusses and further develops all of the points raised in his inaugural lecture of 1933 and the leading ideas of his above research proposals. Following the development of Kelsen's thoughts on 'Peace through Law' until the Holmes Lectures, we can see a threefold line of argument that is ever refined and specified throughout the different steps of the evolution of his argumentation: the distinction between political and judicial communities; the role of a (constitutional) court for a process of centralisation; the road to centralisation safeguarded by the court leads to a world state uniting the member states.

15 For a later elaboration of this aspect see Kelsen (1941).

16 Archives of the IUHEI Geneva, folder 'Echange de correspondence entre W. Rappard et des professeurs de l'Institut concernant une étude sur la paix 1939–1940'. This part of Kelsen's project proposals was reprinted in IUHEI (1967, 57–58).

17 From 1942. In 1945 he was finally appointed full professor of political sciences, from which position he retired in 1952.

18 Published version: Kelsen (1942).

3 *Peace through Law* (1944)

In 1944 Kelsen readdresses, refines and fully develops his theory on the relation of power and law and the use of the special social technique of law for the purpose of (world) peace in *Peace through Law*, his contribution to the field. 'Peace is a state characterized by the absence of force' – Kelsen states at the very beginning. However, in the second sentence he immediately qualifies this statement by saying that within an organised society the absolute absence of force, which means nothing else than anarchy, is not possible (Kelsen 1944a, 3). Instead, Force has to be organised by Law (ibid., 7). Kelsen argues that it is in fact the essential characteristic of law as a coercive order to establish a community monopoly of force (ibid., 3ff). Therefore, for Kelsen the evolution of law from a technical point of view is a continuous process of centralisation (ibid., 21).

Since in Kelsen's monistic view national law and international law form a unitarian legal system headed by international law, interstate relations are governed by law just as relations between individuals. Thus, international law has the same characteristics as state law (see Kelsen 1944b, 385; 1944a, 22). From here it is only a small step to conclude that lasting international peace can be achieved in just the same way as national peace: by applying standards of an established legal order to class international force – namely war – either as an (illegal) crime or as a (legal) sanction against illegal acts. The monopoly to use force as a sanction then has to be conferred on a central agency. Thus, the most effective way to secure international peace would be 'to unite all individual States [...] into a World State, to concentrate all their means of power, their armed forces, and put them at the disposal of a world government under laws created by a world parliament' (Kelsen 1944a, 5).

Being realistic, however, Kelsen comes to the conclusion that no single world government is feasible in the near future, since it is incompatible with the principle of sovereign equality, the idea that all states are equal with regard to their sovereignty, contained in the Moscow Declaration of 1943 (ibid., 9ff., 34ff.). Since no world state is possible at present (1944), lasting world peace can in Kelsen's view only be achieved within the framework of international law. He therefore proposes a confederation of states (ibid., 9). He also provides a draft statute for this confederation, which he calls the Permanent League of the Maintenance of the Peace (PLMP) in the light of the experiences made with the League of Nations, which serves as a model both in a positive (when it comes to the idea of institutionalisation of international relations) and a negative sense (when it comes to the choice of appropriate means to achieve sustainable institutionalisation and centralisation of the legal regulation of global affairs).

Kelsen attributes the complete failure and breakdown of the League of Nations to one decisive cause. Namely, its central organ was not the Permanent Court of International Justice but a kind of international government, the Council of the League of Nations. The Council's decisions had to be passed unanimously, could not bind a member state against its will, and lacked a centralised power to execute them (see Kelsen 1944b, 386; 1944a, 49). Since the majority principle in international relations can only be applied in the procedure of international courts, where it is not considered incompatible with the sovereignty and equality of states, Kelsen suggests that the central organ of the Permanent League has to be the Court rather than the Council (Kelsen 1944a, 21). In support of this position Kelsen refers to his already mentioned theory that the evolution of law from a technical point of view is a continuous process of centralisation. In the progress of forming a centralised state from a de-centralised pre-state, law-applying bodies (courts) are centralised relatively easily and early on, whereas legislation and centralised executive power must form the last step. In early legal societies courts apply (customary) law, but by doing so they also create this law, thus acting in a certain way as legislative bodies as well. In this context Kelsen expressively points out that the term 'parliament' originally meant a court (ibid.).

Since in Kelsen's system the degree of evolution of a legal order is defined through its level of centralisation, international law must be seen as a primitive legal system, in which the principle of self help prevails and every individual (i.e. every state) takes the law into her or his own hands (Kelsen 1934, 244). It could be argued that by placing at the centre of the Permanent League a Court which will apply international law based on custom and agreement and adapt it in its concrete decisions to its actual needs, Kelsen also accepts the possibility that the Court may act as something close to a legislative body. The organisation of the Court is to be based on the Statute of the League of Nation's Permanent Court of International Justice. It is to be the main organ of the PLMP, have compulsory jurisdiction in all conflicts, legal as well as political, and guaranteed the highest level of independence and impartiality possible.

A core feature of the PLMP is that so-called political disputes are not to be excluded from the Court's jurisdiction. In fact, Kelsen rejects the distinction between justiciable legal and non-justiciable political disputes altogether. This distinction is entirely subjective in character, the difference only consisting in the way the parties to the conflict justify their respective attitude (Kelsen 1944a, 28ff.). In accordance with his Pure Theory of Law, omitting any questions on whether a disputed policy, although perfectly legal, may be politically unwise and morally wrong (see Niemeyer 1944, 306), Kelsen maintains that a positive legal order can be applied to any conflict whatsoever. Since 'what is legally not forbidden, is legally permitted' (Kelsen 1944a, 27), all disputes are legal. The declaration that a conflict is political implies only that the declaring party considers positive law as unjust or unsatisfactory (ibid., 29ff.). An important question, however, is how the problem should be solved if a state does not submit to the decisions of the Court or if it resorts to war. In accordance with his theory that lasting peace can be achieved by withdrawing and transferring the right to employ force as a sanction from the injured individuals (here states) to a central agency, Kelsen argues that a centralised executive power in form of a police force would be the most effective solution (ibid., 19).

In Kelsen's view, however, this is again not possible considering the Moscow Declaration on sovereign equality, which forms the reference framework of Kelsen's whole theory on peace through law. Such a centralised executive power could only be achieved if it were based on the obligation of the member states to radically disarm. Thus, decisions of the International Court can only be executed by other states under the direction of an administrative agency (ibid., 20).

As far as the scope of the PLMP is concerned, Kelsen points out that, in contrast to the League of Nations, it should be restricted in its function to the maintenance of peace within the community of member states by settling all disputes between the members through judicial decisions, leaving in general no room for political conciliation for the settling of conflicts. There is also no obligation of mutual protection against aggression from outside and consequently no duty of disarmament for the member states either. The PLMP is therefore to be set up as a legal community rather than a political one (ibid., 66).

In conclusion, it can be said that it is apparent throughout his *Peace through Law* that, unlike many others, Kelsen sees the appropriate means of achieving international order and peace not in political methods but in legal relations. As Zolo points out, Kelsen's belief that in order to prevent the use of force among states it is necessary to centralise the international legal system, particularly its sanctioning organs, and his aim to set up a federal world state, fit well into the tradition of classical and Christian cosmopolitanism as rephrased in Enlightenment terms by Wolff and Kant. Kelsen borrows from Kant both the idea of perpetual peace and the idea of a (Federal) World State (see Zolo 1998, 317ff.).

Kelsen undoubtedly, and even explicitly, based his analysis on value judgements theoretically unavailable to the Pure Theory of Law. Thus, his *Peace through Law* can be seen as an engineering project in international relations reflecting the basic choices of objectivism, pacifism and, consequently, the primacy of international law. However, Kelsen's technique as well as his major premises (e.g. those concerning the distinction of political and legal disputes) still mirror his typical Pure Theory of Law thinking when it comes to the application of the social technique of law to establish and maintain an international legal community, which is based on basic assumptions consistently followed through (see Gordon 1945, 667; Niemeyer 1944, 305).

4 Other views on international peace and security within Kelsen's circle: Verdross and Campagnolo

At the same time as Kelsen developed his theories, some of his students tried to find a solution to maintain world peace as well. Alongside his circle in Vienna, Kelsen taught classes at different European universities. Alfred Verdross, one of the scholars whose views are compared here to those of Kelsen, was among the first fellows in Kelsen's private seminar in Vienna during WWI. The second student discussed below is Umberto Campagnolo who attended Kelsen's lectures in Geneva in the 1930s.

At an early stage of his academic career, Alfred Verdross[19] started to build on Kelsen's Pure Theory of Law (see Verdross 1914), and applied it successfully to international law (see Walter 2004, 39). In 1920, the positions of Kelsen and Verdross began to differ. Kelsen in his *The Problem of Sovereignty* claims that the question of sovereignty cannot be answered with the scientific methods of legal science. So one first has to decide whether international public law or national law is ranked higher. This assumption cannot be made with the help of legal methods. This means that there are two possibilities: the primacy of national law and the primacy of international public law and, according to Kelsen, both ways are equally possible (Kelsen 1920).

Verdross published his habilitation thesis in the same year (Verdross 1920). In this work he reconsiders his former positions and reaches the conclusion that against his original point of view the only possible way to conceptualise the relation of national and international law is the primacy of the latter. According to this theory, national legal systems would have to derive their competence to issue legislation from international law.

Verdross' decisive turn towards natural law became manifest with his work on *The Constitution of the Community of States under Public International Law* (1926). In his argumentation Verdross uses the term *Grundnorm* (basic norm) but in a different sense than Kelsen. For Verdross, the *Grundnorm* is not a scientific hypothesis but an objective and binding norm rooted in the cosmos of values. *Pacta sunt servanda* is the content of his *Grundnorm* (see Durante 1991, 63).

In his further academic development Verdross dealt with general principles of law based on the ethical principle of justice. According to Verdross, the main goal of international public law is world peace which is based on two assumptions. On

19 1890–1980; Kelsen's theories influenced Verdross's scientific approach to international public law, although Verdross rooted international law in natural law. Besides his academic positions Verdross held functions at different international associations and courts: e.g. at the International Law Commission, the Permanent Court of Arbitration and finally the European Court of Human Rights. For an overview on life and work of Verdross see in general Köck (1991); now also the contributions on Verdross by Jürgen Busch, Gerhard Luf and Irmgard Marboe in Olechowski et al. (2011).

the one hand, national law is subordinated to public international law, so legislation that violates public international law cannot be valid in the long term. On the other hand, he defines public international law as a system based on natural law principles, e.g. the principle of justice and, following from that, the principle of peace. As a result, public international law can sustain and secure peace.

Like his former academic mentor and now friend and colleague, Kelsen, Verdross was disappointed with the United Nations. He regarded the principle of prohibition on the use of force as the most important element of a new public international law. At the same time he also criticised the lack of centrally imposed and enforced sanctions for breach of international rules through judicial channels. As a conclusion, it can be said that Verdross's and Kelsen's political goals were the same. Both tried to theoretically elaborate possible ways of a proper constitutionalisation of the international legal order to (better) secure international peace. Kelsen wanted to achieve this through his critical positivistic approach and Verdross through his natural law-based approach. This led them to nearly identical conclusions which had their roots in completely different doctrines.

Apart from Verdross, Umberto Campagnolo,[20] a student of Kelsen in Geneva, also dealt with peace and security. He wrote his doctoral thesis on *Nations et Droit* under Kelsen's supervision.[21] In his thesis he states that a world state can only be achieved by imposing some state's sovereignty upon other states. According to his theory, national law has to be superior to public international law. Kelsen criticised Campagnolo's approach as imperialistic. His theories on international law and world peace were influenced by the political situation after the breakdown of the League of Nations. According to Campagnolo, the League of Nations only used pacifist rhetoric and was never in a position to uphold world peace because it left member states' sovereignty untouched.

In his work *Repubblica federale Europea* (1945), Campagnolo argued that the League of Nations never came into real existence, and that there was only a 'toothless policy' of collective security, demilitarisation and compulsory arbitrary tribunals. He criticised the term 'collective security', stating that it was understood as an individual rather than a collective right. Thus, each state was more concerned with its own national peace than with world peace. Campagnolo's main concern was world peace and in this respect his political goal was the same as Kelsen's. The difference lays again in the theoretical perception of the problem at stake and its

20 He was born in Italy 1904 and emigrated to Switzerland due to his antifascist position. From 1933 he took part in Kelsen's classes in Geneva. Campagnolo's education was more philosophical than legal; nevertheless, he discovered a great interest in international public law during his time in Geneva.

21 The debate between Kelsen and Campagnolo on the latter's thesis was edited by Losano in Kelsen and Campagnolo (1999); see also Campagnolo (2010) and Bersier Ladavac (2004, 181ff.).

possible solution. Campagnolo denied that public international law is a legal system. The only legal system he approved of was the national legal system.

His approach was as follows. If the legal system alone can guarantee peace in a political society, and laws are only made by the state, then to lead humanity towards peace it is necessary to gradually include more and more subjects into this state, by granting citizenship to foreigners. His solution for a peaceful Europe is the creation of a common legal system and, as a consequence, a political community. From his point of view, this is the only possibility for Europe to guarantee its integrity and continued existence. In *Repubblica federale Europea*, he suggests a European Community. He concludes that the European nation shall become a unity not by merging into one singular state, for example the strongest one, but by abolishing borders. He differentiates between state and nation. For him, 'nation' is an affirmative term; he defines it as historically and geographically grown. He sees constant peaceful change and development as one of its conceptual elements. Opposed to this term he defines 'state' as a warlike entity, reaching its objectives through oppression and conquest. He concludes that the only chance of creating a united Europe is through united actions of all its nations. He rejects the possibility of a European state because this would lead to the elimination of the different nations that are seen as constitutive elements of a European political community. He believes that the European community can be built only in a federalist way. Campagnolo sees European peace as a precondition for world peace. In contrast to Kelsen's top-down approach, he follows a bottom-up approach.

5 Outlook: Regional and global constitutionalism

Kelsen has never explicitly dealt with (legal) questions of European integration in any of his writings.[22] Starting with his first book on the theory of state in Dante Alighieri (Kelsen 1905), he was always preoccupied with the idea of the world state. This also becomes apparent in his reflections on a proper constitutional structure for perpetual peace in international relations, as formulated in his research proposals on the future of international peace in 1938 and 1939. However, the similarities between his theoretical insights and those of some members of his circle and the practical realisation of political integration by legal means (integration through law), as they first and foremost took place in Europe after WWII, are striking. They call for further research on the impact of ideas developed at the Institute in Geneva (including Kelsen's ideas shaped there in the 1930s in particular) on the politics of European Integration. The implementation of the European Convention on Human Rights and the establishment of the European Court of Human Rights as well

22 For a detailed discussion of the impact of his legal and political theories on European integration and the EU see Ehs (2008).

as the European Communities (developing into the EU) and the European Court of Justice on a regional, European level, and more recently the creation of the International Criminal Court on a global level are examples of the purposiveness of Kelsen's quest for 'judicial' central organs in international relations. Although legal centralisation in the EU has not (yet) reached the level of a classical federation like the USA, legal 'centralisation', i.e. constitutionalisation, in Europe was shaped from the outset according to the concept of legal domestication of power politics by means of putting it under the control of a central ('constitutional') court and by complementing political institutions with legal institutions. It seems that the reality of European integration has found (or rather circumstances forced it to find) a compromise between Kelsen and his student Campagnolo: a federal structure politically authorised and steered from below, combining elements from the ideals of both a political and a judicial community.

For Kelsen, political communities are by definition legal communities. A political community that unifies its individuals through shared institutions establishes a sound balance of steering political and safeguarding judicial organs, meant to maintain shared core political values like fundamental rights, democracy, and good governance. Such a community does not have to repeat the creation of nation states by means of a far-reaching cultural uniformity at the European level, contrary to the individuality of each EU citizen. What citizens have to have in common in order to ensure stability and peace in regional and global political communities is the will to uphold democracy and the rule of law and to shape the content of law accordingly.[23] Law as such can have any content and will itself never be able to free us from responsibility for the legal domestication of the Gorgon head of sheer power, meaning our responsibility for making an ethical choice for the use of its structures for peaceful purposes. Consequently, in *Peace through Law* and in complementary writings on education and democracy (Kelsen 1913; 1929)[24] it is the politician and pacifist Kelsen, not only the legal theorist, talking to us.

23 For Kelsen the evolution of law towards an ever more complete maintenance of peace has to go hand in hand with the evolution of mankind towards an ever more rational, objective, ever less affective human being (see Jabloner 1999, 269; also Zeleny 2009, 75.)

24 On the interrelation of these writings see Jabloner (1997, 69–70), Ehs and Zeleny (2006, 216–217), Ehs (2007).

Appendix 1

Outline of a research proposal by Hans Kelsen and Paul Guggenheim, answering the Institute's call for proposals on 'Questions concernant la future paix européenne' (November 1939):[25]

I. The material scope of the community or the legal system of the community, meant to define its aims and objectives (such as maintenance of interior peace and protection against aggression from outside)
II. The territorial and personal scope of the community
A. the problem of universality: global or European federation
B. membership to the community: states and other subjects such as organisations, minority groups, individuals; the special problem whether the constitution of the new community shall comprise explicit provisions on minority protection
C. question of the political homogeneity of the community and conditions of accession: democracy, capitalism, ideological character, fight against Bolshevism
D. relationship between a possible European federation and other states
E. law of secession
III. Fundamental character of the organisation: community of jurisdiction or political community?
A. critique of the shortcomings of the institutional structure of the League of Nations: dominance of political organs like council and assembly, their reciprocal relation, composition
B. in-depth critique of the activities of the council and the assembly, starting from the question whether they constitute a community of jurisdiction or a political community
C. the impact of the constitution of the international community on the constitutions of the member states
IV. Sanctions
A. critique of Art. 16 and its application
B. sanctions within the framework of an exclusive community of jurisdiction, sanctions within the framework of a political community
V. Procedural problems
A. majority principle
B. representation of members in the institutions: in particular questions of equal or proportionate representation, compromise between the two of them
C. publicity: in particular the Preamble, now Art. 18.

25 Archives of the IUHEI Geneva, folder 'Echange de correspondence entre W. Rappard et des professeurs de l'Institut concernant une étude sur la paix 1939–1940'; English translation by the authors of this paper.

VI. Necessity of a legislative body?
A. critique of provisions in Art. 19
B. relationship of legislation and jurisdiction with a view to historical experience and the framework of Roman and English law
C. procedure for change of constitution
VII. Disarmament
VIII. Mandates and Colonies
IX. Financial basis of the community
X. Legal technique: separation of constitution and peace treaty, preamble, language of text

Appendix 2

Outline of a research proposal by Hans Kelsen (December 1939)[26]

I. The prerequisites for a pacific international community: a) that all contentious territorial problems be solved according to the principle of self-determination: b) that the rights of minorities be guaranteed under international law
II. The relations between the political and economic constitution of the international community: politics more important than economics
III. Critical analysis of the constitution and activities of the League of Nations with a view to discovering the answer to the following question: could the aims of the pacific international community not be better attained by an organisation of which an international court, and not an international political body, is the central organ?
IV. Compulsory jurisdiction with the exclusion, as far as possible, of contentious territorial questions
V. The objections against compulsory jurisdiction: the imperfect character of the international legal order in the absence of an international legislative organ
VI. The gaps in international law
VII. Legal and political conflicts
VIII. Positive law and equity (justice)
IX. The organisation of an international tribunal: critique of the constitution of the Permanent Court of International Justice
X. Conciliation
XII. An administrative council as executive organ
XII. Sanctions
XIII. Disarmament and protection against threats from without

26 Archives of the IUHEI Geneva, folder 'Echange de correspondence entre W. Rappard et des professeurs de l'Institut concernant une étude sur la paix 1939–1940'.

XIV. Diversity of tasks: the maintenance of peace within and the protection against external dangers from the point of view of the organisation of the international community
XV. Merely a judicial community, not a super-state.

Acknowledgements This paper contains results of the Austrian Science Fund Project P19287-G14, 'Biographical Research on Hans Kelsen' [www.hanskelsen.eu]. Different parts of it were presented by Judith von Schmädel and Kamila Staudigl-Ciechowicz at the *XVth Annual Forum of Young Legal Historians* at EUI, Florence in 2009 and by Jürgen Busch at the *2nd CEE-Forum of Young Legal, Political, and Social Theorists* at Pázmány Péter Catholic University, Budapest in 2010. Chapter 2.3 contains findings of the research carried out jointly by Nicoletta Bersier Ladavac and Jürgen Busch at the IUHEI, Geneva in 2008, leading to a broader basis of sources for the assessment of Kelsen's concept of 'Peace through Law' as it has entered a recent article of Bersier Ladavac (2009) and this paper. The authors would like to express their gratitude for the fruitful cooperation. They are also indebted to Péter Cserne and Miklós Könczöl for a careful review of the paper and valuable comments for its improvement as regards both language and content.

References

Bernstorff, Jochen von. 2001. *Der Glaube an das universale Recht.* Baden-Baden: Nomos.

Bersier Ladavac, Nicoletta. 1996. *Hans Kelsen à Genève* (1933–1940). Genève: Themis.

Bersier Ladavac, Nicoletta. 2004. Hans Kelsens Genfer Jahre (1933–1940). In *Hans Kelsen und das Völkerrecht*, edited by Robert Walter, Clemens Jabloner, and Klaus Zeleny, 169–189. Wien: Manz.

Bersier Ladavac, Nicoletta. 2009. Hans Kelsen in Genf. Die Friedensproblematik zwischen Wissenschaft und Politik. In *Hans Kelsen. Leben - Werk - Wirksamkeit*, edited by Robert Walter, Werner Ogris, and Thomas Olechowski, 289–303. Wien: Manz.

Brunkhorst, Hauke and Voigt, Rüdiger (eds.). 2008. *Rechts-Staat. Staat, Internationale Gemeinschaft und Völkerrecht bei Hans Kelsen.* Baden-Baden: Nomos.

Busch, Jürgen. 2009. Hans Kelsen im Ersten Weltkrieg. Achsenzeit einer Weltkarriere. In *Hans Kelsen. Leben - Werk - Wirksamkeit*, edited by Robert Walter, Werner Ogris, and Thomas Olechowski, 57–80. Wien: Manz.

Busch, Jürgen and Staudigl-Ciechowicz, Kamila. 2009. 'Ein Kampf ums Recht'? Bruchlinien in Recht, Kultur und Tradition in der Kontroverse zwischen Kelsen und Hold-Ferneck an der Wiener Juristenfakultät. In *Turning Points and Breaklines*, edited by Szabolcs Hornyák et al., 110–138. München: Maidenbauer.

Campagnolo, Umberto. 1945. *Repubblica federale Europea*. Milano: Europa Unita.

Campagnolo, Umberto. 2010 [1933–1940]. *Conversazioni con Hans Kelsen. Documenti dell'esilio ginevrino 1933–1940*, edited by Mario Losano. Milano: Giuffrè.

Durante, Francesco. 1991. Die Grundlage des Völkerrechts im Denken Alfred Verdross-Drossberg. *Österreichische Zeitschrift für öffentliches Recht und Völkerrecht* 42: 59–67.

Dyzenhaus, David. 2000. The Gorgon Head of Power: Heller and Kelsen on the Rule of Law. In *From Liberal Democracy to Fascism: Legal and Political Thought in the Weimar Republic*, edited by Peter C. Caldwell and William E. Scheuerman, 20–46. Boston: Humanities Press.

Ehs, Tamara. 2007. *Hans Kelsen und politische Bildung im modernen Staat*. Wien: Manz.

Ehs, Tamara (ed.). 2008. *Hans Kelsen und die Europäische Union. Erörterungen modernen (Nicht-)Staatlichkeit*. Baden-Baden: Nomos.

Ehs, Tamara (ed.). 2009. *Hans Kelsen. Eine politikwissenschaftliche Einführung*. Wien: Facultas.

Ehs, Tamara, and Zeleny, Klaus. 2006. Wissen für alle! Hans Kelsens Engagement für Volksbildung und Demokratie. *Das jüdische Echo* 55: 214ff.

Goněc, Vladimír. 2007. *Skizzen zu mitteleuropäischem rechtsphilosophischem Denken*. Brno: Masarykova univerzita.

Gordon, Murray A. 1945. Review. *Columbia Law Review* 45: 667.

Institut Universitaires de Hautes Études Internationales Genève - IUHEI (ed.). 1967. *Quarantième Anniversaire 1927–1967*. Genève.

Jabloner, Clemens. 1997. Menschenbild und Friedensicherung. In *Hans Kelsens Wege sozialphilosophischer Forschung*, edited by Robert Walter and Clemens Jabloner, 57–73. Wien: Manz.

Jabloner, Clemens. 1999. Verrechtlichung und Rechtsdynamik. *Zeitschrift für öffentliches Recht* 54: 261ff.

Kelsen, Hans. 1905. *Die Staatslehre des Dante Alighieri*. Wien, Leipzig: Deuticke.

Kelsen, Hans. 1913. Politische Weltanschauung und Erziehung. *Annalen für soziale Politik und Gesetzgebung* 2: 1–26.

Kelsen, Hans. 1920. *Das Problem der Souveränität und die Theorie des Völkerrechts*. Tübingen: Mohr.

Kelsen, Hans. 1927. Diskussionsbemerkung: Die Gleichheit vor dem Gesetz im Sinne des Art. 109 der Reichsverfassung. *Veröffentlichungen der Vereinigung der Deutschen Staatsrechtlehrer* 3: 53ff.

Kelsen, Hans. 1929. *Vom Wesen und Wert der Demokratie.* 2nd ed. Tübingen: Mohr.

Kelsen, Hans. 1934. Die Technik des Völkerrechts und die Organisation des Friedens. *Zeitschrift für öffentliches Recht* 14: 240–255.

Kelsen, Hans. 1941. International Peace – by Court or Government? *The American Journal of Sociology* 46: 571–581.

Kelsen, Hans. 1942. *Law and Peace in International Relations. The Oliver Wendell Holmes Lectures 1940–41.* Cambridge (MA): Harvard University Press.

Kelsen, Hans. 1944a. *Peace through Law.* Chapel Hill: University of North Carolina Press.

Kelsen, Hans. 1944b. The Strategy of Peace. *American Journal of Sociology* 49: 381ff.

Kelsen, Hans 2007 [1927]. Selbstdarstellung (1927). In *Hans Kelsen Werke 1*, edited by Matthias Jestaedt, 19–27. Tübingen: Mohr.

Kelsen, Hans, and Campagnolo, Umberto. 1999. *Diritto internazionale e Stato sovrano. Con un inedito di Hans Kelsen e un saggio di Norberto Bobbio*, edited by Mario Losano. Milano: Giuffrè.

Köck, Heribert Franz. 1991. Leben und Werk des österreichischen Rechtsgelehrten Alfred Verdross. *Österreichische Zeitschrift für öffentliches Recht und Völkerrecht* 42: 31–57.

Lepsius, Oliver. 2009. Hans Kelsen und der Nationalsozialismus. In *Hans Kelsen. Leben – Werk – Wirksamkeit*, edited by Robert Walter, Werner Ogris, and Thomas Olechowski, 271–287. Wien: Manz.

Neschwara, Christian. 2009: Hans Kelsen und das Problem der Dispensehen. In *Hans Kelsen. Leben – Werk – Wirksamkeit*, edited by Robert Walter, Werner Ogris, and Thomas Olechowski, 249–267. Wien: Manz.

Niemeyer, Gerhard. 1944. Review. *Harvard Law Review* 58: 306.

Oberkofler, Gerhard, and Rabofsky, Eduard. 1988. *Hans Kelsen im Kriegseinsatz der k.u.k. Wehrmacht.* Frankfurt am Main etc.: Lang.

Olechowski, Thomas. 2008a. Über die Herkunft Hans Kelsens. In *Das Recht und seine historischen Grundlagen. Festschrift für Elmar Wadle zum 70. Geburtstag*, edited by Tiziana Chiusi, Thomas Gergen, and Heike Jung, 849–863. Berlin: Duncker & Humblot.

Olechowski, Thomas. 2008b. Rechtsphilosophie gegen Rechtsgeschichte? Ein Juristenstreit aus der Zwischenkriegszeit an der Wiener Rechtsfakultät. In *Festschrift für Wilhelm Brauneder zum 65. Geburtstag. Rechtsgeschichte mit internationaler Perspektive*, edited by Gerald Kohl, Christian Neschwara, and Thomas Simon, 425–442. Wien: Böhlau.

Olechowski, Thomas et al. (eds.). 2011. *Vetriebenes Recht – Vertreibendes Recht.* Wien: Manz.

Olechowski, Thomas, and Busch, Jürgen. 2011. Hans Kelsen als Professor an der Deutschen Universität Prag 1936–1938. Biographische Aspekte der Kelsen–Sander Kontroverse. In *Československé právo a právní věda v meziválečném období 1918–1938 a jejich místo v Evropě*, edited by Karel Malý and Ladislav Soukup, 1106–1134. Praha.

Pfersmann, Otto. 1993. De la justice constitutionelle à la justice internationale. Hans Kelsen et la Seconde guerre mondial. *Revue française de droit constitutionnel* 16: 761–790.

Rub, Alfred. 1995. *Hans Kelsens Völkerrechtslehre.* Wien: Verlag Österreich.

Rub, Alfred. 2004. Guggenheim und Kelsen: Orthodoxie und eigener Weg. In *Hans Kelsen und das Völkerrecht*, edited by Robert Walter, Clemens Jabloner, and Klaus Zeleny, 191–222. Wien: Manz.

Verdross, Alfred. 1914. Zur Konstruktion des Völkerrechts. *Zeitschrift für Völkerrecht* 8: 329ff.

Verdross, Alfred. 1920. *Die völkerrechtswidrige Kriegshandlung und der Strafanspruch der Staaten.* Berlin: Engelmann.

Verdross, Alfred. 1926. *Die Verfassung der Völkerrechtsgemeinschaft.* Wien: Springer.

Vinx, Lars. 2007. *Hans Kelsen's Pure Theory of Law: Legality and Legitimacy.* Oxford: OUP.

Walter, Robert. 2004. Die Rechtslehren von Kelsen und Verdroß unter besonderer Berücksichtigung des Völkerrechts. In *Hans Kelsen und das Völkerrecht*, edited by Robert Walter, Clemens Jabloner, and Klaus Zeleny, 37–49. Wien: Manz.

Walter, Robert. 2005. *Hans Kelsen als Verfassungsrichter.* Wien: Manz.

Zeleny, Klaus. 2009. Das Recht als Instrument der Friedenssicherung. In *Reflexionen über Demokratie und Recht*, edited by Robert Walter and Klaus Zeleny, 67–75. Wien: Manz.

Zolo, Danilo. 1998. Hans Kelsen. International Peace Through International Law. *European Journal of International Law* 9: 306–324.

The Concept of Cooperation for Development in International Relations: Between International Public Relations and Public Policies

Victor Negrescu

Abstract Cooperation for development is a relatively new field in international relations and has its roots in the Marshall Plan. Initially understood in terms of humanitarian aid, its principles have been adapted and applied to developing countries. Different interpretations of development cooperation result from different conceptualisations of the system of relations between donor countries and recipient countries. Mainly developed by social activists and pushed forward by the public opinion interested in establishing strong and efficient policies in this field, the term has not yet been conceptualised in social science. To what extent can we conceptualise development cooperation today in international relations, given the existing ideological cleavages? This is the question that I try to answer in the paper by using a theoretical framework adapted from international relations theories.

1 Introduction

Cooperation for development is a relatively new domain in international relations that has its roots within the Marshall Plan, realised by the United States in 1948 to support the European countries after the Second World War. Understood initially as humanitarian aid, the principle of international assistance and cooperation for development was adapted and is applied today to developing countries. The concept goes beyond the barriers of humanitarian assistance and also contains principles of economic and social stimulation; both are appreciated as well as criticised for their effects on the beneficiary countries.

Development aid, or development cooperation, is aid given by governments and other agencies to support the growth of developing countries and is distinguished from humanitarian aid because it focuses on fighting poverty in the long run, rather than merely alleviating suffering in the short term. The term 'development cooperation' is used to express the idea that a partnership should exist between donor and beneficiary countries, as opposed to the traditional situation in which the wealth and specialised knowledge of one country dominated the relationship. Most development aid comes from Western industrialised countries and remains governmental, with more than 80% of it coming from public sources and being distributed through bilateral means. This situation implies that there is a direct link between development aid and the national interests of the donor countries.

Studying the concept of cooperation for development becomes even more important due to the apparent competition between the biggest international powers to be acknowledged as the main, or the most important, contributor to development aid. The United States represents the first contributor in terms of total funds spent on development assistance, whereas the European Union is the main donor in terms of percentage of GDP given to international development aid projects. Furthermore, the EU has even assumed the objective to give 0.56% of its GDP by 2010 to development aid. Older member states have to give 0.7% of their GDP by 2015, while states integrated after 2004 have to give around 0.33% by the end of the same year (see Chang, Fernandez-Arias and Serven 1998).

The different approaches given to the cooperation for development are the result of diverse ideological conceptualisations (liberal, realist, or radical) of the system of relations between donor countries and beneficiary countries. These dogmatic perspectives find support in different theories of development designed to underpin the respective ideological positions on the effects produced by the cooperation for development.

Nevertheless, cooperation for development has not yet been conceptualised by international relations doctrines, as promoters of this concept want to dissociate the cooperation for development from power relations and seek to maintain its humanitarian dimension. Despite this, several authors argued that assistance for development is an aspect of soft power politics, a concept elaborated by Joseph Nye; others went even further by saying, in a realist vein, that it is an element of power politics or even a manifestation of national interests.

Our research is intended to establish objective methods for the analysis of development aid policies. The first step is to identify the place of the concept of development aid in international relations discourses. We will attempt to explore the conflicting ideological arguments behind different theoretical perspectives, and to establish empirical data that can be used for an objective analysis of development aid policies. Our paper will, accordingly, start by introducing the key concepts of the cooperation for development domain. Next, we will highlight the differences between the competing theoretical perspectives. Finally, we will try to conceptualise development assistance, focusing on relations between the humanitarian motivation and national and international interests.

2 Conceptual elements of cooperation for development

Cooperation for development requires a relationship of assistance between the developed, donor countries and developing countries. The reference to the concept of assistance implies a hierarchical relationship, placing developing countries in an inferior position. To make the concept of cooperation for development more clear, it seems necessary to give a brief overview of the basic terms that describe this relationship. Therefore, we shall start by presenting the evolution of the concept of 'developing countries' and continue by describing the economic and power relations generated by the assistance for development (see Figure 1).

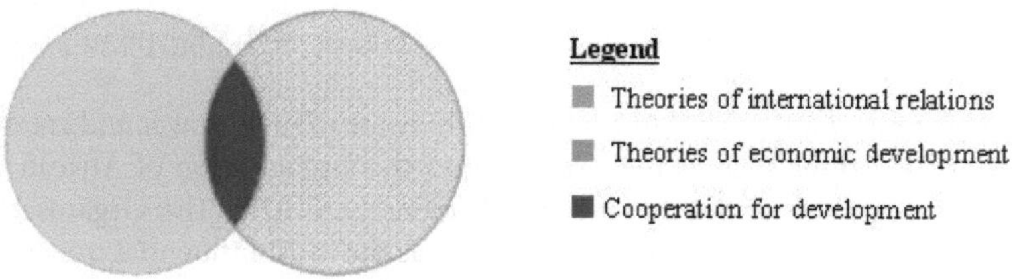

Figure 1: The concept of cooperation for development

2.1 Developing countries, subjects of the cooperation for development

Before 'developing countries', the term most frequently used when referring to countries that had economic deficiencies as a result of their decolonisation was the 'Third World'. It was first used by the French economist Alfred Sauvy in 1952 (see Sauvy 1952, 14), who made a comparison between developing countries and the states that emerged during the French revolution.

It was in April 1955 at the Bandung Conference, Indonesia, held with the participation of twenty-nine countries from Asia and Africa, that the concept became internationally known. The leaders of this conference who announced the appearance of developing countries at an international level were Gamal Abdel Nasser (Egypt), Pandit Nehru (India), Sukarno (Indonesia) and Zhou Enlai (China). Participants of the conference criticised imperialism and colonising countries, and advocated the idea of creating a group of countries wishing to express their interests at an international level beyond the balance and the influence of the cleavage created by the Cold War between the United States and the Soviet Union.

The conference was followed by the reunion hosted by the President of Yugoslavia, Josip Tito, at Brioni. The participants announced the formation of the non-aligned movement, which entailed a common position of these states within the Organisation of the United Nations. The first manifestation of this movement appeared in 1964, when the Conference of the United Nations for Development and Commerce stipulated the necessity of equitable commerce among developed and developing countries.

Thus, there emerged a new actor that was capable of disrupting the bipolar world dominated by the United States and the Soviet Union. One example was the crisis of the Suez Canal in 1956, generated by the nationalisation of the canal by the Egyptian President, Gamal Nasser. His action resulted in a violent reaction from France and the United Kingdom, followed by a military intervention from Israel. Pressure coming from Third World countries, however, led to the withdrawal of the military forces and, consequently, the acceptance of the Egyptian president's decision.

Developing countries became increasingly aware of their power and created regional organisations such as the Arab League, the Organisation of African Unity, and the Association of Southeast Asian Nations (ASEAN). The Organisation of the Petroleum Exporting Countries (OPEC) was the most influential organisation, uniting all the oil exporting countries of the Third World, which represented almost 70% of the oil exports of that time. The OPEC manifested its influence in the 1970s by starting the oil crises aimed at putting pressure on the developed countries and influencing the price of oil.

Despite the increasing power of Third World countries, this region that represented 80% of the world population represented less than 20% of the world's wealth. Moreover, the 1979 Third World Conference, held in Paris, showed the first signs of disorganisation and lack of cohesion within the group (see Friboulet 2004).

Internal tensions, conflicting relations between Third World countries, cultural and economic disparities (the development of some Southeast Asian countries, the so-called 'Asian Tigers'), and the disappearance of leading figures led to the disintegration of the Third World into regional groups with specific interests. The end of the Cold War and the affirmation of capitalism and free trade as the unique way of development has made plausible the idea that a third non-aligned way was no longer necessary.

To understand the political perspective of the great powers of the time, we may refer to the theories of Robert Jervis and Paul Sabatier. The first author contends that international relations decision makers from developed countries have had a strong ethnocentric approach, and that their involvement in ideological conflicts contributed to their subjectivism (see Jervis 1983). Paul Sabatier examined the role of such ideological beliefs in generating opinions regarding public policies in the international relations field. Among his examples was the case of the United Kingdom, who named the Egyptian leader, Nasser 'a second Hitler' or the United States' military intervention in regions where communist doctrine was starting to gain power, as in Vietnam and Korea (see Burchill, Linklater and Devetak 2008).

In the context of the Cold War, we may say that the United Kingdom and France behaved as two former colonising countries that tried to maintain their spheres of influence in their former colonies. The United Kingdom which managed a peaceful decolonisation, imposed its influence by forming local elites based on British education models. In contrast, France refused to decolonise up to the last moment, which led to violent fights, has maintained its influence through French culture and language and economic dependence on the *métropole*. The perception of developing countries at that time was rather sceptical, and maybe somewhat fearful as a result of the Suez conflict. Moreover, while China identified itself as a member of the non-aligned movement, its communist ideology and geographical dimensions isolated it from the other countries. Thus, China could enlarge its sphere of influence only at a regional level, among the Southeastern Asian countries.

The oil crises and the end of the Cold War have generated a change in the explicative model applied to international relations with developing countries. At present, economic and geo-strategic interests seem to influence the relations between developed and developing countries. This means that it is the interest in natural resources and the political positioning of certain countries that, partly at least, determine the relations between the two groups.

The dominant model seemed to be that of the 'rational actor' as described by Graham Allison, where relationships are perceived in terms of costs and benefits, and of power (see Allison and Zelikow 1999). Even so, ideological impacts on the relations between developed and developing countries can be examined from various perspectives, in the field of international relations as well as in development theories. Interpretations become more and more complex and interdependent if one speaks of the relations generated by assistance for development.

2.2 The concept of power in the relations of assistance for development

Relationships between developed and developing countries have generated different explicative models for the power relations within the cooperation for development. Ideological perspectives often determine the interpretations of these relations. The concept of power still remains a central element in the relations generated by assistance for development.

The realistic approach introduced by Hans Morgenthau explains the existence of such relations with national interests of the donor countries, who use assistance for development as a means for exercising their economic power in the world. By offering assistance for development, developed countries place developing countries in their sphere of influence, contributing to the maintenance of power relations at an international level, which could be changed by the emergence of a new power or a group of associated countries. This approach is diluted by Joseph Nye's concept of 'soft power', which refers to the informal mechanisms of exercising influence on developing countries. Two examples are the economic presence of Japan in South America and the massive infrastructural investments of China in some African countries. Such methods are often used by international organisations promoting certain sets of values, too. In this context, non-governmental organisations represent efficient communicational vectors.

The liberal view explains the cooperation for development by invoking the humanitarian desire to help people in need. This conception is based on the interest of developed countries in maintaining international peace, and cooperation for development supports this Kantian objective by expanding democracy and improving the economies of developing countries. In these theories, the concept of power is replaced by the pacifist notion of assistance for development.

Radical theories challenge this point of view, claiming that developing countries have not achieved any considerable development with the help of assistance for development so far, while it maintains their status as assisted countries in relation to the developed countries. Radical authors speak of a 'neo-imperialism' of rich countries using the mechanisms of cooperation for development to generalise their own values to the detriment of national values specific to the developing countries. This prevents economic development by limiting technological and industrial access and, thus, maintaining these countries in the state of 'raw materials producers.'

At the moment, the Millennium Development Goals conceived by the United Nations in 2000 mention a set of objectives for development specific to the developing countries, which includes the allocation of special funds by the developed countries. Cooperation for development as a concept of aid supposes the existence of financial flows between developing countries and developed countries, which will be analysed later on.

2.3 The concept of development economy in relations established by cooperation for development

The main objective of official development aid (ODA) funds is the stimulation of economic development of developing countries by providing financial assistance. In order to analyse the effects produced by ODA funds, one has to understand the concept of development economy and the theories about the ways by which certain economic mechanisms enable the development of an underdeveloped state. In this case, speaking of cooperation for development, we have to take into consideration both the direct effects of the ODA funds and the preliminary condition of market liberalisation, as well as the assumption of free trade, which opens the way for this kind of assistance.

Access to the assistance for development often provokes debates on which economic model should be implemented in the beneficiary countries in order that these funds can bring about the desired effect. Today, three economic models of generating development in developing countries prevail: free market liberalism, protectionist realism, and neo-colonialism.

The first, liberal, conception appeals to the idea that opening the markets of developing countries to international trade can only generate economic development and progress. This model is based on the liberal vision, according to which we live in an international system where peace is maintained through developing trade. The comparative advantages theory introduced by David Ricardo and developed by Heckscher, Ohlin and Samuelson claims that each country has an interest to specialise and to export the products that are the most efficiently produced in the country (see Rainelli 1997). In a broad perspective, the liberal theory perceives trade as an auto-regulating mechanism that enables states to develop by specialising and using their comparative advantages.

Partisans of protectionist realism, in turn, perceive the system of international relations as anarchic. The state of nature being fear and war, international actors are afraid of one another. The economic development of developing countries, as the example of Southeast Asia or even China shows, only brings new actors into the international arena, who can then oppose their own interests to those of the dominant ones. Opening the markets to developing countries on fair grounds can put certain economical sectors of the developed countries in danger. This means an advantage for those countries which can thereby gain importance at the international level and impose their rules of the game (see Montousse 2008).

In the case of neo-colonialism, the relationship between developed and developing states is conceived in terms of dependence. These theories argue that despite the existence of an anarchic system full of risks, the desire for progress of underdeveloped countries can be stopped. In this sense, assistance behaviour and the increasing dependence of developing countries cannot serve future global economic interests. Controlling development ensures a bigger sphere of influence for developed countries but in the long term it also limits the potential sale market for their products.

These three paradigms are equally based on rational actor models and form the basis of policies elaborated by developed countries for dealing with developing countries. Therefore, we cannot talk about a unique theoretical model, even if the majority of the states recognise the advantages generated by international trade as described by liberal theories.

3 Cooperation for development in international relations theories

After this overview of some key concepts related to the cooperation for development we now turn to the different theoretical perspectives. Understanding the different ideological visions on the assistance for development may help us not only to see the mechanisms of this process clearer, but also to conceptualise the cooperation for development as described by theories of international relations. Such an analysis will enable us to define development aid in international relations and it will make it possible for researchers to establish empirical methods of analysis of the relationships brought about by the assistance for development between the donor countries and the developing countries.

3.1 The realist perspective: cooperation for development and national interests

Realist theories start from the premise that, at the international level, states (as the central actors of international relations) act in a Machiavellian manner seeking to satisfy their selfish interests determined by the fear of threats against their territorial integrity. According to the impossibility theory elaborated by Richard Ashley, humanity faces the impossibility to satisfy its needs because of the limitedness of resources in global terms (see Ashley 1982, 226–286). Therefore, states are predisposed to violence and the actions realised are the result of a rational calculation of costs and benefits. The global order is determined by the strongest nations which are imposing the rules and laws at the international level.

From this perspective, cooperation for development is just a selfish mechanism applied by developed countries which use it to demonstrate their influence and power at an international level. Robert Jervis believes that power relations are in fact based on fear, and reciprocity only appears through the hope of receiving something in return for the assistance (as in a contract) (see Jervis 1983, 181).

Realist and neorealist visions merge when dealing with state actions on the international scene. Hans Morgenthau put forth the idea of the balance of power through which the states try to maintain a certain international balance. This desideratum can be explained by what Kenneth Waltz describes in his *International Politics Theory* as the search for security (Waltz 2006, 27–47). He mentions that, at the global level, superpowers act like multinational companies, maintaining control and organising the international system. According to Waltz, a smaller number of strong actors generates more stability. The assistance for development then becomes a simple gate-keeping mechanism limiting the emergence of developing countries in the international arena, by conditioning the economical development with a certain dependence on developed countries and the unequivocal acceptance of the already established international system.

After the end of the Cold War, realism has been subject to more structural criticism that challenged its focusing on states and power relations in the international system. In this sense, several authors developed theories in which international cooperation is at the level of national interests. Stephen Krasner (1983, 372) was the first to write about the possibility of a clearly defined autonomous state and the benefits of international cooperation based on reciprocity. Volker Rittberger (1990, 3) completed this thesis by adding that by its durability the cooperation becomes easier to realise and more efficient. Karl Deutsch (1957, 5) argued that it is only through international cooperation that a security community capable of ensuring stability can be realised. Barry Buzan (1991, 213) went even further by saying that the intensification of international exchange allows for the diffusion of a non-violent culture that will transfer the competition of states to more peaceful domains.

Nevertheless, partisans of offensive realism think that weaker states need to associate with stronger nations because the international political structure is conditioning the latter to assume larger responsibilities, leading them to expansionist diplomacy. The assistance for development is, therefore, the result of a vicious circle in which the developed countries find themselves as representatives of a mechanism of their expansionist diplomacy that they have to apply as a guarantee of the existence of the international system.

By extrapolating this theory to the relationship between donor states and developing states, we may state that assistance for development represents a mechanism of diffusion of the Western model. This process has become more important after the 9/11 events, when developed states realised that what is happening on the other part of the globe can directly affect their interests.

Drawing on the soft power theory developed by Joseph Nye, according to which developed states manifest their power through the diffusion of their own models (cf. Nye 1992, 173), Francis Fukuyama (2005) argues that stronger states have started to reshape the international system. Even though Fukuyama takes into account the military actions of the United States in Afghanistan and Iraq, his notion basically refers to the spreading of Western economic and political models. Cooperation for development becomes a central mechanism within this process of international remodelling determined by the realistic interest of security.

3.2 The liberal perspective: humanitarian cooperation for development

The increasing number of interactions at the international level has led to the growth of interdependence among states as well as between states and other actors. This mechanism was described by Keohane and Nye who pointed out the sensibility and vulnerability of international actors to the changes produced by other states. The originality of this perspective is that it does justice to the diversity of actors who have the means of influencing internal political decisions without being controlled in their external affairs by national authorities (see Keohane and Nye 1977, 10–11).

Robert Axelrod developed his thesis on the advantages of cooperation in his paper *The Theory of Cooperative Behavior* (1992), in which he demonstrates the tendency towards cooperation by two examples. Having organised a computer tournament around the 'prisoner's dilemma', the author arrived at the conclusion that the cooperation strategy is more likely to bring victory than being independent as long as the players are in permanent contact and have the chance to meet more often. The other example used by Axelrod is that of the small English and German military units of the First World War which, despite the directives of military leaders, did not fight a savage war, but imposed an implicit code of conduct, the infringement of which was sanctioned with retaliation. Axelrod concludes that a long lasting cooperation can be established between selfish actors from the moment they discover that it is in their best interest to break the isolation and to establish a cooperative relationship based on reciprocity.

Liberal institutionalism thus conceives of cooperation for development as a necessity, since individuals and states need to cooperate on the international scene. Furthermore, the increase in contacts between developed and developing countries has strengthened their interdependence. Given that the interest of developed states is to maintain peace and security, and to protect their economic and social interests, cooperation for development becomes a mechanism for accomplishing this, as it results in the growth of interdependence among the participating countries.

The liberal school of international relations is based on the Kantian moral law according to which the objective of all states and individuals is to maintain peace. In achieving this goal, Michael Doyle (1983, 205–235) argues, the promotion of democracy is the simplest way of maintaining peace. Advocates of the *pax democratica* sustain two important points: (1) Democracies do not fight against each other. Institutional constraints (Morgan and Campbell), the role of public opinion (Owen), the influence of market democracy (Doyle), and cultural evolution (Maoz and Russet) constrain the warrior activity of democracies. (2) The tendency of democracies to define their interests in a manner that makes cooperation with other democracies indispensable (Owen), conducts them to participate in alliances, the main function of which is to guarantee internal peace (Deutsch), and favours regional stabilisation (Buzan's 'security complex').

Cooperation for development becomes, therefore, a means of propagating the democratic model in developing countries in the service of maintaining international peace. According to functionalist theories, this propagation differs by stages starting with the acknowledgement of the advantages of international and free trade.

The role of social actors in the cooperation is nevertheless understood differently depending on the kind of actors. Andrew Moravcsik (1993, 473–524) regards as social actors those which have promoted on the international public agenda themes of international interest and the benefits of cooperation between states. On the other hand, authors like Samy Cohen, even if they recognise the role of NGOs in the modification of the diplomatic and public agenda, argue that social actors are increasingly dependent on states (see Cohen 2003). In cooperation for development projects, the main funds come from states which finance these projects either through national agencies handling this specific domain or through their ministries of foreign affairs. Nevertheless, it is widely recognised that NGOs have put important issues on the agenda of the United Nations and developed countries, such as environmental protection, the fight against anti-personnel mines, cooperation for development, and have also achieved the promotion of clear commitments and objectives in this field.

Norbert Elias and James Rosenau go even further in the analysis of the actions of non-state actors. The former talks about an individualist society in which a global unity of humankind is based on the desire for survival (see Devin 1995, 305–327). It is one's responsibility to help other individuals, and the assistance for development is the result of such humanitarian actions. Rosenau (1990) completes this formula by adding that alongside citizens, also political leaders and the private sector influence the international scene. Nevertheless, the totality of these actors converges, according to liberal theories, toward the support of developing countries. What animates these theories is the peaceful humanitarian perspective and the belief that only cooperation can maintain international peace. It is precisely this idealistic aspect of the liberal view that radical theories challenge by pointing out the hidden and petty interests of developed states in developing countries.

4 The radical perspective: cooperation for development as a source of imperialism and dependence

Radical theories which focus on the dependence of developing countries generated by developed countries, are some sort of imperialism theories adapted to the post-colonial context. Economist Raúl Prebisch was the first to criticise in the United Nations Economic Commission for Latin America the poor situation of Southern countries. He claimed that the capitalist center bears responsibility for the underdevelopment of South America as it exploits the countries of the periphery.

In *The Politics of World Economy*, Immanuel Wallerstein (1988) adds that unequal exchanges are the result of the hierarchy of states. The weakness of peripheral states is a precondition for the process of exploitation and accumulation by the states of the capitalist centre. These terms refer to Fernand Braudel's theory of the international division of labour modelled as a pattern of concentric circles, according to which developed countries are in the centre of the international system. Starting from this central system, we find circular areas composed of countries that are more or less integrated or developed.

Samir Amin (1988) argues that the international system is dominated by a vicious circle that predestines the countries of the South to be mainly producers of raw materials. This is the reason why these countries remain underdeveloped and cannot benefit from a healthy economic and social development. There are three explanations for underdevelopment: (1) the existence of productivity inequalities linked to the absence of diffusion of technological progress toward the developing countries because of intellectual property protection and the costs of new technologies; (2) economic and development disparities within developing countries limit the possibilities of development; (3) unequal specialisation between the centre and the periphery in the sense that Southern countries are mainly raw material producers.

For radical theories, cooperation for development is a simple mechanism that increases the dependence of the developing countries on the developed countries. This mechanism creates an international assistance regime and underdeveloped states either accept this situation or are at any rate bound by the rules and norms imposed by the developed states. The latter want peripheral countries to specialise in the production of raw materials for economic reasons like low costs and the limitation of competition on high technology markets. Cooperation for development is therefore, in the eyes of the radicals, the result of realist policies based on the principle of negative interdependence – developed countries are imposing their force, culture, and economic interests on developing countries.

5 Conclusion

The conclusion to which we arrive after adapting the different international relations perspectives to cooperation for development is that there are three factors determining the establishment of cooperation for development strategies:

(1) National interests: maximising power;
(2) International interests: maintaining peace and security;
(3) Non-state actors' interests: humanitarian principles (see Figure 2).

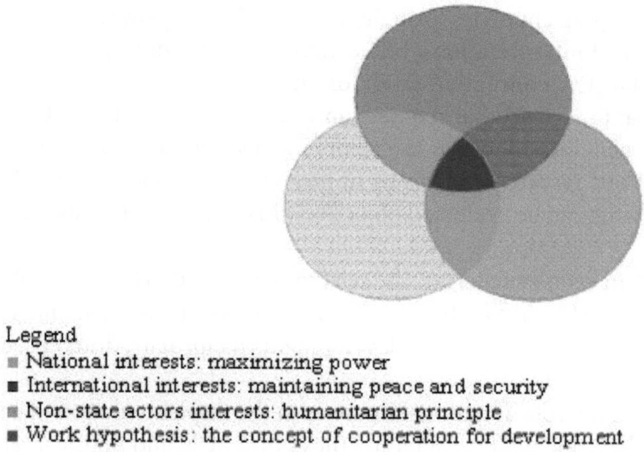

Figure 2: Factors determining
the establishment of cooperation for development strategies

The concept of cooperation for development seems, today, influenced simultaneously by these three different interests, and the influence of each interest differs according to the bureaucratic model of the state providing development aid.

Let us look at just a few examples. In the European Union, even if cooperation for development is still a field covered at the national level, the non-state interests of the different European federations in the field (Concord, Trialog) and the international interest of the EU to appear as a global actor are prevalent in the elaboration of relevant European policies. In Romania, the main beneficiary of cooperation for development funds are Iraq, Afghanistan, Georgia and Ukraine, which shows that the dominant interest is the international interest of the country as a member of NATO and an ally of the United States. In France, the main beneficiaries are the former French colonies, indicating the dominance of national interests in cooperation for development policies. Furthermore, if we look at the commercial balances we see that France actually benefits from this support by receiving important contracts and exporting French goods to beneficiary countries.

The conceptualisation of cooperation for development requires the understanding of the main tensions between the interpretations given to this mechanism by different theories of international relations and development economy. These tensions, alongside the tight link between power relations and economic effects within the cooperation for development, can only underline the complexity of this concept. Ideological perspectives tend to generate subjectivism in the evaluation of cooperation for development policies. More specifically, the relationships between donor countries and developing countries brought about by the cooperation for development can have several interpretations, but a framework of empirical analysis may contribute to an objective conceptualisation of this field.

Development aid is a field that requires an interdisciplinary understanding of the interactions it generates between the actors involved in development partnership. The result of our research enables us to propose some empirical methods of analysis based on what can be evaluated objectively in cooperation for development policies:

(1) Evaluating, in economic terms, the relationships created by cooperation for development between donor countries and developing countries will enable us to illustrate its effects on the beneficiaries' development (reciprocity, domains, effects, etc.).

(2) Determining the role of national interests in the implementation of cooperation for development policies by evaluating the commercial and political relations between donor and beneficiary countries.

(3) Analysing the ability of donor countries to promote their models among the beneficiaries through the cooperation for development, by studying the structural evolution of the beneficiary states' bureaucratic systems and the effects of the projects implemented on the public/leadership opinion of the beneficiary states.

Acknowledgement The author has been the beneficiary of the project 'Doctoral scholarships supporting research: Competitiveness, quality, and cooperation in the European Higher Education Area', co-funded by the European Union through the European Social Fund, Sectorial Operational Programme Human Resources Development 2007–2013.

References

Allison, Graham, and Zelikow, Phillip. 1999. *Essence of Decision: Explaining the Cuban Missile Crisis.* 2nd ed. New York: Longman.

Amin, Samir. 1988. *L'accumulation à l'échelle mondiale.* 2nd ed. Paris: Anthropos.

Ashley, Richard. 1984. The Poverty of Neorealism. *International Organization* 38.2: 225–286.

Axelrod, Robert. 1992. *Donnant donnant: Théorie du comportement coopératif.* Paris: Odile Jacob.

Burchill, Scott, et al. 2008. *Teorii ale relaţiilor internaţionale* [*Theories of International Relations*]. Iaşi: Institutul European.

Buzan, Barry. 1991. *People, States and Fear: An Agenda for International Security Studies in the Post-Cold War Era.* 2nd ed. Hemel Hempstead: Harvester Wheatheaf.

Chang, Charles C., Fernandez-Arias, Eduardo, and Serven, Luis. 1998. *Measuring Aid Flows: A New Approach.* IADB Working Paper No. 387. Washington, DC: Inter-American Development Bank.

Cohen, Samy. 2003. *La résistance des Etats: Les démocraties face aux défis de la mondialisation.* Paris: Seuil.

Deutsch, Karl, and Burrel, S. A. 1957. *Political Community and the North Atlantic Area.* Princeton: Princeton University Press.

Devin, Guillaume. 1995. Norbert Elias et l'analyse des relations internationales. *Revue française de science politique* 45.2: 305–327.

Doyle, Michael. 1983. Kant, Liberal Legacy and Foreign Affairs. *Philosophy and Public Affairs* 12.3: 205–235.

Friboulet, Jean-Jacques. 2004. Tiers Monde. In *Encyclopædia Universalis.* Paris: Encyclopædia Universalis.

Fukuyama, Francis. 2005. *State building: Gouvernance et ordre du monde au XXIe siècle.* Paris: La Table Ronde.

Gilpin, Robert. 1987. *The Political Economy of International Relations.* Princeton: Princeton University Press.

Glasner, Charles. 1995. Realists as Optimists: Cooperation as Self-Help. *International Security* 19.3: 50–90.

Grieco, Joseph. 1993. Understanding the Problem of International Cooperation: The Limits of Neoliberal Institutionalism and the Future of Realist Theory. In *Neorealism and Neoliberalism: The Contemporary Debate*, edited by David Baldwin, 301–338. New York: Columbia University Press.

Jervis, Robert. 1983. Security Regimes. In *International Regimes*, edited by Stephen D. Krasner, 173–194. Ithaca (NY) and London: Cornell University Press.

Keohane, Robert, and Nye, Joseph S. 1977. *Power and Interdependance: World Politics in Transition.* Boston: Little Brown.

Krasner, Stephen D., et al. 1983. *International Regimes.* Ithaca (NY) and London: Cornell University Press.

Montousse, Marc. 2008. *Théories économiques.* Rosny-sous-Bois: Bréal.

Moravcsik, Andrew. 1993. Preferences and Power in the European Community: a Liberal Intergouvernmentalist Approach. *Journal of Common Market Studies* 31:4: 473–524.

Morgenthau, Hans J. 1948. *Politics Among Nations: The Struggle for Power and Peace.* New York: Alfred A. Knopf.

Morgenthau, Hans. 2007. *Politica intre naţiuni. Lupta pentru putere si lupta pentru pace* [*Politics Among Nations: The Struggle for Power and Peace*]. Iaşi: Polirom.

Nye, Joseph. 1992. *Le leadership américain: Quand les règles du jeu changent.* Nancy: Presses Universitaires de Nancy.

Nye, Joseph S. 2005. *Soft Power: The Means to Success in World Politics.* New York: PublicAffairs.

Rainelli, M. 1997. *La nouvelle théorie du commerce international.* Paris: La Découverte.

Rittberger, Volker, et al. 1990. *International Regimes in East-West Politics.* London and New York: Pinter Publishers.

Rosenau, James N. 1990. *Turbulence in World Politics. A Theory of Change and Continuity.* Princeton: Princeton University Press.

Sauvy, Alfred. 1952. Trois mondes, une planète. *L'Observateur politique, économique et littéraire* 118, August 14.

The Millennium Development Goals Report. 2007. New York: UNO.

Wallerstein, Immanuel. 1988. *The Politics of World Economy: the States, the Movements and the Civilizations.* Cambridge: Cambridge University Press.

Waltz, Kenneth N. 2006. *Teoria politicii internaţionale* [*Theory of International Politics*]. Iaşi: Polirom.

Central and Eastern European Forum for Legal, Political, and Social Theory Yearbook

Edited by Jürgen Busch / Péter Cserne / Michael Hein / Miodrag Jovanović / Marta Soniewicka

Vol. 1 Péter Cserne / Miklós Könczöl (eds.): Legal and Political Theory in the Post-National Age. Selected papers Presented at the Second Central and Eastern European Forum for Legal, Political and Social Theorists (Budapest, 21–22 May 2010). 2011.

www.peterlang.de